THE MYSTERIES OF
JOHN THE
BAPTIST

"In *The Mysteries of John the Baptist,* Tobias Churton has produced a remarkably fresh analysis of the 'herald of the Messiah.' The great value of this book is that Churton provides not only a careful overview of the role of John, as handed down in Christian tradition, but gives us a unique and erudite reanalysis of the role of the Baptist using the lenses of Gnosticism, Freemasonry, and other esoteric traditions that have elevated John to a position equal to or superior to Jesus. This book is a truly invaluable addition to scholarly literature on John the Baptist."

THE REV. JEFFREY J. BÜTZ, S.T.M.,
INSTRUCTOR OF RELIGIOUS
STUDIES AT PENN STATE UNIVERSITY AND
AUTHOR OF *THE SECRET LEGACY OF JESUS*

ALSO BY TOBIAS CHURTON

Aleister Crowley—The Biography

The Missing Family of Jesus

The Invisible History of the Rosicrucians

Freemasonry—The Reality

Kiss of Death—The True History of the Gospel of Judas

The Magus of Freemasonry—The Mysterious Life of Elias Ashmole

Gnostic Philosophy—From Ancient Persia to Modern Times

The Golden Builders—Alchemists, Rosicrucians,
and the First Free Masons

The Fear of Vision (poetry)

Miraval—A Quest (a novel)

The Gnostics

Why I Am Still an Anglican (ed.)

The Babylon Gene (under the name Alex Churton)

THE MYSTERIES OF
JOHN THE BAPTIST

HIS LEGACY IN GNOSTICISM, PAGANISM, AND FREEMASONRY

TOBIAS CHURTON

Inner Traditions
Rochester, Vermont • Toronto, Canada

Inner Traditions
One Park Street
Rochester, Vermont 05767
www.InnerTraditions.com

Library of Congress Cataloging-in-Publication Data

Churton, Tobias, 1960–

The mysteries of John the Baptist : his legacy in gnosticism, paganism, and freemasonry / Tobias Churton.

  p. cm.

Includes bibliographical references and index.

ISBN 978-1-59477-474-4 (pbk.) — ISBN 978-1-59477-505-5 (e-book)

1. John, the Baptist, Saint. I. Title.

BS2456.C48 2012

232.9'4—dc23

2012013498

Printed and bound in the United States

10 9 8 7 6 5 4 3

Text design by Jon Desautels and layout by Brian Boynton
This book was typeset in Garamond Premier Pro with Charlemagne and Gill Sans used as display typefaces

To send correspondence to the author of this book, mail a first-class letter to the author c/o Inner Traditions • Bear & Company, One Park Street, Rochester, VT 05767, and we will forward the communication or visit the author's website at **www.tobiaschurton.com**.

I dedicate this book with love to my wife, Joanna, and daughter, Merovée, with thanks to the Brethren of Alexandria-Washington Lodge No. 22, Alexandria, Virginia, and with hope to all the St. John's Men and Women of today and tomorrow.

CONTENTS

ACKNOWLEDGMENTS

This book would not have happened but for the kindness and forbearance of the members of Alexandria-Washington Lodge No 22, Alexandria, Virginia; in particular Past Master Douglas Wood, former Director of Communications at the George Washington Masonic Memorial in Alexandria. This famous Lodge's warm invitations to me to cross the Atlantic to speak have proved strangely inspirational, this book being the first fruit.

Inspiration comes to the prepared mind: a lifetime's study of mysticism and esoteric theology was never in my mind supposed to be buried in the esoteric world alone. I always intended to return to the canonical sources with renewed interest and perception: a golden key to open the mysteries of the kingdom of heaven; such has been the case.

I am reminded of how well I was taught the rudiments of biblical scholarship, both at school and at university. The following names ring out for special mention: divinity teacher Trevor Harding (who encouraged me to return to school with the tantalizing promise of "opening my mind" after I had left for a craft apprenticeship, aged fifteen); Canon Aleric Rose, rector, fine scholar, bibliophile, and sincere Christian; Canon John Fenton, then theology tutor at Christchurch, Oxford; Old Testament specialist Rex Mason of Regent's Park College, Oxford; and master of ancient Near Eastern texts Prof. John Day of Lady Margaret Hall. My wits have been further sharpened by encounters with the late master of Gnostic studies Hans Jonas, the unforgettable Gilles Quispel, the intriguingly provocative Elaine Pagels, and the late head of Uppsala University's theological faculty Jan-Arvid Hellström.

Above all, I thank my late parents, Patricia and Victor Churton. They furnished me with all I needed to embark on a lifetime's theological and mystical quest for truth.

That which inspired John inspired them, and inspired me.

PREFACE

I seldom cease to be amazed by the extraordinary wealth of esoteric knowledge to be found in the Bible. That word *found* is of course the key: "Seek and ye shall find" is a master watchword; do not expect to find anything if you wait to be shown. As I grew up, I was always struck by how much religious instruction came secondhand. No one really wants secondhand parents; likewise we should not be satisfied by anything less than a genuine relationship with the One who draws our imaginations onward to the truth we seek. We need to experience truth in ourselves; if it is not *our* truth, both gift and possession, it is of little value: parrot-talking is the language of the moral bigot who knows what is right for everyone else but does not know himself, fearing exposure to the spiritual light. Laws are walls built to protect us; spiritual truths are doors to the unknown. Hence, the fear of God is the beginning of all understanding: this is the fear that enables us to enter the unknown.

Congregations customarily "receive" the word; consequently the word seldom acquires profound levels of meaningfulness for the receiver. People often hang on to beliefs like talismans, fearing "offense," as if the talisman might shatter if touched by the unknown. Has there ever been a society more fearful of causing or receiving "offense" than ours? The phenomenon suggests to me that our convictions are paper thin, demanding protection of law. Lawyers do well from it all, but spiritual liberty suffers. Meanwhile, sacred mysteries, pregnant symbols, spiritual doors are bandied about like goods in the vulgar marketplace like beautiful love songs on the lips of the lascivious. We take religion for granted, as if we know it all.

We do not.

This insight became very clear to me when I decided to investigate John the Baptist. We think we know who he is, but we have been misled: a flanker has been pulled, rendering us blind. I hope you can share in my journey for the truth of John the Baptist.

Chapter One

THE MYSTERY OF
JOHN THE BAPTIST

*Among them that are born of woman there hath not risen
a greater than John the Baptist.*

MATTHEW 11:11A

I HAVE LONG BEEN FASCINATED by the figure of John the
Baptist, but did not realize how persistent a fascination this was until
I noticed, some time ago, that our home displays no fewer than three
portraits of the mysterious prophet. Each portrait tells a different
story, each reveals something different about the man known to us as
a Christian saint, but who, in his own time, was seen as nothing of the
kind.

Three paintings. They all feature "John," yet they might very well
depict three different people, even though two of the paintings are the
work of the same artist.

First, we see John as a heroic, muscular, commanding figure. He
stands firm, practically naked, towering over the River Jordan with all
the force and passion of Poseidon in his natural element. Fierce and
kind, the Baptist's face and beard are reminiscent of a Sikh warrior
and holy man: an inspired guru, one who knows the world and what is

Figure 1.1. Painting by Louise Ford

beyond it. He has the chest of a Hollywood Hercules, with masterful hands mighty enough to take anyone through anything, from belated baptism to a brick wall.

The background figures, by contrast, seem diminished. They appear as sick, curious, censorious, or violently hostile—like townsfolk nervously watching Clint Eastwood stalking a remote Main Street in a "spaghetti western."

On a hill above the people, Jesus reclines. Perhaps insignificant, a sole spectator of the star performance, Jesus observes the scene below. On the shore, a female figure (a self-portrait of the artist) dips her toe into the waters. Should she "take the leap," or should she not? Should she join the giant in the water's depth and be transformed, or forever cling to familiar, secure territory?

This painting depicts John the Baptist as a figure of massive attraction, at least to the artist. Her watercolor is a kind of fan letter: one from the heart, wrought with the pigments of imagination dipped in the waters of initiation.

Recently, I met the artist, Louise Ford, by chance. Now a quarter of a century since she had been moved to concentrate her talent on the Baptist, just what, I asked, had inspired the work? John, Ford recalled, was for her the man who had *gone beyond*. He was the man with the guts to step outside of society, regardless of peer disapproval and hostility. Heeding a higher light, a purer voice, he entered the wilderness to live in the wild on what nature alone provided: to go without comforts, subsisting on the spirit, to live out his "outsiderness," his consciousness of his difference to the "once-born" children of matter, with all his strength of endurance. Trusting he had done aright, John demonstrated with actions, as well as words, his willingness to pay the price for his audacity and startling holiness. The John-type goes beyond the city walls: the mind-set of his time. And the city, which thinks it knows all, cannot tolerate him; John tells the truth. He is a "voice crying in the wilderness"—a cry the artist long ago heard and clearly longed to hear again, in the feverish vacuum of our collective anthill.

Louise Ford's second vision of John is very different. Wrought in bright poster paints, the painting attempts to fashion a fresh approach to religious art: a kind of psychedelic spiritualism, to capture the spirituality of an event as seen *from within*. The chosen moment is the baptism of Jesus at John's hand. Jesus, having taken the plunge, has arisen, while John also rises from the billowing, quaking waters like a god hewn from a great ship's prow. The beam of his arm extends to his fellow, Jesus. Jesus, no less muscular than his baptizer, stands in a state of sublime reception. He accepts. His arms outstretched, his large hands open, his eyes are closed in mystic union. Above his head we see a divine figure, golden, resembling his physical part, but transfigured. This spiritual figure may be coming from on high—a kind of "Holy Guardian Angel" from beyond this world—or he may be rising from Jesus's head, signifying an inner experience. The overall impression is one of Jesus himself rising, in travail of fire, air, earth, and water—raised, apparently, by the power of John's hand. For all this we still feel ourselves in the midst of a familiar scene, a scene that has defined John's purpose and his status in Christian tradition.

John baptizes Jesus. That is to say—and we are meant to see—John is a secondary figure: one who serves the "main event."

For ancient Christians who favored what would come to be called the heresy of "adoptionism," this baptism signaled the spiritual being of Christ's "adoption" of the mantle of the "man Jesus." The man thenceforth served to cloak the transcendent being: a temporary identification of man and divinity. Whether today's Christian follows the orthodox or so-called heretical scheme here, *John's* position is, in either case, incidental.

Oddly, we might think, John's baptizing of Jesus indicates in Christian tradition not John's mastery, but his subservience. Even the baptism itself is relegated in significance and potency, *before it even happens*. Despite its occasioning the "opening of the heavens" to Jesus's inner vision (Matthew 3:16) and subsequent descent of the "Spirit of

Figure 1.2. Painting by Louise Ford

God" like a dove to Jesus's head, John's kind of baptism is nonetheless regarded in the Gospels as deficient; deficient, that is, when compared to that of a greater one to come "after" him.

John's baptism is only "of water."

Nevertheless, it is difficult to imagine a more effective baptism than this one of John's: a baptism that has inspired artists for nigh on two thousand years! The event is capped by nothing less than a voice from heaven, saying, "This is my beloved Son, in whom I am well pleased" (Matthew 3:17). This divine endorsement of Jesus's significance, apparently a conflation of Isaiah 42:1, Psalm 2:7, and Genesis 22:2, is a statement of religious reflection. Jesus, the Son of God, has come "after" John. Whatever one might make of this account's historicity, John's part in the story is apparently done. Having prepared the way in the wilderness, John ought to retire gracefully. Jesus has no further need of him; the Baptist is redundant; his baptizing the one "after him" is John's spiritual swansong.

Exit John. *Enter* Jesus.

In spite of the early church's determination to ensure that John's significance be confined to that of herald or, if I may say, "warm-up act" for the big star, a very great mystery about John, *the real John,* persists. That mystery kindled the imaginative genius of Leonardo da Vinci. Leonardo painted the third image of John that has hung in my home for many years (see fig. 1.3).

While Leonardo's original *John the Baptist* now hangs before the public in Paris's Louvre Museum, five hundred years ago its viewing required an invitation to the private apartments of François I, King of France. Captivated, perhaps haunted, by the Baptist, Leonardo's royal patron would stare in timeless contemplation into John's enigmatic eyes and androgynous form. The painting became a true *icon* for the king, a window into the beyond. I have been similarly bemused by this great work of art, painted between 1513 and 1516 when Leonardo was in his early sixties. It is perhaps Leonardo's last testament in paint.

Figure 1.3. John the Baptist *by Leonardo da Vinci, Paris, Louvre*

So remote from the image of the unshaven Hebrew prophet, Leonardo's depiction of the "Christian saint" is peculiar. Emerging from blackness, the beautiful figure suggests nothing so much as a pagan "come-on" issued from the cheeky girl/boy face who has borrowed his all-knowing smile from the expressive pallet of the *Mona Lisa* and his left, obscure, and decidedly serpentine arm from the neck and head-form of Leda's divine, impregnating swan, also painted by Leonardo. John's right arm, meanwhile, makes a dramatic gesture, crossing his chest, bending at the elbow to make a "square," then pointing sharply upward—to heaven, presumably. The forefinger gesture is as visually dynamic as Michelangelo's near-meeting of the Creator's index finger and that of Adam on the Sistine Chapel's ceiling.

What does it mean?

Is there a naughty anticlerical double meaning or joke inherent in the finger gesture? John's "model" may have been Leonardo's scurrilous pupil nicknamed "Salai" or the "little devil," so that the gesture may be taken, on one level, as a lewd one: *"Up your ass!"* Leonardo's use of the pointing gesture is, however, a recurring sign in his religious art. But what constituted Leonardo's personal religion, if anything? The slender reed cross was added later. Was it a sop to theological propriety? Though not detracting overmuch from the painting's central action, the cross was probably added to bring Leonardo's puzzling image into securer doctrinal waters. The cross declares this John is a Christian! And, talking of waters, there are none to be seen. This "Baptist" has nothing to baptize with, save his eyes and that suggestive gesture we cannot quite decipher. So strong, indeed, is the pagan, sensual, classical feel of the depiction, rendering it practically unusable, at least at the time, in obviously sacred contexts, we can hardly escape wondering if Leonardo did not see something else hidden in the orthodox, biblical picture of John.

Underlining the ambiguous and arguably pagan inspiration of Leonardo's John is the existence of a similar work, thought to have been painted between 1510 and 1515 by a follower of Leonardo from a draw-ing by the master. The painting has a dual identity. It is known both as *St. John in the Wilderness* and as *Bacchus,* the god of religious ecstasy, wine, and intoxication.

Originally a variant on Leonardo's conception of the Baptist, some *curiosus* in the late seventeenth century chose to add vine leaves to the figure's head and leopard spots to John's hairy loincloth. A vine wreath added to the Baptist's former staff transformed it into a Bacchic *thyrsus,* Dionysus's sacred staff borne by his wine-intoxicated followers. According to Euripides, the thyrsus dripped with honey—a not insignificant detail, as we shall see. We may naturally ask whether this iconographic vandalism resulted from pious outrage at a sensual St. John or whether it was derived from positive insight into the fig-ure's pagan provenance.

We cannot leave this maverick image of John-Bacchus without noting that the characteristic da Vincian finger gesture is stranger still. The Bacchic, or Dionysian, John—if we may call him such—has his right forefinger pointing up at 45 degrees across his chest, while his left forefinger points down vertically to the Earth. With the fig-ure's left leg drawn across his right knee at a right angle to the staff, there is the suggestion of some geometrical conceit, but any suggestion of an injunction to accept the famous, pointedly "Hermetic" princi-ple *as above, so below*—indicating magical links between heaven and Earth—is nullified by the fact that the figure's right hand does not point directly upward, as in Leonardo's more famous painting, but at an angle, as though referring to something off, or right of canvas. The gestures baffle, but they do not compel, as in the single finger gesture of Leonardo's own finished work.

JOHN AS DIVINE MERCURY

Renaissance philosophy revelled in allegories, visual and literary puns, dynamic riddles, and multiple meanings. Renaissance man sought unity of being through the diversity of the world. He confronted chaos and disorder with a faith in hidden harmonies and higher orders on which he depended and with which he could operate. Symbolic links between the pagan gods of the classical period and corresponding "principles" perceived in the church's approved biblical figures were not only high-lighted for moral and philosophical uplift but, in many a learned in-joke, sported with. At least one of these correspondences may illuminate some of the mystery of Leonardo's *John the Baptist,* if not the mystery of "the Baptist" himself.

Less than a decade before Leonardo painted his late masterpiece, the considerably less talented German artist Conrad Celtes adopted the then-current fad for presenting biblical figures as pagan deities. Celtes produced a woodcut wherein, among other obvious correspon-dences, the goddess Minerva appeared as Mary while the Greek god Hermes appeared as a straight stand-in for John the Baptist. There was no mystery or allegorical depth to this cross-identification of John and Hermes. Celtes simply hooked into the idea of Hermes as the divine messenger and made the not-very-startling, or not-very-original, identification of John-Hermes by reference to the ecclesiasti-cally acceptable understanding of John the Baptist as revered "fore-runner" or *herald* of Christ: the one crying in the wilderness. Once appreciated, however, the link of John to Hermes turns out to be highly suggestive.

In ancient times, the "herald" or "ambassador" (Greek: *kērux*) enjoyed an important presiding role at official ceremonies. Like the god Hermes, the herald was the mouthpiece of the sovereign power: the messenger with the message. In Leonardo's day, Hermes was not understood simply as the classical divine messenger with wings on hel-met and feet—a kind of Olympian mailman—he was also seen as the divinity active within Hermes Trismegistus (Thrice Great Hermes), the divine philosopher par excellence and legendary giant of patriarchal sci-ence. Thrice Great Hermes (today we might say *Super-Mega-Awesome*

Hermes) was thought to have been a kind of incarnation of Hermes the god, as well as being the prophet Moses's human contemporary and even inspiration.

Writings attributed to Thrice Great Hermes were collected together as the *Hermetica*. Much later Latin versions of the "Corpus Hermeticum" were also called the "Pymander" or "Divine Pymander." These were named after the first treatise in the collection, called in Greek the *Poimandrēs*. First printed in Treviso, northern Italy, in 1471, the *Pymander* revolutionized Renaissance thinking, pointing the way to the divine mind through *inner ascent* to the heavens. In fact, since at least the late fourteenth century, Hermes had been known as a kind of honorary patron of freemasons (master masons of freestone), a paternal status Hermes had anciently enjoyed in the world of alchemy, the art of chemical transformation and first foundation of modern chemistry. In alchemical "recipes," Hermes often played the role of "psychopomp": leader of souls across the waters of corruption and decay to rebirth and psychic integration: a spiritual-physical ascent-master. It was thought that the "souls" of metals could be acted on by appealing to higher, spiritual influences; man, too, was a "metal" with hidden "virtue" or power.

The Hermetic writings available to Leonardo were composed in the early centuries of the Christian era, probably in Egypt, though nobody in Leonardo's time thought so. They were considered as either antecedent to, or contemporary with, the "philosophy" of Moses. The *Hermetica* appeared to prophesy the "son of God," Jesus. Hermes also spoke of a "herald" (Greek: *kērux*). In *Corpus Hermeticum* IV, this herald was sent by God to mankind with a bowl of *nous* (divine mind) in which men could be baptized if they chose to heed the call and accept the offer of *gnosis* or higher, divine knowledge and consciousness. The "mixing bowl" or *krater* in which the willing initiate could be baptized also enjoyed an alchemical meaning. We see here an obvious link between John the Baptist and the Hermetic revelation: John as Baptist, or spiritual operator and agent of transformation.

Perhaps you have seen old alchemical images of the Hermaphroditic (male/female) *rebis,* the divine Child of the "mysterious conjunction" of the divine Sun and goddess Moon. The rebis was usually illustrated as being masculine on one side and feminine on the other: sometimes rendered as a king and queen in one body. The hermaphroditic rebis symbolized the combination of contrary or opposite principles at a higher level of chemical transformation processes. The very word *hermaphrodite* calls us to observe a spiritually generative conjunction of the gods Hermes and Aphrodite: Mind and Beauty, where Mind is both lunar and mercurial, and Beauty, both solar and Venusian: an ecstatic combination!

Thus, the apparent "androgyny" or Hermaphroditic quality of Leonardo's Baptist may reflect experience of the Hermetic androgyne who points the way to a higher state of being and consciousness. Is this a pointer to a way back to a lost primal condition from which Man had fallen, or a way forward to an evolutionary destiny? It is both. One by-product of the way is the perception that masculine and feminine characteristics will no longer be perceived as being at odds, but unified in joyous harmony: a return to the "One." Leonardo was perhaps looking ahead to a new age. His John pointed the way.

French King François I, who liked to visit Leonardo's apartments at the royal château at Amboise in the Loire Region, stated privately that Leonardo had been not only the most outstanding genius of art and science, but a uniquely gifted philosopher as well: a man to enlighten a king. Did the king get the message?

If he did, he kept it to himself.

That Leonardo's "John" emerges from blackness (ignorance?) may also be significant. The lowest or primary stage of the alchemical art was called the *nigredo* or blackness, from which low material state the transformative principle (sometimes referred to as the "stone"), redeemed the secreted "gold" or hidden virtue of alchemical potential. We are thus at liberty to see Leonardo's *John the Baptist* as an image of the Hermetic principle of spiritual and material transformation:

the "ascent of Man" to a higher stage of psycho-spiritual awareness.

Leonardo's John is therefore not only transformer, but transformed: herald *and* initiator. He is a kind of Christ, symbolizing a higher principle: the divine Self.

He *knows*.

We have come a long way from the image of John the Baptist up to his knees in the Jordan torrent, baptizing Judeans and calling out from the wilderness for national repentance. *Or have we?* I might have thought so until I received an invitation that arrived on the wings of cyberspace around Easter 2010. It was not an invitation to a mixing bowl of noetic baptism, nor to an alchemical wedding: I was invited to bring my own bowl of inspiration to the presence of the Brethren of Alexandria-Washington Lodge No. 22, Alexandria, Virginia, in time for their annual St. John the Baptist Day feast at Gadsby's Tavern in Alexandria. The date: June 24, traditional birthday of St. John the Baptist.

Alexandria-Washington Lodge No. 22 is no ordinary Masonic Lodge. It is one of the oldest Free and Accepted Masonic Lodges in the United States and is famous for once having enjoyed as its Master General George Washington. The Lodge meets today at the remarkable George Washington Memorial in Alexandria, an architectural wonder paid for by Masonic subscription and modeled on the more ancient wonder of the world, the Pharos, or lighthouse of Alexandria, Egypt.

Inspired by the thought of a modern Lodge that linked the light of ancient Alexandria to the modern world and that still honored the age-old link between masonry and St. John the Baptist, the theme for my proposed address came immediately to mind. Would it not be appropriate to delve into just why it was—and is—that the figure of St. John the Baptist holds a special place in Masonic mythology? I anticipated a fairly routine investigation into the usual Masonic sources, with a pleasant mixture of entertainment and, hopefully, a sprinkling of enlightenment for all.

I was in for a surprise.

Though dimly aware that there was more to St. John the Baptist than met the eye, I very soon found my researches taking an unexpected path. What had begun as a literary peregrination into obscure folklore quickly grew beyond the bounds of a forty-five-minute celebratory address into a compelling journey into the shadows of history.

Whether I have emerged from the darkness with pearls rather than "chimaeras of little worth" I must leave for the reader to decide. As the quality of baptisms may certainly differ, so everyone's John will not, and cannot, be the same. I hope, however, that at the end of this journey you will feel you know something of value about the man whose greatness Jesus is reported to have declared unsurpassed by any man born of woman.

Chapter Two

ST. JOHN'S MEN AND THE PASSION OF THE CORN

There were three men came out of the west, their
    fortunes for to try,
And these three men made a solemn vow:
John Barleycorn must die.
They've ploughed, they've sown, they've harrowed him
    in,
Threw clods upon his head,
And these three men made a solemn vow:
John Barleycorn was dead.

They've let him lie for a very long time, 'til the rains
    from heaven did fall,
And little Sir John sprung up his head and so amazed
    them all.
They've let him stand 'til Midsummer's Day 'til he
    looked both pale and wan,
And little Sir John's grown a long long beard and so
    become a man.
They've hired men with their scythes so sharp to cut
    him off at the knee.

15

> *They've rolled him and tied him by the waist serving*
>   *him most barbarously.*
> *They've hired men with their sharp pitchforks who've*
>   *pricked him to the heart—*
> *And the loader he has served him worse than that,*
> *For he's bound him to the cart.*
>
> *They've wheeled him around and around a field 'til*
>   *they came unto a barn,*
> *And there they made a solemn oath on poor John Barleycorn.*
> *They've hired men with their crabtree sticks to cut*
>   *him skin from bone—*
> *And the miller he has served him worse than that,*
> *For he's ground him between two stones.*
>
> *And little Sir John and the nut brown bowl and his*
>   *brandy in the glass,*
> *And little Sir John and the nut brown bowl proved*
>   *the strongest man at last.*
> *The huntsman he can't hunt the fox nor so loudly to*
>   *blow his horn,*
> *And the tinker he can't mend kettle or pots without a*
>   *little barleycorn.*
>
> JOHN BARLEYCORN,
TRADITIONAL ENGLISH BROADSIDE SONG,
SIXTEENTH–SEVENTEENTH CENTURIES

Centrally organized symbolic Freemasonry was allegedly instituted in 1716 when, according to the Rev. James Anderson's *Constitutions of Free and Accepted Masonry* (1738), "Free Masons" from four London lodges met together at the Apple Tree Tavern in Charles Street, Covent Garden, during the second year of the reign of the Hanoverian King George I. These four lodges of Free Masons agreed to form a "Grand Lodge," apparently to "revive" what the writer considered a neglected institution. The Masons put the oldest master mason (or architect-builder) present in the chair to center the union. The Rev. James Anderson's account is the sole record of the proceedings.

On June 24 the following year (1717), according to Anderson, the Goose and Gridiron Ale-house in St. Paul's Churchyard accommodated this "Grand Lodge" of "Free and Accepted Masons" for a midsummer feast, again under the eye of the curiously unnamed, oldest master mason. The presence of the oldest master mason lends some authenticity to the account since it had been established as a rule in 1663 that a Lodge convened without the presence of at least one working stone mason was not properly constituted; it would be Anderson himself who oversaw the "disappearance" of this significant requirement.

From a list of candidates, the Goose & Gridiron's summer feasters elected one Antony Sayer, gentleman, to be "Grand Master" of their "Grand Lodge." New though this Grand Lodge certainly was, the custom of meeting to oversee business—and to feast heartily—on June 24 was long established among the master masons, interested gentlemen, freestone carvers, stonecutters, carpenters, plasterers, painters, glaziers, and tilers who appear to have constituted the greater part of seventeenth- and early-eighteenth-century Free Masons' lodges.

Why did Masons meet on June 24?

June 24 was St. John the Baptist's Day.

Unusual for a saint's day, June 24 was the date Christian tradition allotted to John's birth, not his death. In fact, John's birthday was the accepted date of Midsummer, close to the summer solstice, when the Earth receives her most intimate embrace from the visible source of light and life at our system's center. Seventeenth-century Free Masons called the sun the "jewel" of the Lodge. The Jewel was said to rest first on the Lodge's Master, who, like the Sun and the Square, was called a "Light" of the Lodge, enthroned in the East where the sun rose. The Free Mason works in the day, in the light, in conformity with the pattern of the universe. The symbolic Masonic Lodge is effectively a microcosm, a "little universe": *as above, so below.*

Since time immemorial, St. John the Baptist, who slept beneath the stars, had been an established patron saint of "Free Masons."

In 1723, what is now the City of London's Old Dundee Lodge No. 18 was affiliated to the new Grand Lodge. The Lodge received a number. Taking a number brought it into conformity with the new Grand Lodge's regulations, published that year by Scottish clergyman and dutiful record keeper the Rev. James Anderson. Surviving Lodge minutes show that between 1748 and 1775 brethren received six visits a year from persons signing themselves "St. John's Men." These 162 St. John's Men would *not* be numbered; so they paid a visiting fee, a kind of penalty for having come from lodges outside the Grand Lodge rolls. *Their* lodges had not, would not, or had not *yet* conformed to the new system. Instead, they were distinguished by looking to St. John as their seal of authority. Even though independent of the Grand Lodge, St. John's Men were permitted to visit "regular" brethren accepted by the Grand Lodge. Since London's Grand Lodge did not absorb all Masons at once, and since it certainly encountered resistance to its advances on existing lodges around the country, especially in the north, we may reasonably suppose that there lived around the kingdom, during this period, a goodly number of "St. John's Men" or "St. John's Masons."

St. John appears to have been an identity focus for pre-Grand Lodge fraternities who valued their autonomy. An anonymous "irregular" Masonic catechism called *The Grand Mystery of Free-Masons Discover'd,* published without Grand Lodge authority in 1725, insists on the St. John identity in greeting fellow Masons: "I came from a right worshipful Lodge of Masters and Fellows belonging to Holy St. John who doth greet all perfect Brothers of our Holy Secret; so do I you, if you be one."

Evidence from the late seventeenth century confirms the Baptist's significance to Free Masons, before the appearance of the Grand Lodge. A rare Masonic catechism named after its preserver, the antiquarian and botanist Sir Hans Sloane, is headed "A Narrative of the Freemasons word and signes" (*Sloane Manuscript 3329,* British Library). It contains questions and answers that once passed between fellows and candidates for admission to lodges. Here is an example:

Q: Where was the first word given?
A: At the Tower of Babylon [Babel].
Q: Where did they first call their Lodge?
A: At the holy Chapel of St. John.

We may justly suspect the "holy Chapel of St. John" to have been a euphemism for the wilderness, for that is where St. John the Baptist stood in communion with God, and where he centered his upright spiritual building. The wilderness is the place where the divine voice, or Word, declares that a path will be made straight, as John the Baptist famously declared, echoing Isaiah's ancient prophecy. The voice crying in the wilderness announces the *Way,* the straight way, the way of return to the true Temple of God. On this principle John stood, and endured to the end. And it is worth adding that while we automatically think of John's path in the wilderness as a horizontal road of returning exiles to Zion, that is, a path or even new construction across the earth and stones, we should consider the possibility that enlightened Masons and others may have understood the path to be vertical, to the stars and heavens beyond: a Jacob's ladder or upstanding Square. We may recall Leonardo's John, pointing *upward.* The straight road is a spiritual path and operates in both directions. A path is made so that a higher principle may descend by it as the restored spirit of fallen Man simultaneously "ascends."

Distance from the stain of a corrupt civilization is recommended elsewhere in the *Sloane Manuscript.* A catechism asks the Candidate to consider that the "just and perfect lodge" is to be found "on the highest hill or Lowest Valley of the world, without the crow of a Cock or the Bark of a Dog." This is of course the perfect Lodge. It is constituted in the imagination, as becomes clear when the

Candidate, on being asked, "How high is your Lodge?" is to answer, "Without foots, yards, or inches it reaches to heaven." This ideal, microcosmic Lodge appears to have been enacted in the upper rooms of taverns in the teeming city that emerged in the forty years after London's Great Fire of 1666, when the work of members of the London Masons' Company (formerly the London Freemasons' Company) was in great demand.

The novel Grand Lodge began to assume control of Free Masons' Lodges after 1717, establishing new lodges of its own regulated brand. The Grand Lodge had its own far-reaching, and largely unspoken, agenda. Part of that agenda appears to have been to establish a regulated fellowship where Christian denomination, with all its divisive political consequences, would not influence a lodge's ideal amity and harmony. You must be a brother to a brother regardless of your, or his, religious upbringing, be it Catholic, Protestant, or anything else. While it may be assumed that such mutual tolerance was already a characteristic of some British lodges, the new Grand Lodge went further, asserting that there existed, and had always existed, a "religion on which all men could agree" and "all men" included Jews and Muslims and Hindus and all believers in God. Before Abraham, the Supreme Being or "Great Architect" had made a covenant with all humankind, symbolized in the story of Noah and the rainbow; Man had gone astray, God had stayed the same. This idea answered a specific political, as well as spiritual, need of the time—and perhaps our time as well.

Given this perspective, traditional Christian feast days and saints were perceived by the framers of new regulations as sticking out like sore thumbs, binding British Masonry to its Catholic, prescientific, pre-"enlightened" traditions: a world unreformed, a world conveniently to be cast off as "Gothick," that is, dark, irrational, unenlightened. Overtly Christian references familiar to pre–Grand Lodge Free Masons would be gradually removed from authorized Masonic ritual and commentary.

We can thus understand why those resisting the new order might have made a point of emphasising the "St. John's Men" tradition. They probably felt that their Master—or at the least, sacred patron—was being relegated, even expunged. This phenomenon becomes strikingly visible when we look at some of the critical changes to Masonic regulations that took place in 1723 and fifteen years later, in 1738. One can, I think, see behind the apparently innocuous words to glimpse a distinct anxiety over the stubborn figure of St. John the Baptist.

Ironically, it was on St. John the Baptist's Day, 1721, that the Grand Lodge approved outgoing Grand Master George Payne's General Regulations. Article 22 of these regulations ruled that

> the Brethren of all the Lodges in and about London and Westminster, shall meet at an ANNUAL COMMUNICATION and Feast, in some convenient Place, on St. JOHN Baptist's Day, or else on St. JOHN Evangelist's Day, as the Grand-Lodge shall think fit by a new Regulation, having of late Years met on St. John Baptist's Day.

We see that a "new Regulation" puts St. John the Evangelist's Day (December 27) on a par with St. John the Baptist's Day. For sure, December 27 is very close to the winter solstice and therefore suggests a convenient "harmony" with the summer solstice celebration, if a rather cool one, coming so close to Christmas midwinter feasting and the coldest time of the year. The regulation seems to involve not only a reduction in the traditional significance of the Baptist, but also the downgrading of a specifically traditional Masons' feast. The Regulations proceed to make the case that "St. John's Day," *without now specifying which "St. John" is intended,* shall be for the appointment of the new Grand Master, his Deputy, and Wardens, whether it is agreed to have a feast, either for the "top brass" or all Brethren, or not.

This regulation has led to long-standing and persistent confusion among Freemasons for whom a "St. John" is important. A famous Masonic glyph, for example, shows two parallel lines on either side of a circle with a point at its center. While the circle with a point at its center remains the classic astro-alchemical "sun" symbol, it is worth bearing in mind that Hermetic writings echoed in Copernicus's famous pro-heliocentric treatise *On the Revolutions of the Celestial Orbs* describe the sun as the *second or visible God.* That is to say, the circle with a point at the center may denote the manifest presence of God. Masons are taught that at the center of the circle, they "cannot err."

Masonic symbol-expounders continue to eat their masters' crumbs and suggest, bizarrely, that the parallel lines on either side of the sun symbol represent the "two St. Johns." To this curiosity, the idea is added that the parallel lines somehow represent the bounds of the sun's respective closeness and distance from the Earth (the solstices). In demonstrating such an order, or "harmony"—a concept as central to Grand Lodge ideology as it was to Hanoverian political polemic and Newtonian science—the glyph is said to link the ordered universe and its creator's necessary bounds with the constraints that should morally govern a Mason's conduct. In my book *Freemasonry—The Reality* you may find an internally consistent argument suggesting that the glyph probably represents the Ark of the Covenant with its revelatory staves, once secreted in the holy of holies in the Temple, the centering of God's presence in Zion. Whatever the glyph's original meaning, readers should take the "two Johns" kind of tortured explanation with a pinch of salt. It derives from the confusion that stems from trying to match St. John the Baptist to St. John the Evangelist.

There was considerable political and ideological impetus behind the control-freakery of the new Grand Lodge with its creaking, dryly moralistic, and oh-so-rationally "enlightened" encroachments on old freemasons' lore. The founders of the new Grand Lodge were practically all staunch Whigs, pro-Hanoverian mercantilists and great landowners. Contemptuous of prochurch Jacobite-sympathizing Tories, they were not romantics. Leading Whigs wanted a new, rational order;

their descendants still do. Grand Lodge regulatory activities have long muddied the inherited symbolic waters, bringing many fascinating old masons' traditions and symbols into disrepute, or unnecessary obscurity, among intelligent and spiritually minded people.

The choice of St. John the Evangelist as one of a "pair" of Johns was an astute red herring. We are all familiar with chapter one, verse one of the Gospel generally attributed to John (the evangelist): "In the beginning was the word . . ." First, the use of the evangelist may have been a sop to biblicist Protestants for whom the written "word" of the Bible was religion's sole authority, thus linking the Protestant deity to the mathematically orderly deity of Newtonian science. Second, John's Gospel has much to say about a contrast between "Light" and "Darkness," a symbolism familiar to the language of Masonic initiation as we now know it. Third, the "Mason's word," a secret to die for, is still significant in Masonic mythology. In this case, however, implied reference to the "word" serves primarily to neutralize traditional attachments to St. John the Baptist. The Baptist is generally recognized as a very different figure from St. John the Evangelist. Even in orthodox presentation, the Baptist, unlike the Evangelist, was not a *follower* of Jesus (a "Christian") but a "forerunner."

And John the Baptist was popular: his birthday was once a public holiday or holy day.

Should it be thought I exaggerate the force of apparently minor regulatory changes, it does well to look at *Anderson's Book of Constitutions of 1738.* The book's "New Regulations" supersede even the established "New Regulation" of 1723. From these even newer regulations we can see that the first "new" regulation of 1723 was but a minor pop against tradition. A veritable broadside was on its way. The *new* Article 22 stated:

> The annual Feast has been held on both the St. JOHN's Days, as the G[rand] Master thought fit.

And

On 25 Nov[ember] 1723. it was ordain'd that one of the Quarterly Communications shall be held on St. JOHN Evangelist's Day, and another on St. JOHN Baptist's Day every Year, whether there be a Feast or not, unless the G. Master find it inconvenient for the Good of the Craft, which is more to be regarded than Days.

But of late Years, most of the *Eminent* Brethren [*sic*] being out of Town on both the St. JOHN's Days, the G. Master has appointed the Feast on such a Day as appeared most convenient to the *Fraternity.*

It is hard for us today to grasp fully just what was being both implied and stated plainly here. It is clear that the Grand Lodge, after some fifteen years of activity, had acquired a certain confidence, not to say arrogance, in its dealings with established custom. We need not be surprised. The Grand Lodge was now "well in" with Whig nobility and the Royal House of Hanover, if indeed it had ever been "well out" of it. What matters *now*, the Regulations state, is what the Grand Master "sees fit." And in 1738 the Grand Master was Henry Brydges, Marquis of Caernarvon (from 1744 Second Duke of Chandos), former Master of the Horse to Frederick, Prince of Wales (himself a Freemason), and a Knight, Order of the Bath. The Marquis of Caernarvon was also Whig MP for Steyning, Sussex.

Caernarvon's father, the first Duke of Chandos, had established a great house at Cannons Park, for which Royal Society member Rev. John Desaguliers (1683–1744) was made responsible by the Duke for the engineering of the water gardens. The Duke also supplied Desaguliers with his clerical living; he was the Duke's chaplain and rector of St. Lawrence's, on the edge of the estate.

Desaguliers was in the Duke's pocket. And he was a Freemason.

A French-born Protestant émigré from Louis XIV's vicious anti-Protestant policy, John Desaguliers had trained at Oxford and subsequently become scientific assistant to Sir Isaac Newton. Credited with inventing the planetarium, Desaguliers followed Newton's view that the original religion was the original science. This principle was demonstrated in Newton's mind in the grand design of Solomon's Temple. Newton and Desaguliers believed that religion and science had since been corrupted. Roman Catholicism was held up as prime culprit, whose myriad misdemeanors included, allegedly, the cult of saints and *saints' days*.

We are not surprised, then, to learn that John Desaguliers was the Grand Lodge's third Grand Master and Deputy Grand Master to the Whig peer, the Duke of Montagu, when, in 1723, Desaguliers oversaw James Anderson's composition and publication of the new Constitutions of "Free and Accepted Masons."

The Grand Lodge was a tight ship, with Whigs in the rigging.

High-handedly and with haughty aristocratic disdain for the concerns of older Brethren, the Regulations stated unequivocally that what suited the Grand Master was necessarily for the good of the Craft. *His* will was more important than "Days"; the words *Saints* or *holy* hanging unspoken. The framer of the Regulations could see no rational cause for clinging to mere tradition. Furthermore, the Regulations insisted that since eminent (noble) Brethren found it inconvenient to be "in Town" either for midsummer (heat, stench, and disease) or the winter solstice (too cold, too busy on the estates hunting, and so on), ordinary Brethren should no longer expect a St. John the Baptist (or Evangelist) feast. Such, Brethren were informed, was good for the "Fraternity." What kind of "Fraternity" had emerged was evident to a number of rebel Freemasons. By 1751 they had had enough of the novel, earnest, Whiggish encroachments of the Grand Lodge.

Enter the "Antients."

In 1751, a group of predominantly Irish-born Freemasons met together at the Turk's Head in Greek Street, Soho, London, to form a rival "Antient Grand Lodge of England," claiming to be in accord with the "Old Constitutions" perverted by the Grand Lodge of England. Laurence Dermott wrote the Antients' new Constitutions, called *Ahiman Rezon*. In them, he strongly advocated the Royal Arch degree for Masons.

The Royal Arch ritual, probably of Irish provenance, underscored and illuminated the spiritual Christian content of Accepted Freemasonry. Contrary to the "Premier" Grand Lodge, the Antients declared the Royal Arch authentic Masonry, denied to members of the novel, even if apparently older, Grand Lodge. The Royal Arch caught on fast—Dermott called it the "root and marrow" of Masonry—and the Antients became popular, especially among members of the armed services. Indeed, it was chiefly by that agency that the Masonry of the Antients came to be vigorously transplanted into the American colonies, where it flourished, albeit in tension with Lodges chartered by the older, if not ancient, Order. The Antients' existence fostered a spirit of independence, if not rebelliousness, from Hanoverian government control in the colonies.

It may be inferred that St. John the Baptist had something to do with some American colonists' desire for independence.

Published in 1756, *Ahiman Rezon* gave voice to the significance for Masons of the figure of St. John the Baptist. Page 150 of the book asked Masons to consider how "the stern integrity of Saint John the Baptist, which induced him to forego every minor consideration in discharging the obligations he owed to God; the unshaken firmness with which he met martyrdom rather than betray his duty to his Master; his steady reproval of vice, and continued preaching of repentance and virtue, make him a fit patron of the Masonic institution."

But for the martyrdom, he sounds somewhat like the deified image of George Washington.

The Antients' continued niggling presense eventually forced the Premier Grand Lodge of England to enter into negotiations for amalgamation, although by 1813, when the main negotiations took place, London's Premier Grand Lodge was unlikely to regain loyalty from Masons dwelling in the now independent American colonies. Nevertheless, London continued to charter Lodges in the United States, notably to black-skinned Masons whose aspirations were rejected by indigenous Lodges, whose enlightenment program was racially selective.

It is highly significant that during the discussions that led to the eventual establishment of the United Grand Lodge of England (under the Grand Mastership of the younger son of George III), one of the notable sticking points was the Antients' objection that the so-called Moderns were ignoring Saints Days, in particular the feast day of St. John the Baptist, the day established for the election of Grand Masters. To a limited degree, the Antients appeared to get their way at the amalgamation. From the time of the union of the two Grand Lodges on December 27, 1813 (St. John the Evangelist's Day!), the date of June 24 would be honored for that particular administrative function. Overt consideration of St. John the Baptist himself, however, has vanished from British Craft Freemasonry—just one of many "holes" in the contemporary Order, an Order that has wilfully reduced its ideological and intellectual significance to that of a mere "fraternal society" whose members are distinguished by a powerful— if to outsiders curious—urge to improve themselves morally. To modern observers it must appear that any reference to St. John the Baptist's Day is merely coincidental to the date of Midsummer and the proximity of June 24 to the cosmic solstice, while even that latter relic of science might sound a little "pagan" to contemporary British Masonic authority, keen to scrub itself into a spotlessness verging on the vacuous.

How then can we account for, first, the connection between the Baptist and old Free Masons' customs and, second, the link between John the Baptist and the traditional Midsummer feasting—bearing in mind, as we shall see, that these questions really overlap one another?

ST. JOHN THE BAPTIST AS LORD OF THE FEAST

We have established that St. John the Baptist was important to Free Masons both before and after the establishment of the first Grand Lodge (1716–1723). The Baptist was not important to Free Masons alone. Can we locate what it was about the Baptist that people—and Masons in particular—found so appealing?

This is no simple matter. There were no vox-pop TV or radio interviews in days gone by, asking ordinary people why they liked or did certain things. We can only assemble a rough jigsaw and see if an authentic pattern is discernible within the fragments.

One thing is clear. It did not take Copernicus and the sixteenth- and seventeenth-century scientific revolution to convince ordinary people of the central significance of the *sun* to their lives. Whether the sun went around the Earth or the Earth went around the sun, the sun was still obviously the source of light, and people could see that without the sun, nothing could grow.

Midsummer, when the sun was closest to the Earth and the days were longest was a very special time to our ancestors. Their lives and consciousness were intimately bound up with the cycles of nature. If religion was to have any meaning for this life, its inseparability from nature had to be perceived and acted on. Indeed, most people saw no clear distinction between spiritual and natural activity, except to say that people normally imagined spiritual forces could do for nature what nature could not do alone. Nature could bow to the miraculous. For many people, certain phases of natural processes looked fairly miraculous anyhow; the forces of death and decay had to be overcome. If one failed to thank God and his saints and angels for springtime, sunshine, rain, and harvest, they might not come again, or at least, they might fail, with starvation, death, and disease the result.

So we can perhaps see that the old church's placing of St. John the Baptist's birthday at Midsummer was a masterstroke. Apart from the idea that Luke's Gospel implied that John was born some six months before Jesus (whose "official" birthday of December 25 more or less marked the winter solstice, that is, the beginning of the sun's "return"), the placing of John the Baptist at the crux of the Midsummer festivities gathered all the residual "pagan" ideas of the season and gave them an ecclesiastically solemnized coating and direction. Furthermore, it did not, presumably, pass some smart people's notice that this association of the Baptist with Midsummer was no mere arbitrary placing of an acceptable saint over a pagan (that is, "country") festival; there were certain unmistakable internal resonances between the known figure of John the Baptist and the beliefs of countless ordinary people in relation to Midsummer that magically activated that link.

The first and most obvious resonance between date and saint is the tradition that John was a man who lived "under the sun." The sun at its most witheringly merciless produces the desert; John made the straight path visible in the desert, a place of extraordinary, sometimes blinding, light. It is a place associated with vision, visionaries, and illumination: a place also of purity, of voluntary hardship, and suffering or preparation to receive light.

As a result of his reputation, John was also associated with the so-called "desert fathers": men such as St. Antony, the demon-haunted hermit who established desert life as an ideal in Egypt in the third century, thus inadvertently generating the practice of Christian monasticism, the life of self-denial or asceticism, that is, *training*.

At the twelfth-century Chapel and Hospital of St. John the Baptist in Lichfield, England, for example, the hospital sign today features a *tau* cross (like a "T"), representing the Baptist. This is not a normal sign associated with John. I long wondered if it was the cross with its "head," as it were, removed, since John was traditionally beheaded.

A little research suggested that the symbol may have derived from involvement with the Franciscan friary next door to the hospital. The Franciscan friary was just *inside* the "barrs" or gates of Lichfield; the Hospital of St. John the Baptist was established "outside the Barrs": just outside, in fact. Apart from a fear of disease, this position may also have been significant in assigning the Baptist's patronage to the hospital: the world outside, the wilderness, the world of the itinerant and journeyman. Medieval masons were trade journeymen, not bound to place but free to travel: outsiders who made wildernesses bloom in stone as they journeyed from lodge to lodge and built the monasteries, cathedrals, castles, chapels, and bridges of the Middle Ages: St. John's men.

The Hospital of St. John the Baptist in Lichfield also took pilgrims in at the gates of the city, offering shelter and beer. Pilgrims journeyed great distances to Lichfield to see the relics of St. Chad at the city's cathedral inside its massive protective walls. There is a symbolic connection between the gates to the holy place and baptism, the "password" to salvation. As we shall see, John the Baptist was also linked to healing: the function of holy relics.

St. Francis of Assisi, spiritual father of the friary next door to the hospital, respected the desert fathers, especially St. Antony. St. Antony's staff is usually represented as a "tau" (τ). Franciscans maintain that St. Francis took the tau as a special symbol for his brotherhood because he was impressed by a reading from Ezekiel 9:4–6 (see also Exodus 12:1):

> Pass through the city [Jerusalem] and mark a tav [the Hebrew letter "T"] on the foreheads of those who moan and groan over all the abominations that are practiced within it. To the others I heard him say: "Pass through the city after them and strike! . . . . Old men, youths and maidens, women and children, wipe them out. But do not touch anyone marked with the tav."

The "tav" or "tau" is a sign of the saved, of the redeemed. And, of course, the outward symbol of redemption in the Christian religion has always been baptism. Through the Franciscans and the Order of St. Antony, the "tau cross" became linked to the establishment of hospitals, which were a kind of oasis in the desert of Christian suffering.

The twelfth-century Winchester Psalter contains an illustration of John baptizing Jesus while an angel waits on the riverbank, holding a garment drawn in the outline of a tau—the left and right arms of the "T" forming the sleeves. The garment symbolizes salvation, the "new life" given through baptism. The idea of rebirth is strongly implied, while the holy, healing waters of the Jordan symbolize life and hope flowing into the desert and the deserted.

John is often depicted carrying an image of the "Lamb of God" holding a flag with a red cross on it, the cross of sacrifice. This image derives from the Gospel of John (1:29): "The next day John seeth Jesus coming unto him, and saith, 'Behold the Lamb of God, which taketh away the sin of the world.'"

The idea of the "lamb" derives in part from Genesis (chapter 22) where Isaac asks his father, "Where is the lamb for a burnt offering?" not knowing that his father, Abraham, has been told by God to sacrifice his son: he, Isaac, the son, is the intended offering. As a ram stands in for Isaac's sacrifice, in God's mercy, so the "lamb" that is the messiah will, according to John's text, "take away" the sin that in accordance with God's laws ought to condemn humankind to death. The "lamb" is also the lamb sacrificed at Passover in Egypt when the Lord "hovered over" or "guarded" the homes of those Hebrews whose lintels bore the tav, the sign of salvation from God's judgment, made in the blood of the slaughtered lamb (see Exodus 12:3).

Since sickness and death were seen in medieval Europe to be rooted in human sin, so, in religious hospitals—there were no other kind—healing required sufferers to concentrate on the life-giving powers of the "Lamb of God." John the Baptist pointed the sinner and the sick toward their redemption and healing. The first condition of healing in a religious establishment was, therefore, "Repent!" or turn around to God, let oneself go in faith: the traditional word uttered in the wilderness of parched hopes and spiritual clarity by John, whose hands carried the sinner beneath the healing or "living waters" to the life above them.

Further confirmation of the very personal association of John's word to the fears and the healing of medieval men and women, whether bound to city or village, or at liberty to journey, may be found in some very rare "pendant capsules" discovered by chance in northern England and in the Netherlands. These precious capsules, just over an inch long, are tiny pendants fashioned in gold, precious jewels, and enamel. Originally opened to reveal some holy relic or healing substance, the pendant capsules were inscribed with painstakingly executed images of God the Father, Son, Holy Ghost, Virgin Mary, St. Antony—and

John the Baptist. One example found at Winteringham in North Lincolnshire is in the clear form of a tau cross: a clear call for protection on life's journey from the judgment due to the sinner, and not the only example of its kind.

A diamond-shaped pendant capsule found at Middleham Castle, Yorkshire, dated ca. 1475–1485, has an inscription on the obverse edge that reads *Ecce agnus dei qui tollis* [sic] *peccata* [sic] *mundi miserere nobis,* followed by the words *tetragrammaton ananyzapta.* The first phrase is a Latin rendering of the words attributed in John's Gospel to John the Baptist (John 1:29), "Behold the Lamb of God who taketh away the sins of the world." The words *miserere nobis,* "have mercy upon us," are taken from the eucharistic liturgy and show that Christ's sacrifice for the redemption of sinners is continued through the sacraments of the church where the sinner is pointed toward the "Lamb of God" or *Agnus Dei.* The figure of the Lamb of God, holding the red-cross pennant, is the symbol most associated with John the Baptist. It is clearly depicted below a Nativity scene on the reverse of the pendant. Perhaps the capsule once contained a wax wafer stamped with the *Agnus Dei,* which carried a papal blessing.

It is almost certain that the pendant would also have served as a magical amulet, to ward off evil powers. It features a sapphire, symbol of the pure soul, traditional protector from peril of poisoning or blindness. The reference to the "tetragrammaton" (the four Hebrew letters of God's name) followed by the word *ananyzapta* demonstrates the pendant's magical value. We know from magical texts of the period that the word *ananyzapta* or *ananyzaptus* was widely repeated as an incantation against falling sickness or epilepsy. More prosaically, it was employed as an antidote to hangovers.

THE KNIGHTS HOSPITALLER

The most striking link between St. John the Baptist and the world of medieval medicine may be found amid the extensive activities of the Knights Hospitaller, sometimes called the Knights of St. John. Persisting to this day as the Sovereign Military Order of Malta, based in Rome, the massive medieval organization was first founded in Jerusalem, whence it moved to Rhodes, then Malta.

In 1023, eighteen years after Muslim zealots destroyed a Christian hospital for pilgrims in Jerusalem, a body of Italian merchants obtained Caliph Ali az-Zahir of Egypt's permission to rebuild the hospital on the site of the monastery of St. John the Baptist. The site's sacredness to John appears to explain the adoption of St. John's patronage by the knightly order, which would run side by side with the monastic hospitaller order, founded after the first Crusade in 1113 by Gerard the Blessed. Gerard expanded his order throughout the new Norman Kingdom of Jerusalem, a program augmented by Raymond du Puy de Provence, his successor. Raymond established a new hospital adjacent to the Church of the Holy Sepulchre. When the order began providing armed protection for pilgrims, there emerged a private army and health service combined. Because it attracted chivalry from all over the Western world, the Holy Roman Emperor Frederick Barbarossa granted the expanding order a charter of privileges in 1185. Frederick received the blessings of the Baptist for his pledge of protection.

The Hospitallers have often been confused with the "Poor Knights of the Temple" or Knights Templar who appeared during the same period. The Templars wore a red cross on a white background. Initially distinguished by a black surcoat with a white cross, the Hospitallers adopted a red surcoat with a white cross with Pope Innocent IV's approval in 1248. Complementary colors notwithstanding, Templars and Hospitallers remained institutional rivals, though their differences were glossed over by eighteenth-century Masonic apologists for "Templar-Masonry." That the Templars were dedicated not to St. John but to St. Mary the Virgin, for example, was obscured. However, since the Hospitallers obtained much of the property, and some of the membership, of the Templars after that order's suppression for unholy vice in 1312, it could be argued that there was a quasi-Templar persistense under the patronage of St. John. If Hospitallers in their priories ever wondered at the time whether St. John had redeemed the sins of the Templar knight sinners by extending his care to their collective goods, we know nothing of it.

Where the Rev. James Anderson in London in 1738 supposed that the knightly orders owed their origin to "Masonry" (they had "Grand Masters"–built castles, chapels, and churches and were monastic orders), the pro-Jacobite, romantic Freemason Chevalier Ramsay had declared *au contraire* from Paris the previous year of (1737), that the real Masonic Order was actually derived from the medieval knightly orders (Templars and Hospitallers being implied), whose precepts of chivalry should govern a revived, and almost certainly pro-Jacobite, Masonry. Ramsay's "Oration" would in due course germinate that "Templar Masonry" whose "Knight-Masons" are still with us, albeit strangers to the Middle Ages.

Indeed, all of this eighteenth-century romancing and infra-Masonic pugnacity and one-upmanship was remote from the experience of medieval freestone masons and all of the other, and no less proud, trades and walks of life, for whom the dramatic—and even jovial—figure of St. John the Baptist was close.

Taking St. John the Baptist as one's patron saint in the days before the Reformation carried myriad blessings. The old freestone masons in their guilds, congregations, and chapters were hardly alone in desiring the Baptist's patronage. Nevertheless, the fact remains that all we know for sure about pre-eighteenth-century relations between St. John the Baptist and British freemasons, whether "admitted" persons from genteel backgrounds or associated trades, or working master masons and their companies, is that the Midsummer Feast of St. John the Baptist was important to them. For how long this had been so, or whether other saints days, including that of St. John the Evangelist, meant much to them, we do not know. (St. John Evangelist was patron saint of Edinburgh Stonemasons.) However, since Midsummer festivities were popular throughout Britain and the continent of Europe, we can hardly suppose that freestone masons or "freemasons"—as masons of freestone were called from at least the end of the thirteenth century—made a point of absenting themselves from the general enjoyment. The question of precisely what masons *as masons* saw in the Baptist can only, in truth, be speculated on, though, as we shall see further, there was much resonance between the symbolic figure of John the Baptist and what we know of Masonic ideals, though, in written form, from considerably later in history.

After all the emphasis on hospitals, sickness, Saracens, and salvation, it comes as a relief to know that St. John was probably most associated with the happy, joyous side of life in its naturalness, as well as, if not more than, the deeper meaning of it all.

Before the continental Reformation blew up the Western Christian Church, June 24 was marked in Britain by the appearance of pulpits in the open air, decorated with boughs and green candles. Fires were lit in the open, accompanied, said critics, by "heathen rejoicing." We can be certain that the guardians of Hanoverian *harmony* would not have liked that.

Not only were ordinary folk caught up in sexy, Midsummer frolics of the *Carmina Burana* kind, whole regions and institutions in Europe had cause to celebrate. The Baptist was the patron of Burgundy, Malta, and Provence. He was patron saint of Florence and Amiens, as well as of weavers, tailors, tanners, shepherds, furriers, and of brotherhoods to support the condemned (John had been imprisoned and executed). There were relics of St. John's head in St. Silvestro in Rome (ca. 1400), Maastricht, Quarante, Montpellier (ca. 1440), St. Johann in Aachen-Burtscheid, and St. Bavo in Ghent (built on a tenth-century chapel of St. John the Baptist). John's relics could look forward to an outing for public veneration on the saint's day.

Midsummer Eve was a day of blessing, a lucky day, especially for suckling babes who, weaned on that day, could look forward to a life on the sunshine side; Midsummer was a good time to get married, to conceive a child, to roll sparse-clad on the ground, or to participate, discreetly, in magic rites of fertility and purification. In the German town of Leobschutz in Silesia, John himself blessed the flowers picked in his honor on Midsummer Eve; in Bohemia, a prayer was said to John as "his" flowers were picked before being mixed with animal fodder, while a baby baptized on St. John's Day in the region was more blessed than if the infant had received a thousand thalers.* St. John's Day was a good day for reconciliation of folk in conflict.

A good time was had by all; John's band was a happy band.

HERALD OF THE HARVEST

Why had John the Baptist been chosen by the church to rule over the summer solstice, our closest brush with the sun? Was it only to Christianize pagan solstice feasting and frolicking?

Let us see.

The solstice coincides with what used to be called the "honey moon," the origin of our costly nuptial abandon. The time of the honey moon was the *best* time to harvest honey. A marble figure attributed to Michelangelo's workshop, now in the Kaiser Friedrich Museum, Berlin, depicts a youthful John the Baptist gracefully gazing at a honeycomb held in his left hand (an allusion to John's wild honey diet; Mark 1:6). One wonders if this Midsummer link to honey may have informed the traditional idea of Masons as "busy bees." As we have seen, Midsummer was a favored time both for marriage and for birth.

If we look carefully at the Gospels of Matthew and Luke, we see that John the Baptist is explicitly presented there as the *herald of the harvest*—though John points to no ordinary harvest:

> But when he saw many of the Pharisees and Sadducees come to
> his baptism, he said unto them, O generation of vipers, who hath

---

*[Silver coins issued by various German states from the fifteenth to nineteenth centuries —*Ed.*]

warned you to flee from the wrath to come? Bring forth therefore fruits meet for repentance: And think not to say within yourselves, we have Abraham to our father: for I say unto you, that God is able of these stones to raise up children unto Abraham. And now also the axe is laid unto the root of the trees: therefore every tree, which bringeth forth not good fruit, is hewn down and cast into the fire.

I indeed baptize you with water unto repentance: but he that cometh after me is mightier than I, whose shoes I am not worthy to bear: he shall baptize you with the Holy Ghost, and with fire.

Whose fan is in his hand, and he will thoroughly purge his floor, and gather his wheat into the garner: but he will burn up the chaff with unquenchable fire. (Matthew 3:7–12)

In the ancient East, midsummer marked the time when Tammuz, the comely vegetation god, would be cut as the wheat was reaped and women would weep for Tammuz's separation from his consort Astarte or Ishtar, Venus, the Morning Star of Love, the dawning light in the fields—symbolized in Masonry as the star of hope.

It is undoubtedly significant then that the "spring" wheat harvest in Israel takes place in the third sacred month, Sivan, from May to June, when the Feast of Weeks or *Hag Hashavuot* is celebrated: called "Weeks" because it occurs seven weeks after Passover. Christians celebrate "Pentecost" as the time of the coming on the apostles of the Holy Spirit, but "Pentecost" refers originally to the Feast of Weeks, being the *fiftieth* day (from the Greek *pentēcostē*) from the 14th Nisan, the beginning of Passover. Pentecost is also known as *Hag Hakatzir,* the "Feast of Harvest." Most striking is the name *Yom Habikkurim,* also given to the feast. It means "the Day of the First Fruits," marking the appearance of the first fruits of the summer harvest (see Numbers 28:26).

Leviticus 23:14 ruled that the children of Israel could not enjoy their harvest until the first fruits had been dedicated to God in gratitude for saving the people. At the time of John the Baptist, the Feast of

Weeks was a major festival requiring every covenanted man in the land to visit the Temple in Jerusalem. There the wheat offering would be made in the form of two loaves of leavened bread shown to the assembled in a priestly ritual. An act of atonement was made. Vicarious offering of lambs, bulls, and rams emphasized that an innocent victim was required to remove sin from the people. Sin was a "quantity," and it had *to be seen* to go somewhere to render the covenanted pure before the Lord. The need for blood is made clear in Leviticus 17:11, "For the life of a creature is in the blood, and I have given it to you to make atonement for yourselves on the altar; it is the blood that makes atonement for one's life."

Suddenly, we can see what the historical John the Baptist meant by his attack on his country's religious leaders. We can also see another reason why John's birthday was placed at the auspicious time of Midsummer. John summoned his hearers to offer "fruits meet for repentance." God wanted a first fruits feast-offering not merely of symbolic grain and the blood of dumb animals, but of the living hearts of his people.

The coming "wrath" is the spiritual harvest, the "gathering-in" of God's people; there will be purging, threshing. The righteous, destined for the divine feast, will be winnowed from the unrepentant heading for destruction. Regardless of their ancestors' part in the Mosaic or Abrahamic covenants, should the fruits be unacceptable, the whole tree will be torn up, *roots and all,* as farmers must do periodically if they wish to maintain the health of crops and livestock. If representative of his actual position, John's words would have made a powerful, shocking impression on even the most hard-hearted and stiff-necked of his hearers. As John's message is presented in Matthew's Gospel, there is not an inch of room for compromise. John was on a collision course with the "way of the world."

John the Baptist, if not necessarily the "Lord of the Harvest" (as he must have appeared to our medieval ancestors), is certainly presented in Matthew's text as an overseer and initiator of the divine harvesting process and the stand-alone herald of its completion.

Churchmen in the past presumably read the account of John's prophecy of the great and terrible "gathering into the garner" and observed that its language made most obvious sense around the time of the feast of first fruits, the Feast of Weeks. Since we may surmise that it was not liturgically appropriate to confuse John the herald's message with, arguably, the spiritual fulfillment of that message at the Christian Pentecost, it made sense to place John's birthday at Midsummer. Further justification for positioning the holy day at Midsummer may be found in Luke 1:36 where the angel Gabriel not only informs an astonished Mary that she is about to become pregnant, but tells her that her elderly cousin Elizabeth is already six months gone! Taking six months after John's birthday on June 24 brings us nicely to the traditional Christmas and the hopeful winter solstice as the sun begins to come closer to the Earth once more. The herald's birth and the birth of the promise's fulfillment neatly divide the Christian liturgical year.

If it be cavilled that the date of the Jewish Feast of Weeks and of the Christian Pentecost may fall in late May or early June, it should be considered that the Western wheat and barley harvest occurs in late August and September, with wine being harvested as late as October. In this respect, it seems hardly a coincidence that the Catholic date for celebrating the *beheading*, as distinct from the *birth*, of John the Baptist is August 29, a date that should give us pause, tying in, as it does, the entire body of symbolism that links John the Baptist to the Great Harvest, not only as prophet and herald, but *in himself*, and in his own bloody "fruit": the sacrifice of his life for truth.

John the Baptist's head was traditionally severed from his body, and God accepted his blood, while the shedding of that blood, as we shall see, became a judgment on his and God's enemies. The beheading of John became linked to a profound *archetype*, rooted in ancient conceptions of the head of wheat and barleycorn being severed to fulfill the promise of life and abundance for the people, to provide thank-offering to God, and as the necessary act in the cycle of birth and rebirth, of life and death.

Death is life's door.

English folklore preserves songs both solemn and knowing for the necessary death of the symbolic John Barleycorn. *"John Barleycorn must die"* goes the ballad, known once, tellingly, as "The Passion of the Corn." He—the barleycorn—is beheaded, as the Bible tells us that the Baptist was beheaded at the behest of a maiden fair.

Readers may be familiar with the version of the lyric that opens this chapter. It was set to music by Stevie Winwood and his friends in the group Traffic and has entertained and influenced folk seeking a spiritual harvest rooted more in nature than in orthodox theology.

It seems hard to avoid the conclusion that the "John" of the mythic John Barleycorn is in some profound sense a projection of John the Baptist, who, like Barleycorn, "must die," who though dead, rises again and annually must die to be raised once more:

> *They've let him lie for a very long time, 'til the rains*
> *from heaven did fall,*
> *And little Sir John sprung up his head and so amazed*
> *them all.*
> *They've let him stand 'til Midsummer's Day 'til he*
> *looked both pale and wan;*
> *And little Sir John's grown a long long beard and so*
> *become a man.*
> *They've hired men with their scythes so sharp to cut*
> *him off at the knee.*
> *They've rolled him and tied him by the waist serving*
> *him most barbarously.*
> *They've hired men with their sharp pitchforks who've*
> *pricked him to the heart—*
> *And the loader he has served him worse than that,*
> *For he's bound him to the cart.*

They've wheeled him around and around a field 'til
> *they came unto a barn,*
And there they made a solemn oath on poor John
> *Barleycorn.*
They've hired men with their crabtree sticks to cut
> *him skin from bone—*
And the miller he has served him worse than that,
For he's ground him between two stones.

We can clearly see why the song was once known as "The Passion of the Corn." We have the themes of death, sacrifice, and resurrection played out in nature, just as St. Paul insisted that the "type" for Christian resurrection could be seen in the seed that must first fall to the earth and die before being raised in a new form (1 Corinthians 15:36–44). What held as law in nature was held most true of nature's source and living sustenance, the world of spirit.

Before we leave John Barleycorn raised again in the barley-life of bread and beer and life and joy, we should take a look at a version of the song penned by poet, and Freemason, Robert Burns (1759–1796). Burns's version is very similar to that above, but there are, I think, a couple of Masonic giveaways that make one wonder if Robbie was not himself, in heart at least, one of "St. John's Men." For a start, the necessary attacks on poor John are presented with more emphasis than is usual as being acts primarily of *premeditated murder*. When John begins to look "wan and pale" before harvest, his "enemies" begin to "shew their deadly rage":

They laid him down upon his back,
And cudgell'd him full sore;
They hung him up before the storm,
And turn'd him o'er and o'er.

They filled up a darksome pit

With water to the brim,
They heaved in John Barleycorn,
There let him sink or swim.

They laid him out upon the floor,
To work him further woe,
And still, as signs of life appear'd,
They tossed him to and fro.

The treatment of John has a decidedly ritualistic air to it. One is reminded of the eighteenth-century accounts current after the appearance in Grand Lodge of England lodges of the Masonic Third Degree. Practiced by about 1730, a Third Degree ceremony apparently featured "Hiram Abif," the central hero of Grand Lodge Freemasonry. Hiram Abif was understood as the master craftsman who, having given his best to Solomon's Temple, gave also his life. Refusing to part with his master secrets, Hiram was progressively struck about head and body by three jealous, wicked underlings: a series of three symbolic and finally fatal attacks. Burns's reference to John being thrown in a pit is reminiscent of old Scottish Masonic practice of lowering, or even casting, the Third Degree Candidate into an open grave, a ritual reenactment of Hiram's allegorical death and burial.

The Masonic "festive board" following the ceremony is perhaps suggested in the following lines:

And they hae ta'en his very heart's blood,
And drank it round and round;
And still the more and more they drank,
Their joy did more abound.

John Barleycorn was a hero bold,
Of noble enterprise,
For if you do but taste his blood,

'Twill make your courage rise,
'Twill make a man forget his woe;
'Twill heighten all his joy:
'Twill make the widow's heart to sing,
Tho' the tear were in her eye.

No Mason could miss that last reference to the "widow." Masons have long been known as the "sons of the widow" in honor of master craftsman Hiram, called in the Bible "a widow's son," while also remembering that it was the lady of Tammuz, Astarte or Ishtar, who was left a grieving widow at the annual death of her consort Tammuz, at least for a season or two. Furthermore, we may read of the actual *raising* of the widow's son from the dead by the Prophet Elijah in 1 Kings 17. Elijah is of course completely identified with John the Baptist in Matthew 11, the messenger of the coming "harvest." The widow's son is raised by Elijah's stretching himself over the dead boy's body thrice in a movement reminiscent of modern 3rd Degree ritual. John is profoundly linked to the idea of resurrection and rebirth.

John Barleycorn must die so he may live again, raised in bread and beer.

John must face his 3rd Degree.

We should know that according to the Bible, Solomon's Temple—the House of God first erected on Mount Moriah—was built on the site of a threshing floor bought from a Jebusite, a fitting place to receive the blessing of abundance after the symbolically suggestive process of cutting, threshing, winnowing, chaff burning, and grinding—or separation, rejection, acceptance, and transformation.

In the words of Psalm 24, "Who may ascend the mountain of the Lord? He who has clean hands and a pure heart." Could this explain the age-old practice of Masons wearing gloves? The pointing of a pair of dividers to the heart to assess the heart's purity is a well-known part of the ceremony for taking an "Entered Apprentice" into masonic fraternity.

Would we be wrong to imagine that the old "St. John's Men" might, in such a circumstance, have thought of John the Baptist, Lord or patron of the Midsummer threshing?

The wrathful threshing of which Matthew has the Baptist speak is prefigured in the text of Daniel 2, where we find a reference not merely to "clean hands" but to a stone so supernaturally cut as to be the work of "no hands" at all: "Thou sawest that a stone was cut out without hands, which smote the image upon his feet that were of iron and clay, and break them in pieces." The "image" represented the might of a worldly empire that had turned its back on God. Note that all the power of this world, the iron, the clay, the brass, even the silver and gold "became like the chaff of the summer threshing floors; and the wind carried them away, that no place was found for them: and the stone that smote the image became a great mountain, and filled the whole earth."

Was Jesus thinking of this prophecy, I wonder, when he renamed his follower Simon, "Cephas," a stone? (John 1:42)

The God declared by the Baptist is not content with the *image;* he wants the sacred reality, whatever it takes. In the desert everything is burnt clean to a bareness, a clarity. There is day and night, hot and cold, life and death. It seems that the older freemasons respected St. John. For where did the Masons first call their lodge?

"At the holy chapel of St. John."

The wilderness is where the path will be made straight. *Have we reached it yet?* John stands straight in the wilderness, pointing the way of return to the divine temple. And the path, being really an ascent, may be very hard—though never so hard, in the end, John tells us, as the path of not finding it.

Is John a forgotten "Masonic Exemplar" extraordinary?

It might seem so. But what has history to say of him?

Chapter Three

JOHN THE BAPTIST
IN HISTORY AND
TRADITION

FINDING THE "REAL" JOHN THE BAPTIST is rather like looking for a particular triplet in a crowd of look-alikes. We have already encountered two rather distinct Johns. We have brushed shoulders with the John of mythology whose role is a mythic one, concerned with eternal cycles and subconscious archetypes. This John has something of Hermes, Dionysus, Hiram Abif, and the "Green Man" about him. If his nostrils are not exactly bursting with chlorophyll-pumping tendrils of burgeoning vigor, they are not really filled with the fresh, rushing air of the morning mountains of first-century Judea either.

In addition to "mythological John," we have also become lightly acquainted with "theological John." In Christian theology, John plays a role as "support act," if I may use the phrase, for Jesus. John points men toward Jesus and offers a quick introduction to the imminence of crisis for Israel and the world: a coming judgment. He calls his nation to "repentance" while simultaneously, according to the Gospels, denigrating his own role in the impending drama. In the Gospel narratives, John can't seem to wait to write himself out of the play, as though subject to a theological curfew.

Before his apparently timely departure from this world, John introduces us to the concept of baptism, which, after him, will acquire its status as a fundamental feature of the lives of millions and millions of Earth-born souls.

Baptisms happen because John existed.

For the majority of Christians, baptism is the moment when the newborn receives a *name,* an identity, and a promise. We do not hear much about baptism in the Old Testament, apart from the story of Naaman being healed by seven immersions in the Jordan (2 Kings 5:10–14), but the New Testament is rooted, if not immersed, in baptism. Baptism appears as John's "thing," his *métier.*

The Baptist has become possessed by a church of which, we may presume, he knew nothing.

Now, both the mythological John and the theological John are manifest to us as reflections of the *historical* John. This third John, *the John of historical actuality,* is extremely elusive, as historical figures must be when, already in their lifetimes, they acquire mythic, legendary, spiritual status. Such is the case with the remarkably anti-*status quo* Baptist, the outsider who, like Moses, called the people *out.* Even as he spoke, people, powerful people, asked who he *was,* rather like the soldier on the motorcycle by the Nile who, catching sight of a distant Major T. E. Lawrence in David Lean's film *Lawrence of Arabia,* shouts repeatedly at the prophet-like figure emerging from the Sinai desert: "Who *are* you?" Lawrence himself is not sure how to answer, and neither are we.

People wanted to know who John was even when they could see him with their eyes. His identity mattered deeply to them. *Who was he? Where had he come from?* Questions of history, we might think. Even as he lived, John evoked in people the power of mythic imagination. You would think such a mystery man, such a great man, would stand head and shoulders above the dross of time and compel, if not inspire, the scribe to make historical record of him.

And such is the case.

The difficulty, as usual in such cases, lies in trying to assess the motives of the scribe, who, in this case, is Josephus, Jewish historian and pro-Roman collaborator.

No man looks the same to the enemy as he does to the friend. Men "like John," men who attract a large following, are perennially exploited to serve the interests of other persons and causes indifferent to the authentic nature of the "man himself." It should be observed that in the history of the Middle East, a man is defined chiefly by his adherence to the cause to which he has attached himself, or has been attached; there is little interest in the "hidden man" or self-conscious psyche as has become familiar to the aficionados of modern biography. The archetypal hero has no right to a private life. The life of a saint will tell us of the saintly things we should expect, the devotion to the cause, and not anything that might obscure or detract from that. Saints are censored by their celebrants. In the ancient world, especially in the East, records of people's lives generally tend to portray people as being either good or bad, we hear nothing of ambiguities or *why* they were good or bad. There is no sentimentality about "tragic failures." You're either in or you're out.

Here is just one hitherto unnoticed example of a tension between theological John and historical John. I hope it helps to illuminate the problem faced in seeking the "real John."

In Matthew's Gospel, John declares God can make children of Abraham, that is, inheritors of Abraham's promise, from the stones of the ground if needs be. If the promise is to be fulfilled, the "children of Abraham" must turn again to God. This is all familiar territory.

However, by the "children of Abraham," if the saying's historicity is granted, John would almost certainly have included Idumaean Arabs who were ruling parts of Israel, with the consent and under the control of the Romans. Known as the Herodian dynasty, King Herod the Great and his sons and grandsons were of Idumaean-Arab stock who intermarried with Judean, Nabataean, and Egyptian aristocracy—as well as with their own. They were circumcised and accepted the Jewish religion. As being of Arab descent, they could trace their ancestry to Ishmael, Abraham's first son. You would not notice this inference without hard knowledge about the political facts of Palestine in the first century. It is not apparent from the text of the Gospels.

As a result of the gospel writers' point of view, and that of their audiences, the political facts of the period are, in *very many* important respects, ignored. So, in the case described here, no one who lived after the collapse of the Herodian (Idumaean-Jewish) dynasty, and who was ignorant of the political history, would think of asking the question, *Who was John referring to when he spoke of "children of Abraham" being raised from the stones?* Was it, as we usually take it, an attack on Judean apostasy and alleged sins of Sadducees and Pharisees in particular, or was John specifically threatening the *ruling dynasty*, who, we know, were both proud of and defensive about *their* Abrahamic roots? Or was John warning both rulers and ruled together?

The theological John bypasses such concerns completely.

Indeed, the theological John muddies the issues even more. For if we consider "theological John" as a later Christian reflection on "historical John," we may be inclined to read John's jibe about God being able to make inheritors of the Abrahamic promise *at will*—even, as he declares, out of common stones—less as a taunt to the pride of Judeans or Herodians, and more as a future-seeing encouragement to *Gentile Christians*. If God wills it, Gentiles can become, as from the olive stone, a *new tree*, a holy plantation of the covenanted faithful. Gentiles need not be disturbed by any Jewish taunt that being uncircumcised, they have no right to the promises of Abraham and the prophets on account of the Gentile Church's rejecting, at Paul's instruction, adherence to the Torah or Jewish Law as the means to righteousness.

When brought into the Christian theological perspective, John's attack on the rulers of his time may be interpreted, then, not only as a condemnation of those who reject Jesus as Messiah, but as a *prophecy* of the *Gentiles* receiving the first fruits of God's salvation. It should be remarked that this interpretation may not have been in the mind of the writer of Matthew. Matthew's original audience was probably Jewish-Christian and respected the Law, but Matthew soon circulated throughout the Gentile Church. Among Gentiles, it was doubtless interpreted to support the widespread Pauline anticircumcision position in Asia Minor, Greece, Rome, North Africa, and beyond, even unto today.

In short, the Gospels fail to give us the signifying political context in which the events they describe take place. *Fail,* however, is arguably the wrong word, since there is no sign that conveying political realities was ever an intention of the gospel writers in the first place. The Gospels do not share the priorities of the historian—and *vice versa.* While such a riposte may be employed to defend the Gospels from the charge of fabrication, whether of events or words, it is not altogether certain that the Gospels' lack of conventional historical meat is altogether innocent, as we shall see. It is also doubtful whether the gospel writers—and certainly their readers and hearers—*understood* the nature of the political situation in Palestine during the period of John the Baptist's life anyway. A cataclysm of incalculable proportions had occurred between the time of those events and the sixty-year period in which, in the main, the canonical Gospels came into circulation (70–130 CE).

So where can we find the "historical John?"

JOSEPHUS

If we had asked the Umayyad Caliph al-Walid I (668–715 CE) where we could find the historical John, he would doubtless have pointed us in the direction of his city, Damascus, having informed us with some pride that the head of Yahya (as John is known to Arabs) had lately been rescued from the earth where destruction of the prophet's former resting place had consigned it. It was now placed in a Damascene pillar whose capital was carved into the form of a basket of palm leaves. That head was the most significant part of the historical John, and thanks to the veneration in which Yahya was, and is, held in the Qur'an, pious Muslims preserved it. The grave of Yahya Nabi (prophet) may be seen today in a shrine constructed in the Ummayad mosque in Damascus. John's head, however, is reported to have suffered removal to Aleppo's Citadel in the eleventh century. It was subsequently secreted in the congregational mosque's pulpit, whence blessings accrued to the faithful, to preserve it from Mongol hordes. Not so, according to the guardians of Amiens Cathedral, in France. They claim *their* head to be the true one, as do other places that claim the Baptist's head with all the fervor, if not the intent, of Salome.

What we want is a fairly objective account of John the Baptist, written by someone who was not prejudiced either for or against John, an account preferably written by a contemporary. Such a document, I am afraid, cannot be supplied. The only near-contemporary historian who refers to John in the context of Jewish history's relation to the real world was born about a year after John's death. Still, that is pretty close, if we are not expecting an eyewitness report. Flavius Josephus (37–100 CE) wrote of John in his monumental collection of books called *Antiquities of the Jews.* The context for Josephus's reference to John is his account of the political calamities that befell Herod the Great's son Herod Antipas, Tetrarch of Galilee and Perea (4 BCE–39 CE). Josephus's interest is Herod Antipas, not John.

Josephus's value as an historian must be weighed principally according to whether he was prejudiced for, or against, the Baptist. Discerning any bias in this regard is not easy, for Josephus does not always betray his favorites, though he makes his antipathies clear enough, in the main. Josephus wrote very well about politics because he was a politically minded person, though he sought the truth as a matter of record. Josephus, it is important to recognize, was a Jewish historian who left his country to live in the imperial Roman household in Rome, devoting his time to trying to make Romans understand Jews and to make them see and respect what he considered the best of what Jewish history and traditions had to offer. A Jewish zealot, that is to say a person prepared to kill Roman soldiers and be killed in defense of his patriotic and religious ideals, would have regarded Josephus, for all his patriotic history writing, as a quisling.

Let us take a first draught from what Josephus has to say about John:

> Now some of the Jews thought that the destruction of Herod's [that is, Herod Antipas's] army came from God, and that very justly, as a punishment of what he did against John, that was called the Baptist: for Herod slew him, who was a good man, and commanded the Jews to exercise virtue, both as to righteousness toward one another, and piety toward God, and so to come to baptism; for that the washing [with water] would be acceptable to him, if they made use of it, not in order to the putting away of some sins [only], but for the purification of the body; supposing still that the soul was thoroughly purified beforehand by righteousness. Now when [many] others came in crowds about him, for they were very greatly moved [or pleased] by hearing his words, Herod, who feared lest the great influence John had over the people might put it into his power and inclination to raise a rebellion (for they seemed ready to do any thing he should advise), thought it best, by putting him to death, to prevent any mischief he might cause, and not bring himself into difficulties, by sparing a man who might make him repent of it when it would be too late. Accordingly he was sent a prisoner, out of Herod's suspicious temper, to Macherus, the castle I before mentioned, and was there put to death. Now the Jews had an opinion that the destruction of this army was sent as a punishment upon Herod, and a mark of God's displeasure to him. (*Antiquities*, Book 18, ch. 5:2; Whiston's translation)

The first great revolt of Jews against the Romans began in 66 CE at Caesarea, thirty years after the events described in the quotation above. Josephus took part in the revolt. He was a commander of the Galilean defense against the Roman X (tenth) Legion. But Josephus (the Roman form of "Yusef" or Joseph) soon concluded that neither his own nor his country's best interests were served by protracting the struggle. After escaping ignominiously from a collective suicide pact, Josephus surrendered himself to the Roman General Vespasian, whom he extravagantly declared to be the man prophecy announced as the great ruler who would come out of the East, that is, an imperial savior. Vespasian, founder of the Flavian dynasty from which "Flavius" Josephus took his new name, was made emperor in 69 CE. Josephus backed a winner.

This all makes Josephus's own position in relation to the figure of the John that we think we know somewhat ambiguous. We can, I think, be sure that neither John the Baptist nor any other Jew back in the 30s would ever have come to the conclusion that "the Christ" (Greek translation of the "messiah" or "anointed one") was going to be a Roman general. However, Josephus's profound suspicion of messianic Judaism and its fatal web of enthusiastic zealots were shared in the 30s by the ruling priestly party of Sadducees and their patrons, the Herodians.

One thing we can probably say about John the Baptist with some assurance is that he was in favor of some kind of messianic solution to Jewish problems both religious and political, and one thing we can definitely say about Josephus is that the historian regarded the downfall of his country at the hands of the Romans as the sorry achievement of misguided Jews he calls "bandits," who believed themselves to be the messiah's advance guard. Josephus could see where violent extremism led and, in the end, was proved right.

We have then a slight problem. While Josephus's treatment of John recognizes that John was a thorn in the side of Herod Antipas, the Tetrarch of Galilee, Josephus says nothing of what the Gospels give us to suppose was John's fiery enthusiasm for a messianic solution—though not necessarily of the zealot, military kind. Now Josephus was never slow in accusing individuals of his country of intemperate fanaticism. He was convinced, and wished to convince the Romans, that his country's woes, and those of the Romans with respect to them, were the result of a sect of revolutionary danger-men who brought ruin to the greater good of the Jewish people, whatever religious motives might be claimed in such men's defense. Josephus knew the difference between a "wrecker" and a moderate, and he wanted his Gentile readers to know this too. John the Baptist is described by Josephus in terms that would make a centurion relax his sword grip.

And yet, according to Josephus, something about John's following upset Galilee's old ruler, Herod Antipas, described by Josephus, as if by way of partial explanation, as a man of a "suspicious temper." The implication is that the suspicions might have been unfounded, but this is not stated definitively. We may suppose perhaps that Josephus simply did not know enough about John's large following to come to any conclusion that he could make sense of, either for himself or his readers.

Or maybe he knew only too well.

So, while all of this raises innumerable problems for understanding and interpreting any truth about what Josephus has to say about John, we can at least answer in the negative the question, *Was Josephus prejudiced against John?* As to whether Josephus *favored* John, we are not on such firm ground. Unless Josephus, for reasons either of his own or of his patrons the Flavian dynasty, was trying to rewrite history, we can only say that Josephus recognized John as a *zaddik,* that is, a righteous man. This must mean, given all else that Josephus has to say about his people and their beliefs, that he respected John. He tells us that "the Jews" believed God was displeased at the activities of Herod Antipas with regard to his executing a righteous man, but the historian does not commit himself. This may simply have been political horse sense.

The war to which Josephus's passage refers was fought between Herod Antipas and King Aretas of Nabataea. The war was launched with the explicit backing of the Emperor Tiberius. Tiberius demanded Herod return from the war with nothing less than Aretas's head. Aretas had been a longtime and very expensive annoyance to Roman interests in the region south and east of Sinai.

Josephus would have been on shaky ground with his Roman readers if he had explicitly backed the idea that a war whose loss was detrimental to the Roman interest had foundered as a result of the Jewish God's favor for a Judean baptist. Josephus's solution to this little dilemma was very smart, I think. He implied in his account that Herod's war with Aretas might have succeeded *but* for Herod's persecution of John. Since Herod Antipas was deprived of his position by Roman authority and exiled to Gaul in 39 CE, Josephus was risking nothing by suggesting that Herod Antipas was not always the wisest of rulers, or that he did not always fully discharge his duties to his ultimate political master. We may then conclude that Josephus, as far as the account as we have it goes, could find nothing against John. Josephus then is neither particularly *pro* nor particularly *anti*. In our terms, Josephus must appear fairly objective where John is concerned.

Having established a reasonable basis for thinking Josephus's account is a fair lozenge of history as far as it goes, what do we learn from it about John?

We learn that John was a good man, meaning a zaddik or righteous man, someone separated from birth for God's service, a keeper of the Law, a holy man. He preached to his people. When Josephus says John called on his hearers to "exercise virtue" we should recall he was writing to people of Roman- or Greek-speaking background. The word *virtue* translated back into its Jewish setting could cover a large range of teaching and spiritual instruction, from apocalyptic warnings to ethical social-justice injunctions in the spirit of the prophets Amos and Hosea. Virtue, to a Roman, meant inner strength and vital or virile force, the healthy root of an integrity that could be reflected in the virtuous Roman's social relations and public standing. Virtue also involved the protection of one's family and family name, the courage to face the facts of life, a readiness to die if necessary, to be philosophical, to be impartial in justice, to honor and serve Rome and its ruler, to obey the law, to refrain from avarice or overindulgence in bodily comfort, to live reasonably sparely, and, importantly, to honor the word given. Josephus identifies John for his readers as an upright, honorable man, a *patrician,* even though he did things that might appear strange, at first sight, to Roman citizens.

What would Josephus have meant by the "piety toward God" that John's hearers must demonstrate? The temptation is to go to the Gospels for elucidation, but if we do, we should bear in mind that we enter thereby a theological minefield. We may fairly say, but only in general, that John demanded that his people honor the spirit and the letter of the Law, as the prophets continually recommended, refusing to hold any idol of alien god in reverence, but to love God, obey his commandments, and seek the will of God in all things. Jews should commit themselves to the claims of *zedek,* righteousness toward one's fellows, and *hesed,* pious devotion to God. All of those things, of course, had strong implications as to how to regard the oppressive Roman occupation of Judea.

That Herod "slew him [John], who was a good man" can only really mean that, as an historian, Josephus wants posterity to know that John did not personally deserve the punishment; it was meted out for no wrongdoing on his part. While John was not a criminal, it may have been politically necessary for Herod to have John executed, though a question of honor might hang over such an act.

Josephus's treatment of John's baptism is interesting. The Gospels connect John's baptizing with the general idea that it was "unto repentance." This probably means that his baptism was the definitive act of repentance, after which, backsliding would involve a sin inviting judgment. There is certainly no conception of baptism representing being "born again" or anything like it. Josephus wants it to be known that John's baptism was not any form of mystery-initiation, something with which some of his readers would have been familiar. Of course, if Josephus had come by some of his information on John from Pauline Christian sources, it would have been made clear to him anyway that

John's baptism was "only of water." If such was the source of his information on John's baptism, it is interesting to see what he makes of the idea.

Josephus emphasizes that John's baptism was for washing of the body. He does not mean that it was simply a bath to keep clean. The Romans knew all about baths, of course, though Josephus might well have wished to evoke that familiar concept of civilized bathing to allay any suspicion about John's being a "baptist." *What,* a Roman would have asked, is a "baptist" anyway? Josephus knows a lot more about it, judging from his own autobiographical account of his youthful enthusiasm for asceticism under his "guru," one Banus (who bathed religiously), but he is determined not to distract his readers with complexities, subtleties, and ambiguities. As far as Josephus understands John's activities, the idea is implied, I think, that as the soul had *already* been cleansed by a change of heart and conduct, the body also required some kind of symbolic, or frankly, actual, cleansing: a fresh start to a new day, both actually and symbolically, a manifest sign. Repentance "washes" accreted spiritual pollution away; washing symbolizes that. Clean, one can face judgment with confidence. Josephus does not go into the symbolism. However, since Josephus shows elsewhere in his books a familiarity with the Platonist and Pythagorean idea that the physical body is a kind of "tomb of the soul," and also knows of an extensive party of Jews who shared this belief (the Essenes), there may be more to the idea of a baptism "for the purification of the body" than simply a sign of a moral determination to keep the body free from pollutions, such as fornication, gluttony, drunkenness, and touching things Jews traditionally held to be unclean, such as pigs, the dead, lepers, menstruating women, food that had been offered to idols, foreign gods, bloody meat, and so on.

The idea of mortification may have been involved in John's baptism—and in Josephus's thinking about it—since cold water stills the passions (of most people) and braces the person into alertness. If the Gospels reflect historical fact, then alertness, endurance, and patient *watching* were signal duties of the baptized penitent. Cold water, we know from later accounts of cultic bathers during the next three centuries, was frequently used to still the sexual urges of religious bathing sects whose activities may or may not have been derived from John's activities, or those of his many followers.

Josephus next makes it clear that John had oratorical skills. People liked listening to him; his voice made them curious. He was an attraction. Josephus would not want to say much more about this, lest his readers move naturally to the conclusion that John was a *magician* who by magic of voice seduced his followers, putting them under a spell, making them do things they would not otherwise do. Romans were wary of magicians; so was Josephus, who blamed "false prophets" and sorcerers for many of his country's woes. Josephus would like his Roman readers rather to think of John in terms of an *orator,* a learned and responsible speaker. His words moved people, his presence authoritative. John could command great numbers, sufficient anyway to "put the wind up" the Tetrarch of Galilee, Herod Antipas. This latter fact certainly begs many questions.

What was Herod afraid of? Was it a matter of public demonstrations? General noise and disturbance, public chanting, insults to his family, and the like? Did the ruler fear an armed coup, led by or inspired by John, which might happen once Herod ordered his army to war with Aretas in 36 CE? And if John's following was armed, or ready to be armed should occasion arise, why did Josephus not lump John's following in with the zealot "bandits" (*lestai*), "addicted to liberty" and insurrection at all costs, whom he habitually condemns? This is not a question easily dismissed. When, according to the historian, Herod feared a rebellion, since John's followers seemed ready to do anything he told them, was *rebellion* something John was likely to recommend? He obviously had not done so yet, but was Herod Antipas privy to additional intelligence? Was a plan afoot? We must suppose Herod did not act on hearsay alone. Spies were cheap enough for a king to hire. Were John's exact motives and activities difficult for the tetrarch to interpret, given stressful political circumstances? The presence of holiness could be socially and politically inflammatory.

Josephus, aware of the potential pitfalls in his narrative, would have his readers suspect it was *Herod* who was overzealous in his suspicions, not John. Curiously, Josephus has nothing to say whatsoever about *why* John might have led a rebellion against his overlord. Josephus concludes that John's arrest was basically a precautionary measure, not a remedial one: a political necessity. Herod could not risk even the *possibility* of John's following turning actively dangerous. Certainly he would have had Rome's approval for such a measure. Locking people up, at the very least, was normal Roman practice in such cases. Josephus does not condemn outright Herod's taking John into custody. He does not question the right to rule, nor should we expect him too; he was himself the guest of the ruler and was himself ruled.

Josephus records that John was sent to Herod's castle at Macherus, close to the Nabataean border in the south of his territorial jurisdiction. Again, we are not told why. It may simply have been because Macherus looked, and today still looks, pretty impregnable. Conversely, he perhaps hoped John would escape and, having been given the warning, would go into exile. But excavation has revealed that Macherus was also a *palace* with all civilized amenities, a very comfortable place for those with the liberty to enjoy it. It might have been a matter of John enjoying the "hospitality" of the tetrarch.

Was John executed straightaway? Was that the original plan? We are not told, but it is clear from Josephus's account that John had his liberty, and thereafter his life, taken because of a crisis. That crisis was the war with King Aretas, based at Petra in what is now Jordan. Was Herod concerned that John might be "lifted" from Macherus by Aretas, King of Nabataea? For that is what happened to Herod's wife, Phasaelis, daughter of Aretas, as we shall explore in chapter 5.

And that, loaded with unspoken factors as it is, is the most objective account of John the Baptist that we have. That, we can say, is what straight history has to tell us about John the Baptist.

THE NATURE OF NEW TESTAMENT EVIDENCE

It is a persistent, if unconscious, prejudice of many biblical scholars to think as if the Gospels were written by people like themselves. I try to make no such assumptions. Since we really know nothing of any concrete value from the historical and biographical point of view about the actual personalities who composed the Gospels, we can never be *sure* what precisely their motives were, or how much they really knew that they chose not to make manifest in their writings. Levels of ignorance are very hard to detect.

The Gospels do not debate their contents; they assert them. They never refer seriously to anyone else's writings about their sole subject, Jesus and salvation—other than what is now known as the "Jewish Bible"—and they never express doubt as to a source. They are all conscious of themselves as being in some sense in continuity with, as well as being the fundamental transformation of, holy writings sacred to the Jewish people and respected in parts of the Gentile world. The evangelists borrow style and language from the Greek version of the Hebrew Bible, and they quote from it repeatedly. What is more, the Gospels are full of the certainty that Jewish prophecy prefigures and refers directly to everything they have to say. The evangelists almost certainly had copies of the words of the Hebrew prophets and the Psalms on hand when they commenced dictation. The prophetic "footnotes" *become* the text at practically every opportunity, and the prophecies and declarations of God's demands and future plans do more than illustrate the narrative; they become the raw, pulsing core of it. "Search the scriptures; for in them ye think ye have eternal life: and they are they, which testify of me," Jesus is supposed to have said (John 5:39). The gospel writers did search the scriptures—and how!

The Gospels are written on the assumption that every living word of their contents stands as a stone in an edifice of aggregate and definitive *proof* that the Hebrew prophets were right, even if the prophets themselves were not fully aware of the nature of the eventual fulfillment of the primal *mystery* to which they gave voice. According to the

Gospels, the prophets' promises were fulfilled at every point: such *is* the Gospel. *Looking for the messiah? Hoping for salvation?* Jesus is your man: *Ecce Homo.* This progressive ticking of all the qualification boxes is evident in practically every line of every Gospel. The Gospels are religious texts about religious texts. They are didactic and absolute; to get caught up in them exclusively may do much for the conviction of religious salvation, but little for the critical faculties. The history or story they tell is a spiritual history, not a political history or a social history. They are complex works and unique as literary phenomena, sewn together from disparate sources as they undoubtedly are. They are the work of determined human hands, and it goes without saying that their influence has been incalculable.

The Gospels are not, however, histories in any strict sense of the term. Historical works might inform and even entertain on occasion, but they are not intended to transform lives or reveal spiritual truth, even though we can all learn something from history, such as the fact that people seldom learn from history. Today, the writers are given the dignified term "evangelists." And that says it all. The Gospels are tools of evangelism: preaching and conversion. The Gospels do not "win" because a first-century Roman pot is discovered in Natseret (Nazareth) in Israel, but because a sinner repents and enters the church. Archaeology cannot prove a religion is true.

The Gospels are religious writings. They contain religious thoughts, words, symbols, metaphors, allegories, and stories. Though the setting for all of this is a specific period of history, the point about them is the practice of religion and the presence of spiritual truth; they are concerned above everything with stating what the authors are convinced is shattering religious truth. And what is shattered, be it understood, is the course of *history itself,* both for the individual and for humankind. History is just part of the pallet.

In the case of Luke's Gospel and his Acts of the Apostles, there is a late attempt (ca. 80–130 CE) to dress the *kerugma,* or "proclamation," in historical form, but in spite of Luke's more urbane approach, an approach that has something of Josephus's desire to allay Roman suspicions about it, the point is still the same: Jesus is Lord. Accept it or be damned. We must presume Luke's readers did not object to the hard sell. After all, what they were most interested in was *salvation*. That was what the Gentile churches were offering the pagans. And salvation must mean, ultimately, the end of history. You cannot have salvation without damnation too.

So great indeed is the gospel conviction that history is soon to end that the political structures, which undoubtedly shaped the early first century, pass unexamined and unexplained, time after time. The Gospels are, in a sense, full of missing history. There are Romans in Judea. *So what?* It doesn't matter. Galilee is undergoing a boom in building construction; it doesn't matter. Zealots are being crucified; it doesn't matter. The Emperor nicknamed Caligula is killed by his own guard; it doesn't matter. There's a war between Herod Antipas and Aretas of Nabataea; it doesn't matter.

Jesus is walking on water; *that's* what matters!

History, as far as the gospel writers are concerned, is simply the vehicle by which salvation has been delivered. It is background. As in the Hebrew books of Kings, Genesis, and Exodus, what we get is "salvation history."

John the Baptist only *matters* so long as he plays a part in this.

In John's Gospel this process of spiritualizing history reaches a most otherworldly pitch. We think we are moving in time, but at every moment of the text, we are touching a great eternal circle, the presence of an *aeon,* a spiritual kingdom: *not of this world,* calling us off the Earth, above the waters of flux and change, or history. In John's Gospel we feel that we are leaving *terra firma* altogether—and time with it. As water was a Gnostic symbol for the flux of the material world, we too are walking on water, that is, above it. So elevated is this Gospel's apparent perspective, you might think it had been written by God himself, or one of his angels. But it wasn't. The whole epic magnificence is nonetheless swathed in an aura of heavenly blues and golden bread blended with pale flesh and splashed with glittering blood that threatens to unhinge the story. Jesus's speeches seem to go on forever. He's got all the timelessness in the world. Nevertheless, few would reckon that the narrative lacks bite, or even venom. There are some very vicious things in the "spiritual Gospel" of John, but you need to look carefully to find them. Nevertheless, in the main, we are in the presence, not of mere events, but of divine *signs:* signs to take you *out of time* altogether and upward through a sky-blue infinity to the colorless radiance of eternity beyond.

You are being taken to *God.*

Powerful stuff, as my father used to say.

Great propaganda too.

And history it is not.

The church did not start with the Gospels; they joined the train later. The church started with people. And, according to all four canonical Gospels, the story they have to tell started with *John.* John the Baptist, that is. This is remarkable since no one can be in any doubt that the problem with the Gospels as "historical sources" is that they are utterly Christocentric. Jesus is the star. He gets the dressing room, top billing, and the plaudits. He is center stage even when he is not physically, or metaphysically, present. There is no real room for the supporting cast or bit-part players. They are brought on and off like props. There are no real "character parts." There is no sidekick or moll. Any actor in a biblical epic has a real problem if he or she lands one of these supporting roles; they destroy actors' pride. The names "Peter," "James," "John," "Andrew," "Mary"; you could interchange most of them at any point in the narrative and most people would not notice, even after a lifetime of church attendance. Apart from the historical cameos—Pilate, the Herods, Salome, Herodias—the only figure who really stands out, other than Judas Iscariot, is John the Baptist. He comes in with a big splash at the start, but you quickly feel an impatience in the gospel writers to get him off the stage as quickly as possible. He is almost too *big* for the story. It is no surprise that when the big bucks are splashed out on Jesus epics we find major-league hunks Chuck Heston and Robert Ryan given the role of the "wild man" up to his manly waist in the Jordan in his *One Million Years B.C.* furs, braced with beefy biceps and sun-burnished face and a voice with built-in, heaven-shaking echo. The world is his studio. Surely, this man deserves extra scenes! The producers of *The Greatest Story Ever Told* (1965) duly provided some. Heston/Baptist tells José Ferrer's Herod "what's what" in snappy dialogue that competes with holy writ and turns John's execution into his liberation. Sounds like the scriptwriter had been reading Josephus on the beliefs of the Essenes: canny stuff. They had, note, to *go outside* the Gospels to make the historical context work. In *King of Kings* (1961), the majesty of Orson Welles delivered a better introduction to first-century Palestine than St. Luke.

So, what can we learn about John the Baptist from the New Testament? Well, first we can learn what some people thought about him within a century of his death. If we were writing a biography, we might put this information under the heading of "John's Influence," but that might be misleading if, as it may be suspected, the picture presented has been distorted. It could be that John's real influence has been obscured deliberately, or even falsified through ignorance, arrogance, or malice.

Nevertheless, there must have been things about John that stood out, things that were too well known to reshape or reinterpret, facts that we must presume were not invented. Such may be listed as follows: John existed. His name, "Johanan," means "God comforts," a common Jewish name in the first century CE. He lived in Judea. He kept the Law and was holy. He baptized. He had a following. He may have had something to do with Jesus. He upset the Tetrarch of Galilee and Perea. He was arrested and executed. In death, he still had a big following.

These seem to be irreducible facts.

After that, we have to be very careful indeed in trying to extract historical knowledge from the New Testament. There are things that the gospel writers know but which they are going to ignore. And there are things that the gospel writers do not know and therefore cannot tell. Let us look at what the gospel writers probably do not know or do not care to mention.

From a historical point of view, the Gospels can be viewed as palimpsests. A palimpsest is an old manuscript that has been reused. The old text may just be visible beneath a new, clear text, even though it has been rubbed out. The original text is vague, but it occasionally "comes through" into visibility. I do not mean that the oldest manuscripts of the Gospels that we have are actually palimpsests! What I mean is that there *is* a real historical background to the events described in the Gospels, but the force, implications, and content of that true background seldom come through into the text as we know it. This is in part a result of the Christocentric focus we have already discussed. The problem is that such is the distance of the gospel text from an authentic historical setting that the meaning of the text may suffer a crucial change in emphasis, and therefore meaning. There *is* history behind the text but it is vague; key determinants are missing. Thus, a particular saying attributed to one person may have meant something quite different before being placed in a new context, even if the words of the saying are rendered more or less fairly. I gave an example of this earlier with regard to the meaning of John's tirade in Matthew referring to the "children of Abraham." Until one knows about the grounds for vociferous objection to the Herodian dynasty among pious Jews, one cannot be sure precisely to whom John's words, if they are John's words, were properly intended. And yes, it *does* matter. We may be missing something important, whether or not for one's salvation, I cannot say, but illumination may occur when we get the joins right.

Why is the historical background vague?

The Gospels were written long after the political events took place that shaped the drama of John the Baptist's life. In many respects, they were deemed irrelevant to later generations because almost the entire picture of Jewish life changed so radically between the 30s (John's heyday) and the period after the Romans destroyed Jerusalem's temple in 70 CE.

The critical period may be divided into two: first, from the death of Herod the Great in 4 BCE until John's execution (probably 36 CE), and second, from 36 CE until the beginning of the first Great Jewish Revolt in 66 CE. That entire period consisted of a prolonged ferment of agitation, violence, apocalyptic prophecy, resistance, and repression. Moments fit to enjoy the "lilies of the field" must have been seized eagerly, for they were few. Roman legions trampled the lilies into the earth.

The main protagonists of the infra-Jewish conflict consisted of a number of groups of Judeans and Galileans who believed that the Herodian dynasty was a disaster that, having befallen the nation, spelled anguish for its religion. If Jews did not respond to the crisis, they believed that God would damn them. If they did respond to the crisis, they knew that the Romans would try to destroy them. They put their faith in their religion because that was the only honorable and righteous choice for them as patriots subject to divine judgment.

What all of the most active anti-Herodian elements had in common was a belief in a messianic solution to the crisis. God would send his "anointed one" to redeem the kingdom from God's enemies. We find this messianic fervor abundantly expressed in the writings of the so-called "New Covenanters." The New Covenanters is a name now given to those people who sometime between ca. 160 BCE and perhaps the early first century composed and were uplifted by the original works of commentary and community rule we know as the Dead Sea Scrolls. They were people who subjected themselves to a new covenant with God in the region of Damascus, far from what they considered a corrupted Temple in Jerusalem. Their answer to the crisis was the strictest possible adherence to the Jewish Law, the formation of an ultrarighteous community, and a willingness to fight in a messianic struggle in the future.

Josephus does not mention such a group by such a name, though it is common among contemporary scholars to imagine that Josephus's Essenes be identified with the so-called New Covenanters. Josephus does give us qualified information about so-called bandits: Zealots who fought Romans and collaborators in the uncompromising spirit of the Jewish hero Judas Maccabaeus, the "Hammer" who by force of arms expelled the Seleucid army of Antiochus IV, ruler of Syria, from Jerusalem in 167 BCE. Zealots were sometimes inspired to arms by the idea that if they rose against the invader then their act of faith would trigger the messiah's coming to lead them to final victory. It was a gamble. Others thought the messiah should come first. But it had to be the right messiah. How could one be sure? Some believed there was one messiah; others two: a priest and a king. (Might this expectation account for an authentic political relationship between Jesus and John?)

Meanwhile, in Jerusalem, the Temple precincts echoed to the noise of a persistent, rude, and sometimes violent struggle within the Temple organization for control and influence. One nepotistic high priest followed another, with constant appeals for the deposition of unpopular or allegedly corrupt high priests. As in Iran today, the political tempest of the country was largely fought out in arguments between priests. The conflicts of the priesthood occupy many pages of Josephus's fascinating history of the period. There were poor, "lower" priests who kept to righteousness and pious devotion to the Law: men who romanticized about the golden days of old when Israel was pure and God poured his blessing on the great men of renown, when the dew of heaven fell on the lips of the prophets, and Solomon was arrayed in glory, and God loved his precious people like a shepherd loves his lambs. Then, in the dark corner, so to speak, were the richer priests. The richer priests came from families supported by the Herodians: realists, players, men of the world. They could afford to pay for bullyboys when the occasional riot demanded the heavy hand. The more powerful Sadducees were among these realists of the political situation; for them it was a choice between the Herodians and anarchy: tolerate the Romans or risk having no country at all. And with the Herodians came the power and the glory. If a messiah ever *did* come, it would wreck the whole show.

Needless to say, among the messianic groups, God favored the "poor."

As I demonstrate in my book *The Missing Family of Jesus,* every shred of historical evidence points to these conflicts within Jerusalem's priestly factions as the true setting for the upbringing and self-understanding of John and of Jesus: Johanan and Yeshua. Their background was priestly, and they may themselves have been priests, either practicing as priests in the Temple from time to time or having been trained as priests. According to Luke's account, Jesus's mother, Mariamme, had been a Temple slave girl, given wholly to what many considered a corrupt temple system until redemption by marriage; husband Joseph was probably a priest. The less politically influential and powerful priests of the first century were moved either to support or to denounce groups such as the New Covenanters or the various Zealot factions. Priests—possibly fellow priests—would have watched the activities of John and Jesus with great interest.

Why do the Gospels show so little interest in this priestly background? Admittedly, Luke tells us something about it in his selective narrative of John the Baptist's birth, but the crucial political facts are missing; the setting is fundamentally pacific. Striving to fill out the gospel story as he received it with additional research and fresh material long after the events, Luke pacified the story with Pax Romana soap suds. Centurions could be nice guys.

The fact is that for the gospel writers, practically all of the political setting and much of the authentic religious setting had ceased to exist. In 70 CE, a soldier in Titus's army "accidentally," it was claimed, set fire to Herod the Great's Temple complex in Jerusalem. From that point onward, the Temple system with its twenty-four divisions of priests and six yearly rotations of priestly courses was set at nought. The Jewish Christian community lost for good its established stomping ground (though tradition says that the Jewish Christian community was supernaturally advised to leave Jerusalem before the war erupted). Meanwhile, the center of power of the "Christian" churches had since the 50s been moving westward toward the seat of political power: Rome. Most Christians now appear to have been Greek-speaking former pagans or Jews dwelling beyond Palestine, still fired by the expectations and hopes of apocalyptic messianism. The converts knew that they faced the possibility of persecution and even death. Nero's famous persecution, stimulated by the Great Fire of Rome of 64 CE, which coincided with the Jewish Revolt, was a recent memory. Their religion was very much "of the moment"; they were not disposed to look in too much detail into the past. The words of Jesus were living doctrine concerned wholly and immediately with their lives in the here, now, and hope for the ever-after. Again, salvation was the issue. They were called to witness the triumph of God over the powers of the world.

The great fact for converts and their teachers was that the Christian Church now existed, and you did not have to be a Jew to join it and receive salvation. Consequently, in telling a story of Jesus, its authentic Jewish setting, especially the political setting, could be significantly toned down and in potentially inflammatory areas rubbed out. The polemic grew in force that the Jews had rejected Jesus, even though his coming had been foretold by the prophets and announced by John; Jesus was a prophet without honor in his own country. His "own" allegedly rejected him. Exactly how far this rejection had penetrated his family had not yet coalesced into the later conviction visible in John's Gospel that Jesus's brothers, like Joseph the patriarch's (the one with the colorful coat), were fundamentally against him. The idea of Jesus crucified at the will of his "own," that is, "the Jews," was a convenient untruth to tell Gentile converts: the Jews wanted Barabbas, which is to say, destruction.

They got it.

This point of view, unpleasant as it is to record, does not qualify as anti-Semitism in the racist sense, for it was recognized that there had indeed been a body of righteous Jews, true, though few indeed: a remnant. There was John the Baptist, there were a few miscomprehending disciples, and there was Paul (formerly "Saul") of course. Adopting the Roman form of his name, Paul had announced that the righteous tree of Israel had received a new graft: the believing Gentile who paid his taxes and respected Roman authority was now part of the tree of salvation, promised by the prophets and fulfilled in "Christ Jesus." That the Temple had been destroyed by God's appointed authority (Rome) could only mean that not only was the old prophecy against Herod's construction fulfilled, but that God no longer had any use for either it or its priesthood. There was only one High Priest now: Jesus. He was the last—that mattered. Jesus was a priest of the Order of Melchizedek, and that was supernatural and went on forever (Epistle to the Hebrews 5:6–10).

And with the destruction of the Temple, came the end of the dynasty that had built and rebuilt its controversial precincts. In 68 CE, the last Herodian King of Galilee, Agrippa II, was recalled to Rome and deprived of his kingdom. The Herodians were history too. And history meant "gone for good." So the Gospels were not really bothered about telling converts and catechumens about the facts, mere facts, of first-century Judea and Galilee. The miracles were what mattered, the signs. And the fulfillment of the signs: Jesus reigning as Lord and High Priest over his church. He was gathering in his flock, storing his wheat up in the Great Garner, and before long, the spiritual—and actual—fire would burn up the old husk of the world and reveal a new heaven and a new earth.

Who needed history?

This *was* history.

And, of course, we must not forget about the Romans. The Romans triumphed in Judea. It was the Romans, not the Zealots, who wiped out the corrupt Temple system in Jerusalem. It was the Romans who unseated the Herodians: the entire apparatus was smacked flat by the legions of a man Josephus, for one, reckoned a universal savior (Vespasian).

There was many an inconvenient fact about the presence of the Romans at the time of John and Jesus, some very touchy subjects. Just what level of contact did John and Jesus have with armed resistance to Rome? How far had John or Jesus gone in condemning legal authority in Judea, backed by the will of the senate and people of Rome? What was Jesus really trying to achieve? Who was behind him? Did he pay his taxes? Was he a magician or an inciter of terrorism?

All of these were critically uncomfortable questions. What respectable Gentile would want to join a religious cult whose leader had been executed as a terrorist or pretender "king of the Jews" among terrorists? After the Revolt that brought the Temple to its ultimate destruction, Jews were suspect in the Roman Empire. People paid taxes to pay for the legions that crushed the Jews' futile, fanatical revolt. For many, the word *Jew* was a dirty word; for others it betokened weirdness, magic, astrology. If "Jesus" was to make any headway in the Gentile world, especially in the West, it would have to be made very clear indeed that Jesus had his own scrap with the Jews, his opponents. It was as vital for the evangelists as it was for Josephus to make it clear that there was something decent and honorable and inoffensive, even admirable, in Jewish religion and history and that this skein of righteousness was as far removed from politics and rebellion as could be imagined.

Pilate, it was asserted, could find no fault in him.

And John the Baptist, as Josephus asserted, was really a decent fellow, a virtuous man.

Now, when we take all of this into account and understand the implications of it, we shall find ourselves in a better position to make a judgment about the treatment of John the Baptist in the New Testament as regards its historical value. And there is one final tweak we must apply to our focus. By the time the Gospels were written, John the Baptist had been dead a very long time. We know from Paul's letters however (Galatians especially) and from Luke's Acts of the Apostles (which is really the "Acts of Paul") that John's following continued to flourish into the 40s and the 50s, though we know little about it. From the tiny fragments left to us, it appears John's followers did not share, in the main, the convictions of, well, certainly Paul, concerning baptism and salvation. Paul attacked John's church. Yes, *John's church*. John's followers had their own organization. Paul declared their "baptism" insufficient unto salvation. It was only "of water." The true church—Paul's organization—had the Holy Spirit, and, Paul claimed, he and his followers had "the mind of Christ" (1 Corinthians 2:16).

Problem: *John's baptism had been good enough for Jesus.* Why was it not good enough for members of the new, growing Christian Church? Well, we think we know the answer because we have been told many times that John was only the herald of Jesus. And if we believe the Gospels, John himself said as much, and more. He was his own witness. *"Believe what John himself has to say,"* the Gospels urge.

It is not pleasant to suggest that the evangelists wrote things down that may not have happened. However, it must be recognized that to Christians, living toward the end of the first century, God himself had revealed the facts, that is, the truth. It was simply obvious that John had been the herald, since he was dead and the Church of Jesus, which had "come after," was very much alive. And since the prophet Malachi had said that the coming of salvation would be preceded by the return of Elijah, then was it not obviously true that since salvation had indeed come, then the messenger, John the Baptist, *was* Elijah? And however great Elijah was, he was not as great, nor could he ever have claimed to be as great, as the one whose coming he announced. Furthermore, if it was the case that John prophesied the coming of the messiah or at least a divine intervention, as we should have every reason to suspect, then John would have been familiar with the prophecies (such as *Joel*) that in the day of "the Lord's" (not explicitly the "messiah's") coming, there would be an outpouring of the spirit of the Lord. It only required the gospel writer to be familiar with Paul's arguments about baptism with rival preachers to conclude that John the Baptist must have *foreseen,* since he was the aforementioned "messenger" (*Malachi* means "messenger") that *his* baptism would become redundant! It would be wrong, the believer would I think argue, *not* to make the Baptist's witness clear on these issues, for his role was to serve the Lord. And Jesus was Lord.

The question we must eventually face is whether or not John did in fact either foresee or share, in any respect, Paul's point of view. We must also ask the question, Did the conclusion of some of the leaders of the Gentile Church in the late first century, taking Paul as their authority, *play back* Paul's conceptions of rival baptisms into their accounts of John the Baptist? For if they did not, and John really believed in his own denigration and relative status, how did it come to be that followers of John did not recognize the claim of Paul and *his* followers that John's message had had its time, served its purpose, and was no longer effective?

Did the church reduce John in significance simply because they "got what they wanted" from him, that is, a kind of endorsement, or was it because the existence of John and his followers constituted a very real embarrassment, or even threat, to the followers of Jesus?

We are now in a position to approach the accounts of John the Baptist in the New Testament.

Chapter Four

JOHN AS HERALD
IN CHRISTIAN SCRIPTURE

A FORM OF MARK'S GOSPEL is generally supposed to have been the earliest of the canonical Gospels to appear (ca. 65–80 CE). It opens with an immediate salvo of two quotes from the Jewsih scriptures; both are straightaway applied to John the Baptist. Mark launches his narrative with a slightly misquoted first part of Malachi 3:1. Note the second part of the sentence, omitted by Mark:

> Behold, I will send my messenger, and he shall prepare the way before me: and the Lord, whom ye seek, shall suddenly come to his temple, even the messenger of the covenant, whom ye delight in: behold, he shall come, saith the LORD of hosts.

Malachi proceeds to declare that this messenger will purge the "sons of Levi" (officers in the Temple and guardians of the Law) as gold and silver are purged to make a pure offering of righteousness. "But who may abide the day of his coming?" Malachi asks. "And who shall stand when he [the messenger] appeareth?" (v. 2).

Mark has the messenger preparing the way before "thee" rather than "me." That is to say, in Mark, the Lord is addressing *someone else*. In the original text, "the LORD" (God) is himself the one for whom the way is prepared: a significant detail. Had Mark included the whole quote, the reader or hearer might, understandably, have identified the "messenger" as Jesus, who, according to a tradition, "suddenly" came to the Temple to purge it (John 2:14–17). Certainly, Jesus is presented in the Gospels as the messenger of a coming wrath and a call to repentance: a message attributed first by the evangelists to his relative, John.

The second well-known quote is from Isaiah 40:3. "The voice of him that crieth in the wilderness, Prepare ye the way of the LORD, make straight in the desert a highway for our God."

Again, Mark slightly alters the verse, or his source of prophetic testimonies has altered it. Mark has, "Prepare ye the way of the Lord, make his paths straight" (Mark 1:3). Clearly, the original quotations from Malachi and Isaiah refer to the coming of the *Lord God* to his people. Mark's understanding is that the one who is coming is Jesus; that is, in some sense, Jesus *is* the Lord. "Jesus is Lord" was the earliest statement of Christian faith. The question for us is, If John the Baptist used these prophecies with respect to *himself*, did he understand them to mean that *he* would have to prepare the way for *Jesus*, or would he have to do it for an unnamed or unknown messiah, or was the way to be made for the *Lord God himself*? We should bear in mind that the doctrine of the incarnation, which identifies Jesus as the incarnation of the Lord God Jahveh, did not exist in John the Baptist's lifetime. The Messiah was hardly expected to be Jahveh himself, but rather one anointed by the Lord. In the Gospels, John's baptism of Jesus serves as the anointing of the "Son," though the Baptist has no idea that this will happen.

Given this dizzying ambiguity, we may conclude that a doctrine of divine incarnation, a doctrine that in time would lead to a developed belief in the Holy Trinity, was arguably the sole doctrine capable of resolving the issue of precisely *who* was "messenger" and who was "coming." It may then be argued that the incarnation doctrine itself depended in part on a struggle to place John and Jesus specifically within messianic prophecies. It is hard to avoid the fairly obvious point that to a messianic-minded Jew in the early first century, the Malachi prophecy of a messenger before the Lord would have been taken as a prophecy of the Messiah, who would be in some sense "Elijah returned." By this token, if John was the messenger, then he was possibly the Messiah as well, since the Messiah was understood to be the one who prepared the way of the Lord. And the Lord was God.

Historically, it seems likely that John, if he did see himself as a herald in some way, heralded the coming either of the Lord or of a figure from the Lord. Note that the capital-lettered "LORD" in the Old Testament stands in for the holy name of God, Jahveh, or Yahweh. The use of God's proper name was avoided by scribes wherever possible.

We must also consider the possibility that John was actually proclaiming the imminent arrival of the *herald,* the messenger, the one who would prepare the way for the "Yom Yahweh," the Day of God. In that case the whole idea of John as herald would be a later assumption thrust back in time, based on the idea that if Jesus was the Lord, then an accepted messianic scenario demanded he be preceded by another. After all, the idea that John actually took these prophecies for his own credentials is questionable on account of the potential charge of impious arrogance, even blasphemy, had he done so. It seems most likely then that these prophecies were applied to John *by others,* before or after his death.

We see that, on examination, the "plain truth" of the Gospels is not so plain at all. John has been *interpreted,* both as an individual and with respect to his message.

Mark then tells us that John baptized in the wilderness (he must have been near water) and preached "the baptism of repentance." Perhaps he went to the Brook Cherith, a wild, inaccessible gorge east of Samaria, a tributary of the Jordan's eastern bank. That was where the prophet Elijah was sent by God during a great famine in Israel. There, Elijah was miraculously fed by ravens. There, he would raise the widow's son from the dead (1 Kings 17; Freemasons as "sons of the widow" may note a parallel with their own "raising").

John addressed not a material, but a spiritual famine; God would raise the stricken who turned to him.

John's baptism is indicated by Mark as a baptism by which "remission of sins" was accomplished. The sins would presumably be symbolically "washed away" by baptism, an act of repentance, of turning back to God. The Jordan provided the symbol. Mark says that "all the land of Judea" and of Jerusalem went out to John in the wilderness where they all confessed their sins. This seems somewhat exaggerated! According to this statement, all Judea repented. *Job done,* one might have thought. If all Judea had repented, where was the need for a coming judgment, or even a messiah to initiate it? According to Mark, John called for repentance; repentance he got.

Mark gives us a sketch of John. He wore camel's hair with a leather girdle about his loins. He lived on locusts and wild honey. Behind this literary doodle we get some myth and some credible history. Why the curious dress?

John's outfitter would appear to be 2 Kings 1:8: "He was an hairy man, and girt with a girdle of leather about his loins. And he said, 'It is Elijah the Tishbite.'"

Or is it John the Baptist? Elijah looms large in the John legend. Either John chose to adopt the dress of the ninth-century BCE prophet Elijah (whose name means "Jah is God") or else the prophetic tradition that the "messenger" *was* Elijah encouraged the gospel writer to visually identify John with Elijah. The logic would then be thus: if the Hebrew scripture says that *this* is how Elijah dressed, and Elijah is the messenger, and Elijah is John, then John dressed like this.

But why identify John with Elijah?

The identification was an automatic consequence of reliance on the prophecies of Malachi for knowledge of the "messenger." Malachi 4:5–6 reads:

Behold I will send you Elijah the prophet before the coming of the great and dreadful day of the LORD: And he shall turn the heart of the fathers to the children, and the heart of the children to their fathers, lest I come and smite the earth with a curse.

The story went round early-first-century Palestine that among the many fabulous things that would attend an imminent "day of the LORD" would be the miraculous return of Elijah, last seen by his comrade Elisha heading heavenward in a whirlwind that carried a fiery chariot with horses of fire in 2 Kings 2:11. Remarkably, Elijah had not died; he was biding his time with the heavenly host. From thence he would return, presumably with fire.

I am not convinced that the historical John adopted Elijah's costume, great image though it is. A statement attributed to Jesus to which we shall presently attend suggests a more likely kit. We may have to change our mental image of the Baptist, difficult though it may be. The chances are that John wore the fine linen of a priest, and possibly the distinctive white dress of a mystical Essene. If John was accustomed to take the Nazarite vow, he could at any particular time have been very hairy, the vow period requiring indifference to hair growth, or he could have been clean shaven, a requirement of vow completion.

As for John's rough diet of desert survival fare, it is difficult to believe he would have resorted to the desperate extreme of protein-packed locusts when there were, reportedly, so many people in his entourage. Throughout the East it is still customary for followers of holy men to bring gifts of food to the venerable. These he will generally give to the hungry. It does not look good for a holy man to be seen eating like anyone else; it suggests the dominance of appetite, the weakness of the flesh. "Going without" is a basic mark of holiness. However, holy men must live; reasonable food would have been available to John, though he would have been selective. John was probably a vegetarian since the eating of vegetables or uncultivated food was the diet most associated with the zaddik, the righteous man consecrated to God. Even though vegetarianism was not a requirement of the famous Nazarite vow, whose stipulations in Numbers 6:1–26 give a good idea of the disciplines associated with those "separated" for God, we can nonetheless find authentic background to John's wilderness diet in 2 Maccabees 5:27. There we read of the hero and liberator Judas Maccabeus, progenitor of the Hasmonaean priest-kings who ruled Judea until supplanted by Herod the Great. In 167 BCE, having defeated the Syrian-Greek army of Antiochus IV and secreted the Temple's desecrated altar in the Temple Mount, Judas Maccabeus removed himself from the city, seeking purification:

> But Judas Maccabeus with nine others, or thereabout, withdrew himself into the wilderness, and lived in the mountains after the manner of beasts, with his company, who fed on herbs [wild plants, vegetables] continually, lest they should be partakers of the pollution.

In John's time, Judas was the very model of heroic holiness, that is, zeal for the Lord, and Judas's diet gives a clue as to the inspiration behind John's own wilderness sojourn. John was probably imitating the hero. Holiness was a political act. Holiness led to power: spiritual and political. In Judea, religion and politics were inseparable. And holiness was reinforced by dieting, by self-denial.

The reason for being in the wilderness is made clear. Judas and his company were avoiding the "pollution." The pollution consisted of a Jerusalem desecrated by foreigners, the holy altar of Zion splashed with the blood of animals sacrificed to pagan gods. And *that* is precisely how the revolutionary priests saw the Herodians and their unholy dependence on the pagan Romans. From the height of their Tower of Antonia, indifferent to its God, a Roman garrison looked down on the Temple. We may conclude that John was one such revolutionary, that is, reactionary and traditionalist, priest.

According to Mark, John preached that "one mightier than I" was coming, someone so exalted that John himself, though famed for purity, was unworthy to do for him a menial, slave's task; John refers to the undoing of a man's shoes. In modern parlance, if you will forgive me, John was saying that he was not worthy to lick the shit off the coming one's boots.

This is a fine and effective saying, and we should expect a pious prophet in the first century to hold such an exalted view of either the "messenger" who would prepare the way of the Lord or of the Messiah. But if the story we shall come to concerning John's kinship with Jesus is true, one might hardly expect the real John to say this about a relative, unless, that is, he had reason to believe his relative was the expected one, or was *complicit* in the timing of his cousin's appearance on the scene, that is, that John was *literally* "preparing" the political conditions for a successful messianic takeover. Then, perhaps, we might see John's extravagant language about his own unworthiness as "pumping up," building up his audience's expectation before "laying on" the expectant multitude the real star: "If you think *I'm* big, just wait until you meet your King!" so to speak. "He's coming!" Was Jesus's arrival being "held back" in readiness for the big announcement? Much depends on how, or even whether, the historical John actually presented himself as a "herald."

I do not know if the reader has noticed, but there seems to be confusion about just *who* was expected. You will have noticed that neither the Isaiah nor the Malachi quotations that open Mark's Gospel refer directly to a "messiah." They speak of a "day of God" or a way for God to come, and they speak of one who announces this. Isaiah may himself be the voice crying in the wilderness, or it might be a reference to Elijah who did God's will and brought down fire from heaven and lived in the wilderness. Whoever wrote or uttered the prophecy called "Malachi," he makes it clear, finally, that the messenger will be Elijah. But after Elijah comes the Lord.

We seem to be dealing with different strata of belief about God's big day. The messiah figure expected by first-century CE enthusiasts entered Jewish mythology considerably later than the time of Isaiah, who lived in the eighth century BCE, though different parts of Isaiah's text can be dated between the eighth century BCE and the sixth century BCE. While we know that a number of messianic concepts, such as "he shall be called Immanuel" (God with us) along with profound concepts of God's servant suffering, were taken from Isaiah's text and from other prophets, and *much later* applied systematically to an *apocalyptic* messiah, these concepts now stood outside of their native historical context. Isaiah himself was not aware of the extravagant process-history of imminent destruction of God's enemies combined with the end of the world that lit up the imaginations of New Covenanters, Zealots, and, later again, apocalyptic-inspired Christians. In fact, by the end of the first century CE, the simple promise of Isaiah, that first would come the messenger to prepare the way of God, then cometh God, had been staggered, as a result of aggregate text reading, into a veritable caravan of comings and goings. First the prophecy, then the messenger, then the Messiah, then the *paraclete,* that is, "comforter" or "Holy Spirit," then the *second* coming or return of the Messiah, then, at last, the Lord God in primitive Trinitarian panoply, that is to say, with his Son, who would judge the quick and the dead. A single play had become a long-running series. Preachers still trumpet these prophecies as if they were all saying the same thing.

What this means for us is that John probably did not see *himself* as the personal subject of Malachi's prophecy and, therefore, did not see Jesus as "the LORD," that is, Jahveh. He may have shared extreme views about a messiah with other groups, we cannot be sure, but his own position on who was coming is, at this point of the investigation, uncertain.

According to Mark 1:8, John speaks in the language, that is, in the conceptual framework, of Paul. Mark's John says, "I indeed have baptized you with water: but he shall baptize you with the Holy Ghost."

The background to this distinction appears to be Paul's much later conflict with the posthumous church of John the Baptist. In Acts 19, Luke describes Paul meeting disciples of one Apollos, a learned follower of John, in Ephesus. Apollos, interestingly, came from Alexandria, a notable base for philosophically, as well as apocalyptically minded, Jews.

According to Luke's account in Acts, John's followers tell Paul that they have never even *heard* of the "Holy Ghost." The reason, they say, is because they received John's baptism. But according to Mark, John *himself* preached that he only baptized with water and that one was coming who would baptize with the Holy Ghost. John's disciples had no reason, if Mark's saying was authentic, to be ignorant of the Holy Ghost, or Holy Spirit.

This all raises a host of questions and possible explanations, but let us try to keep to the text. John appears to have preached that a mighty being was coming and this being could do things that neither he nor anyone else could do. John could hardly be expected to know of Paul's later baptism, which, according to Luke, actually produced an ecstasy, an effect of "receiving the Holy Spirit," resulting in powers of prophecy and "tongues." When the Holy Spirit descended on Jesus at his baptism, there were, according to all accounts, no strange phenomena beyond the visionary: no ecstasy, no "tongues," whatever that might mean, no sudden propensity for prophecy. What John *would* have known about was the prophecy of Joel (2:28–29). And he would have associated it with the coming of God and the final end of wickedness:

> And it shall come to pass afterward, that I will pour out my spirit on all flesh; and your sons and your daughters shall prophesy, your old men shall dream dreams, your young men shall see visions: And also upon the servants and upon the handmaids [slave girls] in those days will I pour out my spirit.

This is the nice side of the prophecy. After the spirit comes, the picture changes. The moon will be turned into blood and the sun to darkness, "before the great and the terrible day of the LORD come." Luke knew the prophecy well; he had Peter quote from it at Pentecost in Acts. It will be observed that in the prophecy, the gift of God's spirit is not associated with baptism, not even metaphorically; it is the direct gift of God himself: "*I* will pour . . ." *God* does the pouring out. It is the work of the Lord. If John knew the prophecy, and he employed it, he knew indeed that he who would do these great things far surpassed his own ego.

Furthermore, Luke's view that the "Holy Spirit's" coming was the work of the postresurrection Pentecost and the Pauline view that he, Paul, was the minister of the baptism of the Holy Spirit are not only challenged by the prophetic texts themselves, but by near contemporary references known to us as the Dead Sea Scrolls.

As far as may currently be ascertained, some time in the first century BCE a number of priests ("Zadokites"), Levites, and their followers came together in the "land of Damascus" to make a new covenant of holiness and to establish a perfect rule that would make them fit people to assist God's Messiah when a final apocalyptic war between the "Sons of Light" and the "Sons of Darkness" occurred. Camps were established for training in the "wilderness," possibly the Judean wilderness southeast of Jerusalem, possibly further north, far enough anyway from the "pollution" of Jerusalem: the wilderness south of Damascus for example. The camps were modeled on the wilderness camps of Moses that protected the Law in "booths" or "tabernacles," until the people were sufficiently purified for Joshua (in Greek: *Iēsous* or Jesus) to lead the Israelite army to victory in the Promised Land.

The New Covenanters took guidance from the example of a figure they called the "Teacher of Righteousness." He was opposed and presumably killed by "the wicked priest," known also as the "Spouter" (of lies), a servant of "Belial," a kind of archdemon in human manifestation whose baleful machinations dominated the pollution. A series of conflicts between wicked priests and teachers of righteousness punctuated Jerusalem's history in the first centuries BCE and CE, so there are a number of credible candidate pairs who could be assigned to these archetypical roles in the New Covenanters' accounts.

The historical background to the New Covenanters' conflict with authority undoubtedly lies in the attempts of the Maccabaean high priests, ethnarchs, and kings to maintain control of Judea, first against the Syrian-Greek armies of the Seleucids and subsequently against Roman armies.

In 64 BCE, the Roman General Pompey (106–48 BCE), former comrade of Julius Caesar, crushed the Syrian army of Antiochus XIII. Having established Syria as a Roman province, Pompey headed south via Phoenicia toward Judea. In Judea, Pompey exploited an ongoing civil war. That civil war was fought between Judas Maccabeus's great-great-great nephews, High Priest and King Aristobulus II, and Aristobulus's brother, High Priest Hyrcanus II. Pompey supported Hyrcanus II. Hyrcanus was also supported by the Pharisee faction against Aristobulus II. Aristobulus's support came from Sadducees in Jerusalem.

The Hebrew root of the word *Sadducee* is the same as that of *Zadokite:* zedek, righteousness, particularly toward one's fellow, with the idea of justice, that is, the Law. Josephus speaks of Sadducees as the upper-class Jewish sect who ran the Temple. Dead Sea Scrolls scholar Robert Eisenman believes the Sadducee group split during the first century BCE, broadly speaking into strict-righteousness and realist-collaborationist factions, so that one can think of the "Zadokites," or "sons of Zadok" (the ancient high priest) referred to in the New Covenanters' scrolls as being the *strict* "Sadducees" or "Zadokites" and the antimessianic Sadducees, with their hands on top power in Jerusalem, as being their enemies (servants of Belial). This idea fits the known facts and may help us to identify the Baptist's authentic political background.

The historical circumstances that caused a definitive split among Sadducees may reasonably be sited in the traumatic conquest of Jerusalem by the Roman Pompey. Pagan Pompey entered the holy of holies of the

Second Temple, thus desecrating it, while his soldiers cut down priests in the sacred precincts that soon ran with their blood offering.

Hyrcanus's brother Aristobulus would be poisoned by Cassius and Brutus in 49 BCE. Any political gains Hyrcanus II thought he might have gained through collaborating with Pompey against his brother were, however, nullified after 44 BCE when Aristobulus's killers assassinated Julius Caesar, which plan, we all know, backfired. The famous Mark Antony, in his attempts to shore up power in the civil war that followed Caesar's death, made an alliance with the Idumaean king, Herod. Herod did better from the deal than did the fated Mark Antony. Mark Antony executed Antigonus, Aristobulus II's son, at Herod's instigation in 37 BCE. That is how Herod became "Roman" King of Judea. Seven years later, Herod executed Hyrcanus II. He then proceeded to waste most of the surviving family of the Maccabees, including his own wife, Mariamme, and their two sons. After that, Jewish claimants to the throne were, understandably, in short supply.

This background helps us to understand why the New Covenanters, and many other patriotic Judeans, saw their country and its capital as having been polluted both by foreigners and by their countrymen who had abandoned zedek, righteousness toward one's fellows, and hesed, piety toward God, according to the Law, and who massacred the innocent.

We cannot be sure when, or for how long, the camps established by the New Covenanters existed. The likelihood is that they, or their descendants and example so to speak, were still active at the time of the Baptist, though this is not certain. It must have been a risky business to establish an antiestablishment camp when Herod the Great was ruling, but Josephus recounts a *camp of tents* being established immediately after Herod's death in 4 BCE *within* Herod's new Temple by young Torah enthusiasts, the supporters of two teachers of righteousness, Matthias and Judas, who had been burnt to death by Herod for encouraging the pulling down of a Roman eagle from his Temple. The Roman eagle, a sacrilegious living form on the house of God, was just the kind of abominable pollutant that so incensed the New Covenanters and ideologically related groups.

In painstaking efforts to "keep clean" of the pollutions of life outside the Law, the camps practiced ritual bathing, or baptism. Their view of baptism corresponds well to Josephus's account of the baptism of John. According to the New Covenanters' "Community Rule" or Manual of Discipline, there was a correlation between the state of the inner person and their fitness for the outer rite. The Rule states clearly that the wicked "shall not enter the water . . . for they shall not be cleansed unless they turn from their wickedness" (1QS* v, 13–14). In the words of Dead Scrolls expert Geza Vermes, "True purification comes from the 'spirit of holiness' and true cleansing from the 'humble submission' of the soul to all God's precepts" (*The Complete Dead Sea Scrolls,* Penguin, p. 82). Vermes, perhaps wary of muddying

---

*In the standard English translation, *The Complete Dead Sea Scrolls in English,* translated and edited by Geza Vermes, (revised edition, Penguin, London, 2004), the initial digit of Qumran Scroll abbreviations refers to the *number of the Cave* in which the documents were found (11 caves yielded manuscripts). "Q" always means "Qumran." 1Q means Qumran Cave 1. "S" refers to the Hebrew "Serekh"— meaning "Rule"; in this case the "Community Rule." "1QS" means the Community Rule found in Qumran Cave 1.

"Sa" refers to appendix "a" of the Community Rule; appendix "a" has been called the "Messianic Rule." So the *Messianic Rule*'s full abbreviation is "1QSa." "Sb" refers to appendix "b" of the "Serekh" (Community Rule); that appendix is called "Blessings." The full abbreviation of "Blessings" is then: 1QSb.

The "Temple Scroll" ("TS") was found in Cave 11. So its abbreviation is: 11QTS.

Other abbreviations: a small "p" means a *pesher,* or Bible commentary. "Ps^a" means Psalms Scroll part "a." Its full abbreviation then is: 11QPs^a.

"H" refers to "Hymns."

Where the text has a title included in the abbreviation, as in the cases above, Roman numerals appearing in abbreviations *after* the abbreviated name or manuscript number refer to column numbers, while Arabic numerals after Roman numerals refer to line numbers of words in Hebrew or Aramaic, on the original scroll or manuscript. So the reference abbreviation, 1QS V, 13-14, means: lines 13-14 of column 5 of the Community Rule, found in Qumran Cave 1. However, many texts are identified by manuscript number alone. In such cases, Arabic numerals in abbreviations refer to that manuscript number, *viz*: 4Q390 means: manuscript number 390 found in Cave 4. 4Q521, for example, is the abbreviation for a text known as 'The Messiah of Heaven and Earth' (manuscript no. 521), a name derived by scholars from text contents.

his baptismal waters with religious controversy, carefully uses the term "spirit of holiness." Eisenman, on the other hand, regards a translation of the original Hebrew phrase as "Holy Spirit" to be perfectly accurate. It is the "Holy Spirit" within the purified righteous that is sullied and hurt by unrighteous conduct. God's holy spirit coming alive or springing into the awareness of the person who has chosen the true path of righteousness is clearly indicated in the writings of the so-called Qumran sect as a phenomenon consistent with complete legal cleanliness. It is the power of the holy spirit of the progressively cleansed that makes the person *want* to be righteous, which enables them to see and to desire the righteousness in adhering to the Law, and which enables them to find joy and peace in adhering to the rules of holiness. This holiness brings peace and wisdom and courage.

The Community Rule states (1QS III, 6–9):

> For it is through the spirit of true counsel concerning the ways of man that all his sins shall be expiated. . . . He shall be cleansed from all his sins by the spirit of holiness . . . and his iniquity shall be expiated by the spirit of uprightness and humility. And when his flesh is sprinkled with purifying water and sanctified by cleansing water, it shall be made clean by the humble submission of his soul to all the precepts of God.

If I had indicated that this had been written by a "father of the church," few would find cause to object. The point to be appreciated here is that there is no reason to think that John's baptism was not integral to a turning again of the heart to God's Law. The Law was holy and adherence to it brought purification, which purification opened the inner being to the "spirit of holiness" or the holy spirit. As Genesis states of God's creation, "The Spirit of God moved upon the face of the waters" (Genesis 1:2).

Paul's hostility to this established Zadokite doctrine was that he had experience wherein Gentiles who did not follow every detail of the

Law were nonetheless, after his baptism, exhibiting signs of holy spirit. The Zadokite response was that no one who disobeyed the Law could be considered holy. Paul countered that even while a Jew might be properly bound to the Law, this did not apply to converts after Jesus. Jesus's sacrifice had generated a new covenant. That had been God's long-term intention: the very mystery hidden in the prophecies from the beginnings of time. Besides, Paul argued, no one could be holy by the Law; Man's inherited share in the "sin of Adam" prevented it. The Law put men in condemnation; it did not free them. A new age had come. When it came to the final judgment, only faith in a spiritual communion with Jesus would serve as defense and ground for acquittal. Salvation was an act of grace; it could not be earned by adhering to the rules. Even Jesus, goaded Paul, since he was hanged on a "tree," which the Law declared a curse, was condemned by it. God accepted faith in Jesus's sacrifice as sufficient defense from damnation in the last judgment, as God had accepted Abraham's faith before Moses brought the Law.

The two sides were irreconcilable.

Theologians and rabbis may still discuss the merits or otherwise of the opposing cases, but what is important to this investigation is to recognize that Paul's sundering of God's holy spirit from John's baptism, when that baptism is seen in its broader historical context, appears nothing less than a caricature of it—much in keeping with Paul's and much of the canonical gospels' extreme attack on the Torah as the instrument of salvation—a few passages in the Gospels about not a jot or tittle being taken from the Law being stand-out exceptions to the rule.

It is also important to recognize that long before Mark wrote his Gospel applying Isaiah 40:3 to John the Baptist, the New Covenanters had already taken Isaiah 40:3's "call" to go into the wilderness and make a path straight for the Lord, as *their* special guide and inspiration. *That* was why they established camps in the wilderness:

> And when these become members of the Community in Israel according to all these rules, they shall separate from the habitation of unjust

men and shall go into the wilderness to prepare there the way of Him; as it is written, Prepare in the wilderness the way of . . . make straight in the desert a path for our God [Isaiah 40:3]. This path is the study of the Law, which He commanded by the hand of Moses, that they may do according to all that has been revealed from age to age, and as the Prophets have revealed by His Holy Spirit. (The "Community Rule," 1QS VIII, 10–15; Vermes, *The Complete Dead Sea Scrolls in English,* p. 109)

Robert Eisenman and Michael Wise (*The Dead Sea Scrolls Uncovered,* Penguin, 1993) have examined the fragmentary evidence surrounding the Rule and other key works of the New Covenanters' literary and liturgical material and have drawn attention to remarkable parallels of language between the Scrolls and the New Testament. One fragment of text from the Rule (4Q 286–287, Manuscript B, Fragment 3 [13]) bears the intriguing words, "The Holy Spirit [sett]led upon His Messiah"—which, if nothing else, shows that the idea of the Holy Spirit descending at John's baptism of Jesus has some authentic extra-testamental messianic background to it.

What Eisenman calls a "Baptismal Hymn" and what Vermes refers to less suggestively as "a purificatory ritual and prayers" show that a possible model for John "the Baptist's" activities can be found among the New Covenanters. Were the stakes not so high, most historians would, I think, on the strength of the evidence, be inclined to suspect that if John was not himself of the camp of the New Covenant, then he had, or had had, something to do with the New Covenanter tradition, and was therefore highly unlikely to have echoed the Pauline critique of his baptismal activities, as Mark has him do.

The call to repentance must have meant a call to honor the Law in spirit and in conduct. Otherwise, there would have been no concrete thing to turn again *to,* since God's will was approached through the observance of the Law in faith of him who had long saved his People, when they returned to him.

John the Baptist himself would not have taken his cue from Paul. Mark undoubtedly did, believing Paul to be an instrument in the Lord's salvation. The following quotation from Dead Sea Scrolls fragments may give us an idea of the words that the historical John might have uttered over the penitent receiving baptism at his hand:

> . . . and thou shalt purify us according [to] Thy precepts of holiness for the first, the third and the seventh . . . by the truth of Thy covenant . . . to be purified from the impurity of . . . And then he shall enter the water. . . . Answering, he [presumably the penitent] shall say, "Blessed a[rt Thou, God of Israel] for from the utterance of Thy mouth is declared the purity of all: to be separated from all the guilty men of uncleanness who cannot be purified by the purifying water . . ." (4Q414, Fragment 2 ii 3–4, Vermes, *Scrolls*, p. 398)

The water of purification is holy water. In fact, Mark's Gospel contains a no-less-potent endorsement of the heavenly character of John's baptism. Indeed, it is so strongly linked to Jesus's own *logia* that the saying occurs also in Matthew and even Luke, despite the inference that, read carefully, Jesus's challenge to the chief priests, elders, and scribes absolutely flattens Pauline objections to John's baptism:

> And they [Jesus and his disciples] come again to Jerusalem: and as he [Jesus] was walking in the temple, there come to him the chief priests, and the scribes, and the elders, And say unto him, By what authority doest thou these things? and who gave thee this authority to do these things? And Jesus answered and said unto them, I will also ask of you one question, and answer me, and I will tell you by what authority I do these things. The baptism of John, was it from heaven, or of men? Answer me. And they reasoned with themselves, saying, If we shall say, From heaven; he will say, Why then did ye not believe him? But if we shall say, Of

men; they feared the people: for all men counted John, that he was a prophet indeed. And they answered and said unto Jesus, We cannot tell. And Jesus answering saith unto them, Neither do I tell you by what authority I do these things. (Mark 11:27–33; Luke 20:1–8)

Jesus and John receive authority from the same source; who dare question it?

MATTHEW'S GOSPEL

Matthew's Gospel is usually dated ca. 80–100 CE. Scholarship generally concludes that its primary audience was Syrian-Jewish Christian and that it may have been composed in Edessa. It is believed that Matthew probably had either a copy of Mark to work with or a source common to both.

Where the Baptist is concerned, Matthew deviates from Mark straightaway.

After the baptism, *Mark* has Jesus going straight into the wilderness to be tempted of Satan and to live among the wild beasts while being cared for by "angels." We then hear that John has been put in prison, whereupon Jesus enters Galilee, saying, "The time is fulfilled, and the kingdom of God is at hand: repent ye, and believe the gospel." Matthew 3:2 makes this latter conviction the opening salvo of John the Baptist, *not* Jesus, who, preaching in the Judean wilderness, says, "Repent ye: for the kingdom of heaven is at hand. For this is he that was spoken of by the prophet Esaias [Isaiah], saying, The voice of one crying in the wilderness, Prepare ye the way of the Lord, make his paths straight." Matthew has John personally identify himself with the voice in the wilderness. Mark had the quote, then the appearance of John. The reader was supposed to link them together. Matthew seals the identification.

Matthew makes it clear that the "Repent" message of Jesus is identical to that of John, who utters it first. Matthew's John is closer to Jesus than Mark's. For example, when Jesus, after the Temptation in the wilderness, goes into Galilee, it is because he has heard of what happened to John:

"Now when Jesus had heard that John was cast into prison, he departed into Galilee" (Matthew 4:12)—and it is *from that time* that he began to preach the same message as John (Matthew 4:17). John's arrest is *causative* of Jesus starting to preach. Mark 1:14 associates the two events, but only chronologically. These may seem fine points but they are suggestive. Jesus moves with reference to John: the operation is a concerted operation. This closeness is manifested again in Matthew's interesting conversation between John and Jesus, which takes place after John's aforementioned speech, aimed at Pharisees and Sadducees, about God being able to make children of Abraham from the stones, and that even those with deep roots would be torn up and burnt if they failed to bring "fruits of repentance" at the coming apocalyptic harvest, or, more prosaically, imminent Feast of Weeks.

Matthew has Jesus coming all the way from Galilee to be baptized by John. His arrival occurs just after John declares that "he that cometh after me is mightier than I." We then get the comment about John's unworthiness to "bear" his shoes (slightly less forceful than Mark's reference to undoing the coming-one's shoe "latchet") and the proclamation that the one who is coming will "baptize you with the Holy Ghost, and with fire" (3:11). Mark, note, does not have the telling "fire" reference.

This fire might be a reference to the Pentecost story of the Holy Spirit appearing like flames on the apostles' heads, or it could refer to the judgment of the previous verse (3:10) when the bad tree is "cast into the fire." The latter seems most appropriate, given the context. Elijah was known for calling down fire from heaven on God's enemies. Thus Matthew's "baptism of the Holy Ghost" that is greater than John's of water may not have that intimate, philanthropic flavor of Mark: quite the opposite. The Holy Baptism of *fire* would truly sort out the wheat from the chaff! In other words, the baptism of the Holy Ghost looks more in Matthew like a metaphor, not for "Paul's baptism" but for the coming judgment itself, the rain of fire and the waters of destruction, from which the sole protection would be, presumably, the redeemed character of the baptized penitent.

Nevertheless, while the source detail suggests that it is God's judgment that is coming, the arrival of Jesus from Galilee appears to be the intended fulfillment of John's prophecy concerning "he that cometh after me." This does seem a little forced on the material. John prophesies, then, *hey presto!* Jesus appears.

The problem lies in that phrase about the one who is coming after "me." As we have seen, the original prophecies refer to God, the Lord. However, Jesus can only "come after" John with some forced narrative; that is, John makes the speech, then, afterward, Jesus comes from Galilee. Furthermore, the reader or hearer probably knows that John the Baptist died, and *afterward,* Jesus's church began. Jesus appears to "come after." And Matthew's Gospel seems to want you to get that message because Matthew tells us later that John was cast into prison and "from that time Jesus began to preach" (4:17). This all chimes in neatly with the idea—or propaganda—of John as herald of Jesus.

However, apart from the fact that Jesus and John were probably contemporaries, and one did not "come after" the other, it would seem from the nature of their dialogue in Matthew 3:14–15 that the two may have known one another. John may have been surprised to learn his days on Earth were numbered, as indeed were Jesus's: maybe only a year between them, as we shall see.

Jesus comes to be baptized, but John forbids it, saying, apparently in the sense of the water/Holy Ghost duality that "I have need to be baptized of thee, and comest thou to me?" There is no hint that John has suddenly recognized the Messiah, which, one would think, would be a pretty astonishing thing to happen to him. Jesus says, "Suffer it to be so now: for thus it becometh us to fulfill all righteousness." Having heard this curious statement, John duly "suffered him" and did the business (3:15). According to Jesus's statement about righteousness (zedek), Jesus wants to stand within the rules prescribed for the righteous. There was, please note, no prophecy that "the messenger" should baptize the Messiah. But there *does* appear to have been an expectation among New Covenanters that the Holy Spirit would descend on the Messiah. And this is what happens next in Matthew's account. According to this line, Jesus identifies himself with the whole righteous community as a prelude to his being anointed by the Holy Spirit.

There was no prophecy of the messenger baptizing the Messiah, no, but there was certainly a prophecy applied *to the Messiah* that the spirit of the Lord would "rest upon him." We have seen this very prophecy in the New Covenant baptism hymn being slightly reworded to apply to "His Messiah." The prophecy is Isaiah 11:1–2:

> And there shall come forth a rod out of the stem of Jesse, and a Branch shall grow out of his roots:

> And the spirit of the LORD shall rest upon him, the spirit of wisdom and understanding, the spirit of counsel and might, the spirit of knowledge and of the fear of the LORD.

If there is any historical actuality in Matthew's account, it would appear that John and Jesus were, if only for a time, *working together,* perhaps consciously, to enact the prophecies. The descent of the Holy Spirit, its "resting" on the promised leader, has little to do with the Pauline "baptism of the Holy Ghost." Were it otherwise, every baptized Christian would be a messiah, but it does have much to do with the *one* who must accomplish the work of the Lord, which work is clear from the picture in the verses of Isaiah preceding those quoted above. These verses seem to have directly informed the content and flavor of the speech given to John the Baptist concerning the apocalyptic harvest:

> Behold, the Lord, the LORD of hosts, shall lop the bough with terror: and the high ones of stature shall be hewn down, and the haughty shall be humbled. And he shall cut down the thickets of the forest with iron, and Lebanon shall fall by a mighty one. (Isaiah 10:33–34)

A mighty one would come. But who would it be?

LUKE

Luke's Gospel is in no doubt. The mighty one is Jesus, Lord and Savior. "Luke" or Luke's writer was a 100-percent "Paul man." His Gospel bears all the signs of a Pauline education in Jewish history. Whether the author received his instruction from Paul himself is uncertain. The famous "we" passages in Luke's Acts of the Apostles (such as 16:11) suggest he may have traveled with Paul for a time (ca. 58 CE). In that case the general dating spectrum for his Gospel of 80–130 CE seems a trifle late at the top end. However, the Gospel may have been linked to a Luke who knew Paul, whence the first-person plural material derived. The complete work may have been composed by someone else.

Luke is usually dated after Matthew for he appears to use Matthew's Gospel where it suits his purposes. Luke offers lots more information about John the Baptist than Matthew does. He may have got this inside information from Paul. Paul was well informed about affairs in and around the Temple, in which world, we assume, John was brought up. We receive a fascinating account of John's birth and his family. We learn that John was related to Jesus and that their mothers were friends. We shall explore this startling aspect of Luke's John in chapter 6.

Luke gives us some straight history too. He tells us that it was in the fifteenth year of the Roman Emperor Tiberius (29 CE) that John, the only son of priest Zacharias, received the "word of God," being in the wilderness at the time; in Jerusalem, Luke tells us, Annas and Caiaphas were high priests. Was John steering clear of high priestly pollution? Luke gives us the now-standard quotation from Isaiah 40:3 about the voice in the wilderness. He takes Matthew's speech about the messianic harvest and the stones of Abraham. He aims it, however, not at Pharisees and Sadducees, as Matthew does (Sadducees were hard to come by after the Temple's destruction in 70 CE), but rather at the "multitude" who have come to John for baptism. This seems a bit rich; John has, after all, called the people to repent. Furthermore, and for no apparent reason, John calls the undifferentiated multitude a "generation of vipers." *Who,* he asks, has warned them to flee the wrath to come? Who indeed? So, having come, they should bring forth "fruits worthy of repentance" and humble themselves utterly.

Luke is now off on his own tack. Impressed and conceivably at a loss, the "people" ask John, "What shall we do then?" John gives them an itinerary of the duties of zedek: righteousness toward one's fellow. Whence Luke obtained this nugget of John's social teaching we know not:

> "He that hath two coats, let him impart to him that hath none; and he that hath meat, let him do likewise."
>
> Then came the publicans [tax collectors] to be baptized, and said unto him, "Master, what shall we do?" And he said unto them, "Exact no more than that which is appointed you."
>
> And the soldiers likewise demanded of him, saying, "And what shall we do?" And he said unto them, "Do violence to no man, neither accuse any falsely; and be content with your wages."
>
> And as the people were in expectation, and all men mused in their hearts, whether he were the Christ, or not. (Luke 3:11–15)

This all sounds like Paul's general good-neighborly, Pax Romana advice. *Why Paul?* First of all, Luke has omitted Matthew and Mark's references to John's living on a wild diet of locusts and honey. This is almost certainly because Paul told his opponents who insisted on the Mosaic Law for holiness that vegetarian diets were for the "weak"; real men (Gentiles?!) knew God was not against eating flesh. Out goes Judas Maccabeus's wilderness diet of herbs! Luke's John does not advertise his diet, only to say that anyone who has meat should share it.

We now come to the tax collectors. Where the taxes raised were specifically for Rome, pious Jews of the New Covenanter stamp held it blasphemous to give pagans the fruit of God's holy land. Taxes caused wars. Tax collectors were hated people. In the Pauline spirit, Luke's John advocates the view that so long as the amounts levied were fair,

God would accept the work of the tax collector. Since tax collecting in this period was simply an opportunity to extort sums for oneself (that being the "pay"), the demand was somewhat unrealistic, though that may have been the intention. God's forgiveness would not come cheap, and was nonnegotiable.

Likewise, the reference to soldiers has the ring of Paul about it, and if these were Roman soldiers, then particularly so. Asking a soldier not to do violence was quixotic in the extreme. Paul, however, advocated the view that Roman soldiers did the work of God, keeping order. He was not at all in step with his patriotic countrymen here, who had to stop themselves from reaching for a weapon whenever a Roman soldier appeared. When Roman Senator Cyrenius and Coponius of the Equestrian Order came down from Syria to supervise a tax census over Judea in 6 CE (Herod's son Archelaus had been recalled to Rome by Caesar Augustus), the occasion gave their unpaid soldiers an opportunity to supplement their meager income by grabbing what they could, bullying Judeans and destroying their homes, robbing, pillaging, and crucifying opponents. Galilee was in uproar, and a rising was only suppressed with great savagery. Luke omits such incendiary "anti-Roman" facts.

To ask a soldier to be content with his wages and not to accuse people falsely would undoubtedly have been an otherworldly Godsend for the people, but to ask it of a soldier would, historically and realistically speaking, have been regarded as something of a sick joke. In Luke's account of the taxation period, where he mistakenly places Jesus's birth (see my book *The Missing Family of Jesus*), everything is sweetness and light. Joseph and Mary make their way to Bethlehem as good citizens—having no Roman citizenship they still had to pay—and their sole obstacle is an inn too full for comfort. In cleaning up the history for Gentile audiences, Luke did all but give the couple a kindly Roman escort. Luke took the Pauline view; indeed, to do anything else would have made his Gospel a seditious document and its holder liable to execution.

THE ESSENES AND JOHN

John doubtless had a message of righteous conduct suitable for a penitent, but it is doubtful if he expressed it like this. There is one detail, however, that bears comment. That first injunction: that a man with two coats should give to he who had none, and if he had meat, he should share it, suggests not only a sense of social justice (zedek), but a whole attitude to life, where material welfare was deemed secondary to spiritual welfare. We find precisely this attitude in an account written by Josephus of a Jewish sect called the Essenes. Hear this from the eighth chapter of Josephus's second book of *Jewish Wars*:

> These men [Essenes] are despisers of riches, and so very communicative as raises our admiration. Nor is there any one to be found among them who hath more than another; for it is a law among them, that those who come to them must let what they have be common to the whole order, insomuch that among them all there is no appearance of poverty, or excess of riches, but everyone's possessions are intermingled with every other's possessions; and so there is, as it were, one patrimony among all the brethren.

> They have no one certain city, but many of them dwell in every city; and if any of their sect come from other places, what they have lies open for them, just as if it were their own; and they go in to such as they never knew before, as if they had been ever so long acquainted with them. For which reason they carry nothing at all with them when they travel into remote parts, though still they take their weapons with them, for fear of thieves. Accordingly, there is, in every city where they live, one appointed particularly to take care of strangers, and to provide garments and other necessaries for them. But the habit and management of their bodies is such as children use who are in fear of their masters. Nor do they allow of the change of shoes till be first torn to pieces, or worn out by time. *Nor do they*

either buy or sell any thing to one another; but every one of them gives
what he hath to him that wanteth it, and receives from him again in
lieu of it what may be convenient for himself; and although there be no
requital made, they are fully allowed to take what they want of whom-
soever they please. [my italics]

And truly, as for other things, they do nothing but according to
the injunctions of their curators; only these two things are done
among them at everyone's own free will, which are to assist those
that want it, and to show mercy; for they are permitted of their
own accord to afford succor to such as deserve it, when they stand
in need of it, and to bestow food on those that are in distress; but
they cannot give any thing to their kindred without the curators.

It should be noted that the Essenes had priests among their number.
Some of them worked as stewards for an order that numbered some
four thousand, according to Josephus. It remains something of an
open question as to whether John was, or had been, of their number.

There is a telling detail that links the Essenes' extraordinary
piety (hesed) to the picture we have of John. The Essenes practiced
ritual washing for purposes of purification:

And as for their piety toward God, it is very extraordinary; for
before sunrising they speak not a word about profane matters,
but put up certain prayers, which they have received from their
forefathers, as if they made a supplication for its rising. After
this every one of them are sent away by their curators, to exercise
some of those arts wherein they are skilled, in which they labor
with great diligence till the fifth hour. After which they assemble themselves together again into one place; and when they have
clothed themselves in white veils, they then bathe their bodies in
cold water.

The purification was a privilege of members fully admitted; neophytes could not be "partakers in the waters of purification" until they had observed sect discipline for a year.

So striking is this linkage between cold bathing and the Essenes that for many years scholars presumed that on the basis of this link and because of the exclusive and self-exalting character of the community documents of the Dead Sea Scrolls that the authors of those documents must have been Essenes, and the whole conception of Qumran-Essenes-Dead Sea Scrolls sprouted and grew. It was quickly presumed that because the Dead Sea Scrolls were found in some of the caves of Wadi Qumran on the western side of the Dead Sea, and since archaeaology showed there had once been a small settlement and cemetery at Qumran, then there must have been an "Essene monastery" there. The idea of the "monastery" appears to have come in part from the imaginative world of Dominican monks engaged by the Catholic Church's École Biblique to translate the texts. They knew of numerous monasteries in Palestine with libraries of old texts and put two and one together and came up with a mystical sect of unorthodox monks somewhat addicted to ritual bathing. Tourists to Israel are still told about the "Essene monastery" at Qumran. It seems to suit the authorities: a convenient but unproven theory.

Josephus puts the Essenes in towns and private homes, with stewarded agricultural land, not in the Judean wilderness. I wonder whether a stone-built community of anti-Herodian, anti-Sadducee messianic holy men ready at the first significant trump to join a messianic war against "Belial" and all his minions would have been tolerated by Herod the Great, or any of his family, for more than the time it would have taken them to lay a second course of stones.

According to Josephus, an Essene called Simon was an advisor to Herod the Great himself. Hardly a spiritual renegade, Simon the Essene was given to famously accurate prophecy. Perhaps he advised Herod concerning Matthew's "Christmas" Magi reported to have visited Jerusalem most probably in 7 BCE, inspired by the famous messianic Star Prophecy (Numbers 24:17, 19).

Philo of Alexandria, the Baptist's contemporary, also puts the Essenes in towns, but maintains they preferred villages on account of the dissolute types to be found in towns and cities. The outsider, as regards Essene whereabouts, is the Roman historian Pliny. Pliny, who died amid the volcanic ash that smothered Pompeii and Herculaneum in 79 CE, wrote a voluminous classic, the *Natural History*. The *Natural History* (5:18:73) refers to Essenes on the western side of the Dead Sea, inland a little, near En-gedi. En-gedi is some twenty miles south of Khirbet Qumran:

> By the western shores [of the Dead Sea], but away from their harmful effects, live a solitary people, the Essenes, wonderful besides all others in the world, being without any women and renouncing all sexual desire, having no money, and with only palm trees as companions. Their assembly is born again day by day from the multitudes, tired of life and the vicissitudes of fortune, that crowd thither for their manner of living. So, for thousands of ages—strange to say—a people, in which no one is born, is eternal, so fruitful for them is the repentance of others for their life! Lying below [*infra*] these was the town of En Gedi, once second only to Jerusalem in fertility and groves of palm trees, but now like the other, a ruin. After that, Masada, a castle on a crag, itself not far from the Dead Sea, is the end of Judaea.

En-gedi was destroyed in 40 BCE during the conflict that brought Herod the Great to power. Since it was rebuilt by the time of the Jewish Revolt, Pliny's information presumably derived from Roman surveys made around John the Baptist's lifetime. Stephen Goranson of Duke University has made the interesting observation that Pliny's reference to the "fruitfulness of their repentance" is rather suggestive when seen next to the account of Matthew 3:7–8 of John's attack on Pharisees and Sadducees coming for baptism, "You brood of vipers! Who warned you to flee from the wrath to come? Bring forth therefore fruits meet for repentance. . . ."

Pliny tells the charming story of the Essene community's numbers being perpetually replenished over the generations by penitents (*tam fecunda illis aliorum vitae paenitentia est*). The fruit of that repentance was a community that enjoyed a kind of "eternal life," which itself rather justified the Essenes' abstention from sexual desire!

Could it not have been the case that a body of New Covenanters had at some time taken refuge among Essenes, as may be implied by Pliny's account, when under pressure, secreting their "library" nearby?

Josephus speaks of Essenes being tortured by Roman soldiers, presumably for interrogation purposes. I speculate of course, but could it not have come to the Romans' attention that Essenes were hiding more radical countrymen among their number, on the basis that they had made full repentance of all sins and were thus eligible for their own washing for purification? Thus you could have at Qumran, or further down the coast, an Essene community of some kind becoming, in the tumult of war, a temporary refuge for unarmed eschatological radicals who owed their inspiration to the Teacher of Righteousness, the *Damascus Document,* the *Manual of Discipline,* and sundry works and prophetic commentaries, some of which, anyway, would not have been alien to what we know of the sympathies of the Essenes. We seem to find such openness to the repentant of different and conceivably more radical backgrounds in the accounts of Jesus (whom we know had Zealots in his entourage); may we not also see such a situation with regard to John, perhaps a sometime Essene who had left the community proper on receiving his call in 29 CE?

Proponents of the Essene-Qumran theory take Pliny's statement as support for their advocacy of Qumran as an Essene base, even though the archaeology at Qumran hardly adds up to a town, more like a trading post. While the debate will doubtless rattle on, the fact seems to be that the Dead Sea Scrolls material does not accurately reflect the spiritual priorities of the Essenes, as Josephus describes them. Nor does the word *Essene* feature in any of the scrolls; one might consider that a significant fact. Nevertheless, as I have suggested, more radical bodies may have left or stored their writings in the caves near to an Essene base in desperation, or in hope that the Essenes themselves might not have suffered persecution. One can certainly imagine an Essene keeping a blind eye to such a scenario.

Why some scholars are so keen to force the issue seems to be a deep matter. It may arguably have something to do with (a) a desire to keep the nonbiblical Dead Sea Scrolls material in the "sectarian" bracket, and therefore no serious challenge to modern Judaism and broadly accepted Jewish history, and (b) a desire to keep the dangerous idea at bay that the New Covenanter material may represent an authentic "proto-Christian" messianic movement and even, as Eisenman believes, *the* works of "primitive" Jewish "Christianity" *itself* as against a "heretical" attack on it, instigated by Paul, which gave birth to the Orthodox and Catholic-Gentile Christian traditions. The Dead Sea Scrolls are still political hot potatoes, something you can tell by the hysterical level of invective that surrounds deviance from mainstream opinion since their first reappearance to the angry world of 1947.

While Josephus's account gives us little to identify the Essenes with the legal puritanism and messianic fervor of the New Covenanters, there is a flavor to be gleaned from his presentation of Essene living that does not seem out of place with what we know of John, or, for that matter, of Jesus.

Philo of Alexandria's glowing account of the Essenes is less philosophical than Josephus's. In his *Quod Omnis Probus Liber Sit* ("Every Good Man is Free"; 12:75–87) the Jewish philosopher Philo makes it clear that Essenes advocate social equality, loathe anything that renders people covetous or makes them want to get ahead of their fellows, and insists that the Essenes, which he takes to mean "holy ones," draw most inspiration from the Law:

> . . . and leaving the logical part of philosophy, as in no respect necessary for the acquisition of virtue, to the word catchers, and the

natural part, as being too sublime for human nature to master, to those who love to converse about high objects (except indeed so far as such a study takes in the contemplation of the existence of God and of the creation of the universe), they devote all their attention to the moral part of philosophy, using as instructors the laws of their country, which it would have been impossible for the human mind to devise without divine inspiration.

Now these laws they are taught at other times, indeed, but most especially on the seventh day, for the seventh day is accounted sacred, on which they abstain from all other employments, and frequent the sacred places, which are called synagogues, and there they sit according to their age in classes, the younger sitting under the elder, and listening with eager attention in becoming order.

Then one, indeed, takes up the holy volume and reads it, and another of the men of the greatest experience comes forward and explains what is not very intelligible, for a great many precepts are delivered in enigmatical modes of expression, and allegorically, as the old fashion was; and thus the people are taught piety, and holiness, and justice, and economy, and the science of regulating the state, and the knowledge of such things as are naturally good, or bad, or indifferent, and to choose what is right and to avoid what is wrong, using a threefold variety of definitions, and rules, and criteria, namely, the love of God, and the love of virtue, and the love of mankind. (vv. 80–83)

One has no difficulty in seeing either John or Jesus at home, at least for a time, among such persons.

We may, I think, imagine a certain fluidity of movement among individuals who turned away from the corruption surrounding the Temple system of formal religion. Sincere seekers might go from one group to another, following their destiny; thus practices and ideas might be found outside of their source bodies. For example, one might today like some of the ideas of Freemasonry without joining a Lodge. Or one might have once been a member and since "moved on," keeping to some insights that were personally meaningful. One might keep up a "working relationship" with the system, drawing on it in times of need. The Essene system, while being closed in terms of membership, did not "lock up" their members in closed communities; they traveled from place to place with a mutual cooperative system that seems to have functioned in a manner analogous to Freemasonry.

One thing we find in no account of the Essenes, however, is any enthusiasm for, or reference to, messianic solutions to Israel's woes. This must be significant. However, what we have in the early first century is a widespread reaction to the Herodians and their chosen priests. This reaction was explosive and took a number of forms. In practice there was bound to have been interaction as well as mutual hostility between groups on points of doctrine. One is reminded of the invective spat on the "Judean People's Front" by the "People's Front of Judea" in Monty Python's satire on messianism, *The Life of Brian* (1979).

The Essenes, for example, had their own differences with the Temple system. According to Josephus's account in his *Antiquities of the Jews* (book 18, chapter 1), Essenes would not make sacrifices in the Temple in Jerusalem, even though they still sent produce dedicated to God there. They had, according to Josephus, "more pure lustrations of their own." Philo insists the Essenes would not sacrifice living animals. As a result, the Essenes were apparently excluded from the common court of the Temple, whether by choice or prejudice against them, Josephus does not make clear. He nonetheless points out that the Essenes were "better than other men" in their course of life. Righteousness, they believed, was its own reward.

Essenes did give to those outside their number who were in need, and even took in unwanted children, while being themselves, in the main, unmarried. There is no reference to them calling the whole nation to repentance however, and Josephus has them for the most part occupied with husbandry and their own rituals and business.

Josephus had himself been trained by a holy ascetic, one Banus, when a youth. Would it be surprising if John likewise had received early training among such persons? His specific "calling" came to him, after all, in his thirties, according to Luke's dating. Josephus does not say that John was an Essene. It is possible that since John had serious trouble with the authorities, Josephus did not wish to "rub it in." In his account of the interrogation of Essenes by the Romans during the revolt, they never broke nor cursed their torturers. As he admired the Essenes so much, Josephus may have been unwilling to give any grounds for thinking they could be "rabble-rousers."

If John was, or had been, among their number, Josephus's account may give us an idea of his real dress. The Essenes wore white clothes, bound with a girdle at the waist, and a white veil. They believed in the immortality of the soul. The soul's "enticement" into the body constituted the soul's imprisonment; death was a release, a consummation devoutly to be wished: a point made strongly in Charlton Heston's portrayal of John in the film *The Greatest Story Ever Told,* based on Fulton Oursler's bestseller of 1949. The film script has Heston replying to Herod Antipas's threat of execution: "You'll be freeing me!"—clearly inspired by Josephus's account to which the sensational discovery of the Dead Sea Scrolls had doubtless alerted the scriptwriters.

Essenes eschewed fornication. According to Josephus, they partook largely of silent suppers—no one spoke over anyone else—with bread and equal measure of meat, in private rooms, served by persons engaged for the purpose. This sounds familiar, doesn't it?

> They dispense their anger after a just manner, and restrain their passion. They are eminent for fidelity, and are the ministers of peace; whatsoever they say also is firmer than an oath; but swearing is avoided by them, and they esteem it worse than perjury for they say that he who cannot be believed without [swearing by] God is already condemned. They also take great pains in studying the writings of the ancients, and choose out of them what is most for the advantage of their soul and body; and they inquire after such roots and medicinal stones as may cure their distempers.

There are also those among them who undertake to foretell things to come by reading the holy books, and using several sorts of purifications, and being perpetually conversant in the discourses of the prophets; and it is but seldom that they miss in their predictions.

Josephus elsewhere illustrates this with the aforementioned account of the Essene called Simon who served at the court of Herod the Great. Simon predicted that Herod's successor would reign in Judea for ten years, which was the case. So, clearly, there were Essenes who did not spend all their time with their brethren. We should also note that Josephus, to a degree, plays down the legalistic side of his subjects. Nevertheless, Essenes were particularly strict about the Sabbath and about ritual washing. If juniors touched senior members, they had to wash. People who broke the rules were kicked out with no support. Josephus says that members so ejected kept to what they had been told. Rejects had been known to try to live on grass or had starved to death in misery. Josephus then says that such former members were taken back in, just before they expired. The consequences were considered ample recompense for sin, and they could begin again. One might think of the famous story of the rich young man who came to Jesus, impressed. When Jesus asks if he would sell all he had to follow him, the man made his excuses and left. He might have expected similar treatment from Essenes who held all things in common, as Acts records also of the post-Pentecost assembly of Jesus's followers in Jerusalem during the late 30s.

Frankly, it is astonishing that Christian scripture forebears to mention the Essenes. This would not be so startling if, in some way, the church had emerged out of some kinship or association with the Essenes, a name, by the way, whose derivation is unknown.

With nothing to say of the Essenes' eschatology, or ideas about the end of the world, Josephus's accounts seem clear that they were not, apparently, obsessed with waiting for a messiah to redeem Israel. Josephus does say, however, that they held books of "angels." The one significant book of the period to feature lists of angels was the remarkable Book of Enoch. The Book of Enoch does look to a final judgment, though it is less a judgment on humankind than on the wicked "Watchers" or rebellious angels who, in primordial times, had insinuated themselves into the bodies of humanity out of ancient lust for the daughters of men. This was an esoteric interpretation of the account of the "Nephilim" in Genesis 6:1–4. Esoteric tradition suggested that the fallen angels had become guardian angels of the Gentile nations. Before the Gentiles could be saved, the fallen angels—their national guardians, or "types"—would have to be judged. Clement of Alexandria (ca. 180 CE) believed this justified Paul's mission to the Gentiles. If the fallen angel doctrine was a favored doctrine of the Essenes, Josephus either knows not of it, or does not wish his readers to know of it. He wants his readers to think of the Essenes as exemplary men of philosophy and virtue, and this undoubtedly colors his presentation.

I have to say that while evidence for a direct link between John and the Essenes is insufficient to deliver conviction, I find it difficult to think of John and not think of them.

For all Luke's extra information, his presentation of John is, when all is said and done, still only that of a secondary figure and typically colorless as to John's personality. Luke's concern is with Jesus as the Son of God; John played his part.

Luke has the "people" ask themselves whether *John* was the Christ. *Why* they should do so is by no means clear; *that* they did so is significant. John had not done all that a messiah was expected to do. John did stand up for God's Law against religious and political authority. He demonstrated exemplary personal righteousness and piety, but, unlike Elijah, he had not raised the dead, unless we take "raising of the dead" as a metaphor for inducing a spiritual awakening in those formerly dead to the word of God and the divine life. Nevertheless, the suspicion must lurk that people afterward *did* take John as a messiah, and Luke is preempting (or postempting) the issue. He lands the now familiar line about the distinction between water and Holy Spirit baptism right on the nail of this issue. According to the tradition dear to Luke, John cannot be the Christ because his baptism is not powerful enough. Luke adds Matthew's "fire" to the Spirit baptism. The coming one will baptize with Holy Spirit and with fire. Nevertheless, Luke clearly understands the fire as referring primarily to the fire of the messianic harvest: "the chaff he will burn with the fire unquenchable" (3:17). Luke has his cake and eats it. He links the Holy Spirit baptism he knows about from Paul directly to the fire of judgment, as Paul himself did.

In Luke's account, Jesus's part in his own baptism is confined to himself. There is no conversation with the Baptist: "Now when all the people were baptized, it came to pass that Jesus also being baptized, and praying, the heaven was opened, and the Holy Ghost descended . . ." (3:21–22). It may be the case that Luke wants to be sure that none confuse the water and spirit baptisms. That is, *John's* agency in the baptism, which brings the Holy Spirit on Jesus, is muted. The opening of the heavens seems to have as much to do with Jesus "praying" as with the now almost incidental fact that he was being baptized by John "when all the people were baptized." The reason people did not get the Holy Spirit was because John was not given the gift —as, Luke believed, Paul was. And yet, the uncomfortable tradition existed that John baptized, and Jesus received the Holy Spirit. Another fairly obvious point coming out of this distinction is that there *is* no account of Jesus baptizing with water and the Holy Spirit (or fire) anyhow. When Jesus baptizes in John's Gospel (3:22–24), the idea that Jesus was himself baptizing people is actually *denied* in the chapter following (John 4:1–3)!

Chapter Five

JOHN AND JOHN

BUT FOR THE LONG TRADITION that John's Gospel was named, rather confusingly, after the "beloved disciple," who "wrote these things" (21:24), and who was then, tautologically, identified as "John," disciple of Jesus, from the Gospel's existing title—and supposed to be John the "apostle," or "evangelist"—one might conclude that the Gospel was originally named after John the Baptist. Yes, *John the Baptist.* That is not to say that the Baptist actually wrote it, of course, but that its contents are bound up with the figure and alleged testimony of John in a powerful, determinative, mysterious way.

If this sounds a trifle eccentric at first hearing, take a look at the following remarkable feat of verbal acrobatics from chapter 1, verses 29–34:

> The next day John seeth Jesus coming unto him, and saith, "Behold the Lamb of God, which taketh away the sin of the world. This is he of whom I said, 'After me cometh a man, who is preferred before me: for he was before me. And I knew him not: but that he should be made manifest to Israel, therefore am I come baptizing with water.'" And John bare record, saying, "I saw the Spirit descending from heaven like a dove, and it abode upon him. And I knew him not: but he that sent me to baptize with water, the same said unto me, Upon whom thou shalt see the Spirit descending, and remaining

on him, the same is he which baptizeth with the Holy Ghost. And I saw, and bare record that this is the Son of God."

The whole story is presented as coming from the Baptist who "saw" and "bore record," that is, who testified in his own words, what happened at the baptism: "And I saw . . ." In complete contradiction to the synoptic Gospels, John says it was *he* who saw the Spirit descending: "And John bare record, saying, I saw the Spirit descending like a dove, and it abode upon him" (v. 32). This alone would seem to me to explain how this maverick Gospel, beloved of mystics, a veritable "half-way house to Gnosticism," as Rudolf Bultmann's study of John called it, came to acquire the title of the Gospel of *John*. It is there, staring you in the face if you care to see it.

John is doing the testifying. John is "bearing the record"—at least to start with.

Common sense suggests that someone read that direct testimony from John in the first chapter and titled the work "The Gospel according to John," unless it was so titled from its beginning. *John* is announcing the good news: *this* is the "herald's" role: the kērux of the divine ceremony.

On this reckoning, John the Baptist *is* John the Evangelist! And who is John testifying *to*? It seems to me that "John" is addressing an elect body in an eternal setting. The text is then delivered, as it were, to the seekers below: *us*.

The Gospel is the truth in which we are called to "dip": the mixing bowl in which we may be spiritually baptized. A Neoplatonist philosopher would undoubtedly recognize John's role here as one incarnating the divine Hermes, the psychopomp leading the soul upward through the waters to a higher life, or, if the Neoplatonist were Hebraic in outlook, across the waters to the Other Side and on toward the Promised Land: a new Moses, preparing the way for the new Joshua-Jesus.

The Gospel of John's treatment of the baptism story is extraordinarily peculiar. Yes, we see some of the familiar lines about John's unworthiness to undo the shoe latchet of one coming after him, but the whole essence is different; it is deep. There is bizarre wordplay; the *real* message is for those who can see behind the apparent sense. Let's just take the verses above.

"This is he of whom I said, "After me cometh a man, which is preferred before me: for he was before me." Note the play on *"after me* cometh," followed by "for he was *before me.*" This seems a flat contradiction, but it is a gnostic riddle: *how can he who comes after be he was before?* The answer is in verse 26:

> I baptize with water: but there standeth one among you, whom ye
> know not.

There is one who *stands*. This almost suggests a giant. This being stands when all else falls. This being has *always stood.* You did not see him. This being is the one "whom ye know not." Verse 31 then informs us that John also, *he* knew him not: "And I knew him not: but that he should be made manifest to Israel, therefore am I come baptizing with water."

John's job is to make the one whom we, *and he,* knew not, manifest to Israel. And he does this by baptizing with water. Without John, the being is not made manifest. Without John, we cannot *know.*

John knows.

In verse 33, John repeats that line for emphasis; it is crucial: "And I knew him not [he does now!]: but he that sent me to baptize with water, the same said unto me, Upon whom thou shalt see the Spirit descending, and remaining on him, the same is he who baptizeth with the Holy Ghost. And I saw, and bare record that this is the Son of God" (John 1:33-34).

John has received a message from "he who sent me" (*ho pempsas me*). This Greek phrase is used with great emphasis by Jesus later on in the Gospel: "he who sent me." "He who sent me" is *"the Father."*

The Father sent John.

John *saw,* and "bare record."

What did John see?

John saw the "Logos." The "Logos" is translated as the "Word" (John 1:1) but English does not do the Greek justice. The Logos was understood by Greek philosophy as the intelligence, the Mind, by whose order the universe was created. That is why "he" was before John. "He" had *always* existed. For anyone saying, "John came first; Jesus copied him," John's Gospel says "No!" John *himself* testifies that he did not really *know* the one who was before him, who yet came "after." This figure is a cosmic, eternal principle, ever-present but unseen; now manifesting in flesh.

Those seeking understanding of the universe need to find the Logos inherent in the creation-design, just as a Taoist seeks the Tao, or as an ancient Egyptian sought Ma'at: goddess of justice and balance. The Hindu equivalent of the Greek word *logos* is the Sanskrit *vāk,* or divine sound: the manifestation of the soundless. When the primal conditions emerged in the ultimate *soundless* God for the creation of the universe, a divine sound became manifest. Thus: "in the beginning was the Word."

In the deepest sense, the universe *is* sound, or vibration, and making union with that sound is the basis and goal of mantra yoga (where the Sanskrit *man* means "thought," and *tra,* "liberation"); thus: the "truth will make you free." The carnally inaudible (or unseen) vāk or logos may reveal the existence of the soundless, invisible source of creation. In pictorial terms, the primal God's utterance contains the divine formative intelligence: the "word" is creative and *in* creation; the "word" was "with us from the beginning."

At the time John was baptizing, a Jewish philosopher living in Alexandria called Philo (ca. 20 BCE–50 CE) identified the Greek *logos* with the Hebrew *Hokmah,* or Divine Wisdom. The Divine Wisdom was philosophically identified as God's cocreator or "Son" (not to be taken literally!), *a part of himself,* the means by which intelligibility was infused into primal chaos, and the means by which that intelligibility and meaning could be discerned by the "children of wisdom." While the Logos could be seen as a manifestation of God's profound nature, men, by and large, could not see it.

The *Word* of God should not be, as it so often is, confused with the *words* of God or written scriptures, however exalted or profound they may be. The Voice or presence of the Spirit—the divine breath itself—is far more important than letters and words. Far beyond mere words exists the divine vibration; *that* is what must be experienced and known for true spiritual liberation to take place. This spiritual tradition was almost entirely obliterated in the bibliolatry of the Western Reformation, which divorced the words from the Word and Music: the divine sound to which the carnal world is deaf—and blind.

The hymn, which opens the Gospel of John, famously leaps to a tremendous affirmation:

"And the Word was made flesh, and dwelt among us" (John 1:14).

That is to say, the "divine word" became, temporarily, audible, "enfleshed" to those who had ears for it. This Logos is the one that the people among whom *he* was standing *knew not*. The Logos was there, but not manifest; the Logos went unseen. And the answer to this riddle becomes plainer still. The Logos was indeed, as John the Baptist declares, "before me." The Gospel's prologue makes it plain that the Logos was *preexistent*. It was both *with* God as being an aspect of God, and it "*was* God" since God is not divided but manifest according to the perceiver's capacity. To make the situation plainer still, the hymn or prologue begins with a direct echo of Genesis 1:1: "In the beginning God created the heaven and the earth." John begins, "In the beginning was the Word . . ." There was no heaven and earth without the Word, the Logos. And the Logos appears as a Man!

We need to look closely at the famous prologue to John's Gospel, for John the Baptist is revealed in its words to be *second only in significance to the Logos*. John occupies a very important place in the divine scheme. It is extraordinary that this inference has so rarely been grasped. So full have commentators been with the idea that John was, according to "John," secondary, they have been blinded to the import of what he was secondary *to*. If John's Prologue is a hymn to the Logos, the Son of God, it is also a hymn to John:

> In the beginning was the Word, and the Word was
>   with God, and the Word was God.
> The same was in the beginning with God.
> All things were made by him; and without him was
>   not any thing made that was made.
> In him was life; and the life was the light of men.
> And the light shineth in darkness; and the darkness
>   comprehended it not.
> There was a man sent from God, whose name was
>   John.
> The same came for a witness, to bear witness of the
>   Light, that all men through him might believe.
> He was not that Light, but was sent to bear
>   witness of that Light.
> That was the true Light, which lighteth every man
>   that cometh into the world.
> He was in the world, and the world was made by
>   him, and the world knew him not.
> He came unto his own, and his own received him not.
> But as many as received him, to them gave he
>   power to become the sons of God, even to them
>   that believe on his name:
> Which were born, not of blood, nor of the will of the
>   flesh, nor of the will of man, but of God. (1:1–13)

There is, of course, an entire religion in these words.

It is generally held by scholars that the references to John, *viz*, "He was not that Light, but was sent to bear witness of that Light" were a deliberate attempt to scotch residual beliefs among John's followers that he, John, was the Messiah. If so, those beliefs must have been very strong indeed. If we accept a date of ca. 90–130 CE for this Gospel, those beliefs must have been remarkably persistent. According to this view, John was being taken by followers to be "the Light," the one who revealed the essence of salvation, long, long after his death.

John's Gospel, then, trumps this view with nothing less than the testimony of *John the Baptist himself*! This explains with satisfying economy why the fourth Gospel takes the name of *John:* John the Baptist.

John was the true Evangelist.

John himself elucidates why the Son of God must take primacy over him. It is because the Logos came "before him." The Son is a power, the wisdom, behind the universe: the only one who can ultimately create and save, the only one with the right and the means to destroy.

However, John's Gospel does not deny that John was sent by God to make the Son manifest to Israel. John begins as the *center* of religious interest. Priests and Levites leave Jerusalem to go to John. His testimony opens the Gospel on completion of the prologue. He is temporary narrator and subject:

John bare witness of him, and cried, saying, "This was he of whom I spake, He that cometh after me is preferred before me: for he was before me." And of his fullness [*plērōmatos*, a term favored by Gnostics for the Father or Godhead] have all we received, and grace for grace. For the law was given by Moses, but grace and truth came by Jesus Christ. No man hath seen God at any time; the only begotten Son, which is in the bosom of the Father, he hath declared him. And this is the record of John, when the Jews sent priests and Levites from Jerusalem to ask him, "Who art thou?"

And he confessed, and denied not; but confessed, I am not the Christ.

And they asked him, "What then? Art thou Elias?" [Greek form of Elijah]

And he saith, "I am not." "Art thou that prophet?" And he answered, "No." Then said they unto him, "Who art thou? that we may give an answer to them that sent us. What sayest thou of thyself?"

He said, "I am the voice of one crying in the wilderness, Make straight the way of the Lord, as said the prophet Esaias." And they, which were sent, were of the Pharisees.

And they asked him, and said unto him, "Why baptizest thou then, if thou be not that Christ, nor Elias, neither that prophet?"

John answered them, saying, "I baptize with water: but there standeth one among you, whom ye know not; He it is, who coming after me is preferred before me, whose shoe's latchet I am not worthy to unloose."

These things were done in Bethabara beyond Jordan, where John was baptizing.

The neutral voice of the narrator now reappears, but John is soon back with his "Behold the Lamb of God" speech and the ensuing drama flows from John. After the baptism, two of John's disciples, one named as Andrew, brother of "Simon Peter," leave John. They follow the one the Baptist has called a second time "the Lamb of God." Andrew's brother then joins them. Having been informed that his brother and the unnamed disciple of John have "found the Messias," Jesus gets his operation going.

John showed them the way.

How much historical fact might lie behind this extraordinary, cross-pollinating narrative is anybody's guess. It does not read like history and it is not meant to be history; it is really *meta*-history. The essence of the "events" takes place on another plane: a higher plane. Such may be hinted at in the otherwise prosaic-looking statement of the gospel writer that "these things were done in Bethabara beyond Jordan, where John was baptizing" (1:28). *Beth* is the Greek transliteration of the Hebrew for "house" and *abarah* is the Hebrew for a ford or crossing place. While on the one hand we may be talking of a convenient spot on a tributary east of the Jordan, the "ford" and the "house" suggest the presence of a ferry. Symbolically, the "ferryman" may then be seen as John-Hermes. Hermes, remember, was seen in Hellenistic tradition as a "psychopomp": literally a guide of souls through the darkness of death to the other side, the herald of another world attainable only through death. *Johanan* means "God comforts." Hermes bridges boundaries from the divine to the human: in Jungian terms, from the unconscious to the conscious and back again. Greeks would make a sacrifice to Hermes before going on a journey.

Think again of Leonardo's John, with his upwardly pointing finger. May we not also see this as a *beckoning finger,* indicating the words: *"this way"*—and is not this way "across the ford," through the darkness from which John emerges? There is of course a well-known link between the passage of symbolic death, rebirth, and baptism.

The baptismal events in John's Gospel illustrate spiritual insights of great depth; one is reminded of Brecht's dictum that "realism does not consist in reproducing reality, but in showing how things really are." Dramatic truth transcends journalism. Even so, it has long been recognized that the fourth Gospel does contain unusual pieces of authentic period background unrecorded in the synoptic (or broadly similar) Gospels. We meet new characters, such as Nicodemus; new events, such as the wedding at Cana; new miracles, such as the raising of Lazarus from the dead. In fact, we get a new perspective altogether, *so* new in fact that John was not accepted by all churches as authoritative scripture for some time. What is more, John flatly contradicts the assumptions and plain statements of both Matthew and Luke that the Baptist was a prophet—that he was Elijah—the prophesied messenger, returned.

When in Matthew 11, John hears, even though in prison, what Jesus has been doing, he dispatches two disciples to ask, "Art thou he that should come, or do we look for another?" This sounds credible, possibly even historical. John's John of course would hardly need to enquire. He has seen the Logos in the flesh!

However, it is not entirely clear whether the imprisoned Baptist is asking whether Jesus is the "messenger," that is, Elijah, or whether he is the one for whom Elijah must make straight the path. In trying to explain matters to his disciples, Jesus emphasized it is *John* who "is Elias, which has for to come." If, that is, they "will receive it," meaning, if the disciples can understand the teaching and deal with the statement's import. According to this account, John was Elias returned, but perhaps did not realize it himself!

One might have thought that it was clear by now to Matthew and Luke that John was the messenger, but Luke's account of the visit of John's disciples to Jesus to find out who he is leaves the question hanging in the air.

Luke prefaces his treatment of John's disciples' visit with a stupendous miracle. Coming to a city called Nain, southwest of the Sea of Galilee, near the Judea-Galilee border, Jesus is called to a widow's grief. The widow's son, a young man, has died. Jesus raises the widow's son from the dead. The significance here is that the story is an almost precise repeat of Elijah's raising of the widow's son from the dead in 1 Kings 17:17. In Luke's account, this parallel is not at all lost on the people who observe it. The implication is clear; they take the miracle as a sure sign that Elijah has returned. The miracle man in Nain must be the great Prophet! The time of the Messiah has come:

> And there came a fear on all: and they glorified God, saying, "That a great prophet is risen up among us; and, That God hath visited his people." And this rumor of him went forth throughout all Judaea, and throughout all the region round about.
>
> And the disciples of John shewed him of all these things. And John calling unto him two of his disciples sent them to Jesus, saying, "Art thou he that should come? or look we for another?"
>
> When the men were come unto him, they said, "John Baptist hath sent us unto thee, saying, Art thou he that should come? Or look we for another?" And in that same hour he cured many of their infirmities and plagues, and of evil spirits; and unto many that were blind he gave sight.
>
> Then Jesus answering said unto them, "Go your way, and tell

John what things ye have seen and heard; how that the blind see, the lame walk, the lepers are cleansed, the deaf hear, the dead are raised, to the poor the gospel is preached. And blessed is he, whosoever shall not be offended in me." (Luke 7:16–23)

Luke's account leaves John's disciples in no doubt. They need look no further for the one who is to come. Jesus has ticked all the expected boxes of what the Messiah should do, including the raising of the dead.

John's disciples having left, Luke has Jesus say that John is "much more than a prophet" (v. 26), though he does not say why. Unlike Matthew, he does not, for some reason, say directly that John is Elijah either. He seems to hold something of that dignity in some sense to himself (see also Luke 4:26*ff.*). Instead, he alludes to the messenger prophecy of Malachi: "Behold, I send my messenger before thy face, which shall prepare thy way before thee," without Malachi's conclusion, that is, that the messenger was Elijah. Luke cannot bring himself to repeat Matthew's words about Elijah because of what he *next* takes from Matthew: "For I say unto you, Among those that are born of women there is not a greater prophet than John the Baptist: but he that is least in the kingdom of God is greater than he." Luke's slap-in-the-face caveat might not have been thought appropriate for Elijah, but it was, apparently, appropriate for John. One cannot help thinking, in reaction, that we are in the Pauline territory of distinguishing between the alleged two baptisms, of water, and of the Holy Ghost, with John being given a theological kiss-off.

There is no doubt that this switching here and there about John's real status is puzzling. It perhaps explains why the author of John's Gospel, as if having the last word, wipes aside all doubt and ambiguity: *John was not the Christ*. John was not Elijah. John was not a prophet. John was quoting a prophet, Isaiah: "I am the voice [or sound] crying [or shouting aloud] in the desert." John is the sound, the only sound, in the emptiness.

We should perhaps look more closely at the magical poetry of John's quotation from Isaiah. Taking the "desert" as a metaphor, that is, as an image for a bare, empty, hard, lifeless, perhaps even spiritless place, may we not see "John" as the cry, the embodied sound, the mantra emitted from within and beyond that world: the long pain of the world, longing, yearning for spiritual rain? Then John is the anguish of the world. Thus is he greater than a prophet, for no ordinary prophet could stand for so much, and yet the smallest one who has already entered the kingdom of God is greater than he who is crying *outside* of it, a voice in the wilderness. And, mark, it is not as though John's message was unheard, as we usually think when we use the phrase about someone being "a voice crying in the wilderness," as was employed of Winston Churchill, for example, when his warnings about Germany during the 1930s went largely unheeded and which times in his life came to be called "the wilderness years."

John *was* heard, even by them that did not see, in the wilderness.

John's Gospel is unique among canonical Gospels for showing a most unexpected scenario. John and Jesus are shown as both baptizing, possibly even in the same place, apparently at the same time. Again, there is no mention of Jesus's baptism being any different from John's:

> After these things came Jesus and his disciples into the land of Judaea; and there he tarried with them, and baptized. And John also was baptizing in Aenon near to Salim, because there was much water there: and they came, and were baptized. For John was not yet cast into prison. (John 3:22–24)

Aenon is only a couple of miles west of the Jordan, on the opposite bank to the Brook Cherith where Elijah is said to have sojourned during the great famine described in 1 Kings 17, some twenty miles south of the Sea of Galilee in what was the Decapolis. Whatever they were up to, the plain statement that Jesus baptized is contradicted at the beginning of the following chapter:

When therefore the Lord knew how the Pharisees had heard that Jesus made and baptized more disciples than John, (Though Jesus himself baptized not, but his disciples,) He left Judaea, and departed again into Galilee. (John 4:1–3)

This all sounds peculiar, and the lacuna is not picked up in any way; the narrative runs on elsewhere. The explanation may be because the author has realized the theological implications of Jesus and John baptizing. If their baptisms were of the same nature, as this little story suggests, then in what way could it be justified that John's baptism was allegedly deficient, as it is presented in Matthew, Mark, and Luke? If we look carefully at John's account of Jesus's baptism, however, it is *not* there stated that one comes after John who will baptize with the Holy Spirit. He does not seem to be very interested in the Pauline baptism distinction. "He who sent him [John]," having been sent by the Father, was *sent* to baptize with water. It was God's will. The gospel writer's understanding of the Holy Spirit comes later. The "Comforter" will be sent "in my name" some time in the future (John 14:26). So Jesus does not baptize with the Holy Ghost and with fire, for the Holy Ghost has not yet been sent. Jesus baptizes with water, as do his disciples. They are doing the same as John.

We seem to have something of a competition between John and Jesus in the baptism stakes; Jesus seems to be winning, in terms of numbers anyway. Again, the authorities seem to be trying to work out which of the two is greater, or perhaps more dangerous: Jesus or John, a competition that must look most unedifying to us today, but which is a significant concern for the gospel's writer. Indeed, John gives us a rather odd conversation about the matter (3:25–36). The debate takes place originally between a group called "the Jews" (a habitual expression in the fourth Gospel) and some of John's disciples (*were they not Jews too?*), before abruptly switching to a debate between "the Jews" (or properly, the Judeans—possibly in distinction to Galileans) and John himself. The subject is ostensibly an academic one about "purifying": a subject we have examined in detail.

The subtext of the debate involves "the Jews" (or Judeans) trying to put a wedge between John and Jesus. They sneer by implication that Jesus has taken John's baptism and is now attracting bigger crowds than John. John's answer is to say that he is a friend of Jesus; he applauds what is clearly God's work. Jesus is entitled to the prize; John's joy is fulfilled. Jesus's success is his success. John then gives a classic "Johannine" speech, aimed straight at the questioners and their real nature, which the Baptist perceives. *They* are of the earth; they do not see or understand heavenly things. If they did, they would not ask such stupid questions! If they fail to see "the Son," they will deny themselves eternal life. They will find the wrath of God abiding in them instead, for God is eternal life, and he is wrath; it depends on the will, as well as the capacity, to receive truth, as to what of God a man will experience:

Then there arose a question between some of John's disciples and the Jews about "purifying." And they came unto John, and said unto him, "Rabbi, he that was with thee beyond Jordan, to whom thou barest witness, behold, the same baptizeth, and all men come to him."

John answered and said, "A man can receive nothing, except it be given him from heaven. Ye yourselves bear me witness, that I said, 'I am not the Christ, but that I am sent before him. He that hath the bride is the bridegroom: but the friend of the bridegroom, which standeth and heareth him, rejoiceth greatly because of the bridegroom's voice: this my joy therefore is fulfilled.

"He must increase, but I must decrease.

"He that cometh from above is above all: he that is of the earth is earthly, and speaketh of the earth: he that cometh from heaven is above all. And what he hath seen and heard, that he testifieth; and no man receiveth his testimony. He that hath received his testimony hath set to his seal that God is true. For he whom God hath sent

speaketh the words of God: for God giveth not the Spirit by measure unto him. The Father loveth the Son, and hath given all things
into his hand. He that believeth on the Son hath everlasting life:
and he that believeth not the Son shall not see life; but the wrath of
God abideth on him." (John 3:25–36)

This is John's testimony, according to John, and such is its power that I
have myself little doubt in ascribing the title of the Gospel to John the
Baptist, a long overdue ascription.

As for its historicity, or of its value as telling us about the "real
John," well, it is hard to imagine that the author's idea of what was *real*
about John was what would interest a historian. There can be little
doubt that the author was convinced truth was being conveyed. Since
John was a messenger of truth, he could hardly object. I do not think
we are receiving verbatim reports of John's words or anything like them.
They are too contrived for that.

I have always been struck, however, by that line: "He must increase,
but I must decrease." Apparently taken in the above context for a kind of
"bowing-out" line, as John practically volunteers to leave the scene, this
luminous logion may have been lifted from a very different context. As it
stands of course, it is straight propaganda against anyone still under the
sorry impression that John was to be preferred to Jesus. Again, John testifies to his own alleged deficiency. Whether he did or not, it is impossible,
on the basis of the evidence to tell for sure. I suspect he did not, though
he may have had "plans" for Jesus, and there may have been some kind of
key assignation of roles, as we shall examine in due course.

The saying "He must increase, but I must decrease" seems to me a
straightforward piece of mystical advice on the lines of "He who tries
to save his life will lose it, he who loses his life for my sake will save
it." The aphorism appears as an authentic insight of contemporary wisdom. If we swap the word *ego* for *life* we get near the mark, I think.
"He" (God) must increase, but I (ego) must decrease. The carnal mind
is enmity against God, as St. Paul knew. The rational mind cannot

reach the spiritual mind of its own will. The True Will, of which we are unconscious, knows best. That is where the "call" comes from. God cannot be present when the "I" is raving, nor can we be in the divine presence. The true "I" is in fact "he," but men cannot see it. He stands among us and we know him not. "He" is the voice crying in the wilderness. He is the still small voice that Elijah heard amid the earthquake, wind, and fire. He becomes flesh and dwells among us. So long as we live below, he will come from above.

John points the way.

Chapter 6

WHY MUST JOHN DIE?

MANY OF US ARE FAMILIAR with the story of how John the Baptist's head came to be on a blood-soaked platter at the behest of the slimy Salome and the harridan Herodias, the maiden's malevolent mother. Coming as it does with the archetypal striptease, the legendary (and unbiblical) *Dance of the Seven Veils,* it is a legend that has cut its way into films, orchestral scores, a play by Oscar Wilde, and an opera based on Wilde's play by Richard Strauss.

There's something about it we like.

Looking at the description above you will realize that we are not going to run away on a romantic quest. We are going to do something far more interesting. We are going to find out how the romance has been triggered by some seriously exciting history, history that, when taken to its logical conclusion, will surprise us all. It should lead to a fundamental rethink on how we view John the Baptist, Jesus, and Paul: the "Big Three" of the New Testament. We might even get some insight into the hectoring of Herodias and saucy Salome too.

One might have thought that Luke would have been the Gospel with the most to gain from the gory story of John's beheading. Luke's has been called the "romantic Gospel," and it tends to fill out Mark or Mark's source where it can. But no, Luke eschews virtually the entire story. Perhaps he did not believe all that stuff about Salome. Anyhow, he reports merely that Herod Antipas, reproved by John for marrying his brother's wife, added to "all the evil things" he'd done by shutting up John in prison. Luke does not even commit himself to a motive for imprisonment. There is no causative link between John's reproving Herod and his being shut away (Luke 3:19–20). John's beheading is only mentioned in passing later on. Perhaps Luke knows the true story and finds it too strong, too politically sensitive, for his Gentile audience. It is impossible to escape the conclusion that Luke is avoiding both the story as related in Mark and what he might have been informed to be the true story, or something like it.

So we must turn to Mark for the juicy tale, for Mark's is the longest account, even though it appears in what is the shortest Gospel and probably the earliest. Matthew's telling condenses Mark's nourishing draught into a hasty dram.

Mark's story starts with Herod Antipas being so surprised to hear of all the miraculous things Jesus is doing, and especially the numbers of people who are following him, that he declares John the Baptist returned from the dead. Herod has no problem with the idea of resurrection—or is it reincarnation?—unlike the temple Sadducees who, as a group, were sceptical of the soul's immortality. Others opine to Herod that the latest Galilean phenomenon must be Elijah or one of the prophets, or someone like a prophet. Herod says "No, you're all wrong"; he can tell: it's John the Baptist all right, "whom I beheaded: he is risen from the dead" (6:16). Matthew 14:2 adds an intriguing little detail to Herod's firm conviction: "That is why these powers are at work in him." It is because John is in a *risen* state that he can now do miracles: most interesting. If Elijah departed with fire, John has returned with it. John has returned with power. Might one wonder whether John had himself told Herod that such was the likely outcome of chopping his head off?—something on the lines of, "You won't see the back of me that easily, Herod. *I shall be raised!*" Had the beheading truly set the real John free? As far as the Tetrarch of Galilee was concerned, John was now more alive than ever! Cut at the head, he was back from the dead!

It is a great story, but it has been won by the complete annihilation of the political context and the concrete historical forces at work on the issue. Was this because the readers were not interested in the politics of the situation, being removed from them by many years, or because the facts were too embarrassing, or because Mark himself was ignorant of them? Whatever the real reason, we lose a great deal by not attending to the political realities.

The missing context here is that Herod Antipas was about to fight a war.

And the war had quite a lot to do with his marriage.

Mark has to backtrack to explain how it came to be that John was beheaded. After all, Mark had been following Jesus's operation, not John's. Unlike Luke, Mark lays most of the blame on the women of the story. Herod himself is "exceeding sorry." He knew better than to chop a popular zaddik:

> For Herod himself had sent forth and laid hold upon John, and bound him in prison for Herodias' sake, his brother Philip's wife: for he had married her. For John had said unto Herod, "It is not lawful for thee to have thy brother's wife." Therefore Herodias had a quarrel against him, and would have killed him; but she could not: For Herod feared John, knowing that he was a just man and an holy, and observed him; and when he heard him, he did many things, and heard him gladly.
>
> And when a convenient day was come, that Herod on his birthday made a supper to his lords, high captains, and chief estates of Galilee; And when the daughter of the said Herodias came in, and danced, and pleased Herod and them that sat with him, the king said unto the damsel, "Ask of me whatsoever thou wilt, and I will give it thee." And he sware unto her, "Whatsoever thou shalt ask of me, I will give it thee, unto the half of my kingdom."
>
> And she went forth, and said unto her mother, "What shall I ask?" And she said, "The head of John the Baptist." And she

came in straightway with haste unto the king, and asked, saying, "I will that thou give me by and by in a charger the head
of John the Baptist." And the king was exceeding sorry; yet
for his oath's sake, and for their sakes, which sat with him, he
would not reject her. And immediately the king sent an execu-
tioner, and commanded his head to be brought: and he went and
beheaded him in the prison. And brought his head in a charger,
and gave it to the damsel: and the damsel gave it to her mother.

And when his disciples heard of it, they came and took up his
corpse, and laid it in a tomb. (Mark 6:17–29)

Let us look first at Herod Antipas's marital situation, the only real
clue we get from the gospel records. What do we find? Well, if this
were a soap opera, rather than a blood opera, we might be forgiven for
describing the situation as a mess.

Herod Antipas's father, Herod the Great, died in 4 BCE. Having
enjoyed numerous wives, as Arab custom permitted, and having executed one of them, as well as the two sons issuing from that marriage,
he left many children and grandchildren. Let us look at the children
and grandchildren of just four of Herod's marriages, inheritors of pieces
of his great kingdom.

Herod Antipas, Tetrarch of Galilee and Perea (4 BCE–39 CE)
issued from Herod's marriage to Malthace, a Samaritan. Antipas's half-
brother, also called "Herod" but confusingly named "Philip" in the
Gospels, was the son of Herod the Great and Mariamme, the daughter
of High Priest Boethus, who came from Egypt. Another half-brother of
Antipas was properly called Philip. Philip was Tetrarch of Trachonitis
and Batanea, the region north and east of the Sea of Galilee. Philip gave
his name to the new city Ceasarea Philippi, built near Paneas, the biblical "Dan." Philip died in 34 CE, not long before the following drama
began.

Herod the Great had another wife of the name Mariamme (Mary).

Mariamme was the granddaughter of the Maccabean King and High Priest Aristobulus II. Aristobulus II was poisoned by Cassius and Brutus in 49 BCE. This equally unfortunate Maccabean princess was executed by Herod in 29 BCE, having borne him two sons, both of whom were executed by their father. One of these sons, Aristobulus, half-brother to Herod Antipas, Herod, and Philip, married Bernice, his half-sister from Herod the Great's marriage to Costobarus, an Idumaean. Aristobulus and Bernice's children included their daughter Herodias.

Herodias was thus the "half-niece" of Herod Antipas, Philip, and Herod.

Herodias married her "half-uncle" Herod ("Philip" in the Gospels) and they had a daughter, Salome. Salome, in her turn, married her father's half-brother, Philip, who died in 34 CE. Salome would go on to marry her mother's brother's son, that is to say, her cousin.

Now things start to get a little complicated.

The strict chronology vouchsafed by Josephus is a little hazy as to when precisely the following event took place, but it looks most likely to have been some time after Philip's death in 34 CE. Herod Antipas was in Rome, presumably trying to settle his late half-brother's legacy with the emperor, Tiberius. Herod the Great's sons and grandsons always had to travel to Rome to discuss any redistribution of the Herodian inheritance, and these occasions always involved the plotting of brother against brother or half-brother against half-brother. Whatever the sons or grandsons of Herod the Great deliberated, the emperor always got his way.

On this occasion, Antipas was lodging with his half-brother, Herod, who was living the high life in Rome, having had no share of his father's kingdom. The married Antipas "fell in love" (as Josephus puts it) with Herod's wife, Herodias, and it was agreed between the lovers, and Herodias's husband, that if she was to be divorced from Herod, Herod Antipas would divorce his own wife, Phasaelis. Herodias was not prepared, apparently, to be part of a coterie, like her grandmother. It may not have been an altogether romantic liaison; Herodias stood to secure real territory for herself and her now widowed daughter, Salome.

Herod Antipas returned to his tetrarchy, probably to his sparkling new city, Tiberias, named in honor of the emperor, on the western coast of the Sea of Galilee.

He had a problem.

His wife.

Phasaelis, the daughter of Aretas IV, the King of Nabataea, had been Herod Antipas's wife for many years. A wealthy Arab kingdom, supplying the empire with incense from its lucrative contacts in southern Arabia, Nabataea bounded Herod Antipas's tetrarchy to the south, east, and northeast. What was more, Aretas (the Greek form of "Haritha") did not respect the borders of the late Philip's tetrarchy, especially in the region of Gamala, due east of Galilee. In short, Aretas had an interest in who should rule "Gamalitis," as Josephus describes a large chunk of Philip's old tetrarchy, right up to its border with the Roman province of Syria. Wanting it for his own kin, Aretas was suspicious of his son-in-law's intentions in the region now that Philip was dead. The son-in-law was equally suspicious of the father-in-law. Antipas's wife Phasaelis had every reason to be suspicious of her husband.

Antipas found himself on the horns of a dilemma, a political dilemma aggravated by the fact that his marriage to Phasaelis had been secured by his half-Nabataean father, Herod the Great. The marriage had settled long-running conflicts between his kingdom and Nabataea. Maintaining reasonable relations with Nabataea suited the Romans. The Romans knew the Nabataeans duplicitous in protection of their trade with Arabia but appreciated that they could, occasionally, be useful. For example, the Nabataean King Aretas IV had offered his army to Quintilius Varus, governor of Syria, when Varus invaded Judea in 4 BCE after Herod's death, an act of not entirely unselfish generosity to be expected from one whose father Obodas had fought against Herod five years earlier over the still disputed territory of Trachonitis, after Nabataea gave asylum to some forty "bandit chiefs" who raided Judea and Syria.

King Aretas was no pushover. Known as Philopatrus, "lover of his people," Antipas's father-in-law considered himself *no one's* subject. During Aretas's long reign (9 BCE–40 CE), his capital Petra's embellishments flourished as Nabataea's wealth increased. Visitors to Petra today are astonished by the extraordinary carving of a temple out of rose-red rock undertaken during Nabataea's golden age under Aretas IV. It was used for the climax of the film *Indiana Jones and the Last Crusade* (1989). Aretas IV would, perhaps, have been flattered.

Herod Antipas might have chosen a less able opponent. He felt, however, that he could rely on qualified Roman support, as well as the will of his wife-to-be, the formidable Herodias, a woman who knew what she wanted, regardless of consequences.

It must have been hard to keep the affair between Herodias and Antipas a secret because without Antipas's knowledge, Phasaelis, daughter of the Nabataean king, got wind of her husband's plans to divorce her and, without letting on, asked her husband if she might go for respite to their "all-mod-cons" palace at Macherus, high on a crag five miles inland from the Dead Sea's eastern shore, some eighty miles to the south of Tiberias: her home away from home so to speak. Macherus was barely a half-hour's walk from Nabataea. Before departing for the mountain palace, Phasaelis organized her "lifting" from Macherus, an exercise accomplished by Aretas's general-in-chief, who ordered his officers to convey Phasaelis southward to Petra in stages.

Having secured his daughter's safety and acquired all the facts, Aretas announced to his son-in-law that divorce meant war. We may assume that it was about this time (35–36 CE) that the news hit the streets that Herod Antipas was divorcing his wife to marry his half-brother's wife, who was herself his half-brother's daughter, whose own daughter had been his half-brother's wife, with the likely consequence that a war would ensue involving Galileans and Nabataeans—and most likely Romans—in slaughter and destruction.

Into this historical picture walks a man called John. And John, a popular and powerful figure, declares that Herod Antipas, having done the deed, is a sinner before God. He should repent and put off the sinful woman. At least, that is the gospel account; it is not the account of Josephus the historian.

We now observe a curious coincidence. The gospel record informs us that John, for opposing the marriage of Antipas to Herodias, and for hurting Herodias's pride thereby, was sent to Macherus a prisoner. Since there is no talk of a dungeon, he was probably under "house arrest" in a gilded cage: a precautionary, politically sensitive measure. According to Matthew 11:2, John, in custody, was able to send messengers to Jesus, enquiring as to *who he* (Jesus) *thought he was.*

Ten miles due west across the Dead Sea from the vicinity of Macherus is the wilderness of Judea. Some ten miles north of those shores is Qumran; ten miles to the south is En-gedi, both sites linked to the Essenes and to the New Covenanters.

According to Matthew (4:1*ff.*), after being baptized by John, Jesus was led into the "wilderness," where he was tempted. One of the temptations was that Jesus should seize power, take on the world, and win. "Then the devil leaveth him, and behold, angels [or messengers] came and ministered unto him."

"Now when Jesus had heard that John was cast into prison, he departed into Galilee." Jesus quit the wilderness, apparently, on hearing of John's imprisonment. He headed north: a move suggesting a variety of possible motives. According to Matthew, it was, "From that time Jesus began to preach, and to say, Repent: for the kingdom of heaven is at hand" (4:17). He seems to have picked up where John left off. The obvious conclusion to the objective historian from these coincidences would be that Jesus was in some sense deputizing for his arrested comrade: carrying on the struggle, with a possible hint of "mission creep."

To recap: John is arrested; Jesus starts up on his own, with John's message. And by the way, New Covenanter documents suggest the purest of the community in the wilderness camps were to be in some way "angels" that they might involve celestial angels in their struggle (*viz:* War

Scroll VI:3–6; 4Q274; CD XV). Jesus experienced a profound crisis in the wilderness, then "angels" came and ministered to him. This is all very curious in the light of the historical resources now available to us.

If we put Matthew's account into historical context, we must add significant facts. When the war broke out between Herod and Aretas, Aretas's army poured into Gamalitis and Perea and raided even as far as the western banks of the Dead Sea in the region of Qumran. Such events would have provided ample incentive for Jesus to hotfoot it north to Galilee. Judea was in the bottleneck of a crisis: "Repent: for the kingdom of heaven is at hand." The cry makes sudden sense.

This is it!

The war was possibly taken as a sign. If so, it was a mistaken one, as events transpired, though as we shall see, this war was not without long-term significance. Its complexities, however, were of no use to the gospel writers; it was "off-message."

One astonishing fact is that the very case that the Gospels insist John laid against Herodias and her new husband was one made in an important New Covenanter text called the *Damascus Document* found in the caves of Qumran just across the water from the palace where John was to be executed. The precise sin John is reported to have criticized Herod for, namely marrying his brother's wife, Herodias, and, according to Mark, lusting after her daughter, Salome, is related in the *Damascus Document* as being that sin that defiles "their holy spirit," opening the sinners' mouths "with a blaspheming tongue against the laws of the Covenant of God, saying, 'They are not sure.'" This latter phrase refers to princes who claimed to interpret the Law as they found fit:

> And concerning the prince it is written, He shall not multiply wives to himself. [Deut. 17:17]

> And each man marries the daughter of his brother or sister, whereas Moses said, "You shall not approach your mother's sister; she is your mother's near kin." [Leviticus 18:13]

> But although the laws against incest are written for men, they
> also apply to women. When therefore a brother's daughter uncov-
> ers the nakedness of her father's brother, she is (also his) near kin.
> (*Damascus Document* V8–12)

Herodias was the daughter; Aristobulus was her father; her father's
(half) brother was Herod Antipas. Had this text appeared verbatim
in the Gospels, spoken by John, we should hardly have been surprised.
Furthermore, in the same section of the *Damascus Document* (thought
to have been composed in the first century BCE and held dear by the
New Covenanters), we read of the "builders of the wall" (Ezekiel 13:10).
The epithet "builders of the wall" fits the Herodian builders of the
Temple neatly. Rejected by the righteous "sons of Zadok" of the Dead
Sea Scrolls, the Temple organization was also condemned by Jesus, who
foresaw woe to those who ignored the righteousness of God (Mark
13:3). Jesus apparently quoted a similar prophecy (Psalm 118:22): "The
stone the builders rejected has become the head of the corner." What
the "builders" reject becomes the basis for a new, purified holy building.

In the *Damascus Document,* the "builders of the wall" are accused
of having followed a "Spouter" who "shall be caught in fornication twice
by taking a second wife while the first is alive," whereas the principle of
creation is, "*Male and female created He them*" (Genesis 1:27). This quotation was of course the essence of Jesus's reply to gambits about the legality
of divorce (Mark 10:1–12). Might we suspect the divorce issue was originally put to him because it was the central issue for which John suffered?

Before we look again at Josephus's account of John, putting it this
time in the context of the war, one important point should be observed.
Much is made of Herodias's antipathy to the voice of John. However,
John was, as far as we can tell, neither born nor had lived under the spe-
cific jurisdiction of Herod Antipas. He appears to have been a Judean.
Judea was until 37 CE under the jurisdiction of the prefect, Pontius
Pilate. Had John wished to avoid ensnarement by Herod, he need only
have crossed the Jordan to the west. If there is any truth to the Gospel

of John's account of the Baptist and Jesus baptizing in the area of Salim and Aenon, it should be noted that these places were in the Decapolis, the "ten cities" region that enjoyed autonomy under Roman protection. So it remains something of a mystery as to how a major figure like John came to be arrested by Herod Antipas, unless John had more to do with Galilee (Antipas's territory) than the Gospels are prepared to admit, or that John was a habitual frequenter of Herod Antipas's court—or even a regular visitor to Macherus, a friend perhaps of Queen Phasaelis. Had John been an associate of Phasaelis, then Herodias's alleged personal hatred for John would become clearer still. After all, Herodias was taking Phasaelis's place, and if Phasaelis knew John, it may have been she who informed him about the divorce plans, specifically to generate a political and legal defense of her position. Thus, John might conceivably have been party to Phasaelis's "escape" from Macherus. He might have been at the palace when he was arrested. His execution then could conceivably have been connected to Macherus's proximity to Nabataea.

If there was a chance of Aretas getting hold of John as a political and religious mascot, such a fear might have necessitated the execution that Herod must have known was politically very risky on the home front; not taking action also involved risk. There is also the real possibility that the nudge to execute John came from Rome; John was putting himself in the way of imperial policy, a policy that, literally, demanded Phasaelis's father's head. Since John's opposition was obstructing this policy, the Emperor Tiberius would expect the Baptist troublemaker's head to roll too. Niceties about John being a Judean would not have thwarted such an intent. That Rome might have been the critical, if covert, voice in John's execution would not have suited the gospel writers one little bit. Paul had taught Gentile Christians that Rome's authority was benign, a Godsend in fact. If Josephus knew more about the case, he would have probably felt compelled to hold the party line. Herod Antipas gave the order for John's execution on the grounds of political expediency; that could mean simply "on Rome's orders." *Somebody's* head was going to have to roll.

It should be stressed that Josephus says nothing about John being "in the wilderness" at any time, only that he baptized. He could have done that anywhere. If we understand the "voice in the wilderness" as a true poetic metaphor, and not as description of habitual place, we may imagine a considerably more mobile figure than we are used to imagining, with followers all over the region. The Gospels' placing of John "in the wilderness" is clearly based heavily on the most literal interpretation possible of Isaiah 40:3, one into which I fear we have all been taken in. There is not a lot of water in the wilderness. One might imagine a man of John's archstature in religious history would have enjoyed the most profound spiritual understanding of the inner nature of Isaiah's ancient prophecy. Any man who could formulate a movement of the scope he achieved was unlikely to have been one whose imagination was bound by the materialistic literalism of the peasant—or the average and below-average religious teacher.

From this observation, another flows. If John was perceived by Herod Antipas as a political liability, for whatever reason, then we may be sure that King Aretas IV of Nabataea would have been "on the case." If the Gospels are correct in attributing part of Herod's objection to John as being due to the latter's opposition to the marriage with Herodias, then we can see that, as far as Aretas was concerned, John was standing up and putting the legal case against Aretas's errant son-in-law. This would immediately give John the kind of political status enjoyed fifteen hundred years later, in England, by Archbishop Cranmer when that distinguished churchman provided a legal-religious case for Henry VIII's divorce of Catherine of Aragon. A corresponding parallel would then lie in the case of St. Thomas More, who for reasons of piety declared against Henry VIII's supremacy of the church in England. More was beheaded. And it should be noted here with some emphasis that *beheading* was a form of execution reserved for persons of rank. John was clearly such a person, and his death, as much as his life, would be the cause of deep embarrassment to Herod Antipas, at least, and perhaps to other political players as well.

The legality or otherwise of Herod's marriage would have provided the legal basis or *casus belli* on which Aretas could justifiably have disturbed the Pax Romana and fought a war. In that case, John would certainly have been a dangerous figure to have in the corridors of power and, more particularly, among people at large.

We cannot also therefore discount the real possibility that John may have been in contact with Aretas, having been seen by the Nabataean king as a significant ally. Therefore, anyone who served Herod's family would, in such a case, have been concerned to neutralize John and, were there any chance of it, to prevent him from getting under the direct protection of Aretas. In this respect, the sending of John to Macherus is problematic. One could perhaps imagine the value of removing John far from his followers, but that would be to presuppose his greatest following was to have been found in Galilee, which the Gospels seem to be curiously quiet about, referring only to a scenario wherein all the people in *Jerusalem and Judea* "went out" to hear John. That puts him down south. Then why, when Jesus does miracles in Galilee, does the gospel Herod declare that John is back from the dead? Did the gospel writers wish to separate jurisdictions, as it were: Jesus of Galilee and John of Judea? One feels John has been "decreased" as Jesus has been "increased." It does seem odd that a man as Josephus presents him should have been confined when, after all, his message was, as far as we assume, offered to all who had an ear for it.

Now, let us look at Josephus's account of the war:

So they [Herod Antipas and Aretas] raised armies on both sides, and prepared for war, and sent their generals to fight instead of themselves; and when they had joined battle, all Herod's army was destroyed by the treachery of some fugitives, who, though they were of the tetrarchy of Philip, joined with Aretas's army. So Herod wrote about these affairs to Tiberius, who being very angry at the attempt made by Aretas, wrote to Vitellius [Lucius Vitellius, President of Syria] to make war upon him, and either to take him alive, and bring him to him in bonds, or to kill him, and send him his head. This was the charge that Tiberius gave to the president of Syria. (*Antiquities* XVIII.5)

Dead Sea Scrolls scholar Robert Eisenman has suggested that that reference to Aretas's head being desired by Tiberius went through a curious inversion when the Gospels were composed, and it became John's head that was removed. Extreme as this sounds, it is curious how in Josephus's history, John the Baptist suddenly appears, but only in the context of the war. The marriage is not mentioned, and Josephus does not say by what means the Baptist was put to death:

> Now some of the Jews thought that the destruction of Herod's army came from God, and that very justly, as a punishment of what he did against John, that was called the Baptist: for Herod slew him, who was a good man, and commanded the Jews to exercise virtue, both as to righteousness toward one another, and piety toward God, and so to come to baptism; for that the washing [with water] would be acceptable to him, if they made use of it, not in order to the putting away [or the remission] of some sins [only], but for the purification of the body; supposing still that the soul was thoroughly purified beforehand by righteousness. Now when [many] others came in crowds about him, for they were very greatly moved [or pleased] by hearing his words, Herod, who feared lest the great influence John had over the people might put it into his power and inclination to raise a rebellion, (for they seemed ready to do any thing he should advise,) thought it best, by putting him to death, to prevent any mischief he might cause, and not bring himself into difficulties, by sparing a man who might make him repent of it when it would be too late. Accordingly he was sent a prisoner, out of Herod's suspicious temper, to Macherus, the castle I before mentioned, and was there put to death. Now the Jews had an opinion that the destruc-

tion of this army was sent as a punishment upon Herod and a mark
of God's displeasure to him.

To attribute the loss of an army to the execution of John gives us a good
idea of the status John enjoyed in his own country. Disappointingly, we
do not learn when the Baptist was put to death. The context suggests
Antipas was under pressure. One would not want a rebellion or riot
occurring when one's army was engaged with an enemy. Antipas may
well have wished to go to war without fear of an organized fifth column
behind him. But as we noted before, Josephus offers no clue as to *why*
John might have wished to raise a rebellion. John's hold over the popular imagination is very clear; he appears to have no rival.

The overall impression one gets from the limited, though highly
suggestive, sources is that John had involved himself in the tetrarch's
affairs to a considerable degree and his activities put him under official
suspicion, even if not entirely justified in terms of active, presumably
armed, political opposition. What Herod did recognize was the power
John wielded over his followers' minds. If those minds were enflamed
by messianic fervor, Antipas had grounds for concern. The Herodian
dynasty's corruption of the temple system was a constant target for messianic invective.

Can we fix a date for John's death?

All indices suggest that the battle between Aretas and Antipas took
place in 36 CE. That is the most likely date for the Baptist's execution.
Other than the appointment of newly made Consul Lucius Vitellius
as governor of Syria in 35 CE, the only certain date we have that ties
the historical record, such as it is, together is the death of the Emperor
Tiberius. Tiberius died in 37 CE.

But have you noticed something rather surprising? In most books,
the date of Jesus's crucifixion is given as sometime between 30 and 33
CE. After plowing through the arguments for these dates on many
occasions, none of them, in my judgment, compels assent. They exhibit,

I think, a tendency or desire to avoid a salient issue. The majority of commentators treat the Gospels as reliable or fairly reliable historical records. There are heavy vested interests. The crucifixion of Jesus was not recorded at the time it happened by anyone whose record has survived. The main marker has always been that it occurred under Pontius Pilate. Pilate was relieved of his duties in 36 or 37 CE, having governed Judea and Samaria, according to Josephus, for ten years. In this regard, study of the events around the death of John the Baptist has caused private dismay among some committed Christians. Since the "ministry" of Jesus (I prefer the word *operation*) is generally accepted as having begun after the Baptist's arrest, and as it is generally accepted that it lasted some years (two or three usually), then, if John died in 36, and Jesus was active for another three years, then he could not have been crucified "under Pontius Pilate." It would throw all the creeds up in the air. For this reason, Christian commentators cannot help themselves but to find every possible reason to suppose that John was arrested much earlier than 36—even earlier than the time of the death of Philip (34 CE), when the destiny of Herodias's daughter's tetrarchy became an issue (Salome was married to Philip) and marriage to Herod Antipas would strengthen their hand: vainly as it turned out. Whatever one makes of that, the execution of John is removed as far back as possible from the war with Aretas; the whole issue is fudged.

This might calm nerves where evangelism is concerned, but on a purely historical basis, arguments *against* putting John in the context of historical actuality, derived from an urge to preserve articles of religious belief (or what has come to be associated with religious belief) can only appear to the objective eye as being profoundly biased, even misguided. Again, John is *decreased!* There is a curious disquiet when the theologically "decreased" are restored to historical proportions.

My own survey of the evidence provides not only ample time for the key events to take place, keeping the creedal formularies of the faithful intact, but provides powerful insight into what in all probability happened and why. The key to opening the picture comes from recognizing the true significance of John the Baptist.

FROM JOHN'S EXECUTION
TO JESUS'S CRUCIFIXION

The years 36 to 37 were tumultuous and confused for the eastern Roman Empire. Newly made Consul Lucius Vitellius, a rising star, had been sent by Tiberius to Syria to deal with the threat of a Parthian invasion of the strategically vital province. Vitellius had four crack legions at his disposal. In spite of the fact that the Syrian legions were the last resort in the case of rebellion in Judea to the south, the Parthian threat from the east and northeast was Vitellius's chief concern. The last thing the empire needed was a war with Aretas IV and a breakdown of order in Palestine.

Prefect Pontius Pilate occupied an unenviable position. He had no automatic jurisdiction in Herod Antipas's territory but knew perfectly well what was going on and the threats posed to order in Judea and Samaria. If the worst should happen, and the Parthians should unite against Rome, the whole eastern border could collapse. Herodias's egging on of her ambitions through her husband must have appeared to Roman eyes distinctly irritating, if potentially exploitable.

The Emperor Tiberius had decided to join the late Philip's tetrarchy to Syria, unwilling to let it go to Antipas and Herodias. Tiberius doubtless held it as a bargaining prize. Had Antipas defeated Aretas in 36, instead of the other way around, Antipas might reasonably have expected it to go to him. This would explain why, if there is any truth in Mark's story of a "dancing Salome," Philip's widow had gone to live with her mother and her mother's new husband. To put Salome back in her late husband Philip's inheritance, Antipas needed a victory. If John's word had blunted the will to win against the Nabataeans, little wonder John found himself in custody. John would probably have found himself being investigated at a deep level, by someone like Saul of Tarsus, who according to Acts, specialized in zealously investigating unto death religious leaders who threatened the Herodian religious order. There is no reason whatever to think that Saul only came "on the job" in time for the beginning of the Acts of the Apostles narrative. Indeed, Eisenman wonders if the Christian Paul was not "Saulus," grandson of Costobarus, Idumaean wife of Herod the Great. This would explain why Saul went to "Arabia" after he was parapsychologically confronted by the realization that he was still pursuing the "Son of God," who was supposed to be dead, finished, politically neutralized. It would also explain Saul's Roman citizenship and influential political positioning.

By joining Philip's tetrarchy to Syria, instead of giving it to Antipas, Tiberius must have realized he had made Antipas a potential ally of Artabanus II, the anti-Roman king of Parthia, whom the emperor was keen to unseat permanently when the time was right. Tiberius's chief instrument of policy, Vitellius, brought a Roman-backed Parthian prince, Tiridates, to north Syria. Many Parthians backed Tiridates. It is no surprise to find that when Tiridates crossed the Euphrates with Roman escort on his way to Parthia, Herod Antipas was there to greet him, assuring his own loyalty to Rome by joining his welcome to that of pro-Tiridates Parthian nobles.

Defeated by Aretas, Herod Antipas's begging letter to Tiberius came in the context of both Roman success and continued threat from Parthia. Tiberius meant to show iron will on the eastern border and was determined to teach Aretas a final lesson for daring to go war with Rome's approved Tetrarch of Galilee and Perea. Flush from a propaganda coup in Syria, Vitellius received orders from Tiberius to deal with Rome's enemy in the south. Everyone who served Rome in the region was sensitized to the need to quell the least signs of rebellion; Tiberius was watching. If John had made a case that suited Aretas, then John would have to go; it was a question of authority.

Pontius Pilate doubtless felt discomfited by all the news pouring into his Judean and Samarian jurisdiction. If he could avoid it, Pilate probably did not want to have to call on Vitellius's legions to deal with unrest in his territory. He would have sought the emperor's approval not by calling on his aid, but by showing he could be trusted to do the right thing with the resources allotted him. He had kept insurrection down for ten years by brutal force. With the emperor's eye on Syria, with fighting between Aretas and Antipas to the north, east, and south, with the threat of more instability, an occasion soon presented itself that called for Pilate's firm hand.

It is at this point in Josephus's record of events that his narrative begins to mirror the instability of the times. This is partly because he has two chapters dealing with two separate political stories, which happened at roughly the same time (*Antiquities,* Book 18, chapters 4–5). The first is an atrocity wrought on Samaritans by Pontius Pilate. The second is the war between Aretas and Antipas. The problem is that for Josephus's narrative, the consequences of both accounts are the same, and in both narratives, the death of Tiberius in 37 CE spoils the intended plans that conclude each story. Not only that, each account involves a visit to Jerusalem by Vitellius, governor of Syria, *both* involving attendance at Jewish religious festivals, *both* involving news of the death of Tiberius, and *both* posing a question mark over the future, and indeed the whereabouts of Pontius Pilate. It looks quite possible that *one* visit to Jerusalem by Vitellius has been split into two because the journey to Jerusalem was bound up with two crises. If the crises were more or less simultaneous, then it is likely that there was one visit, though not all the details match. There is a discrepancy over the names of high priests appointed and disappointed. In trying to deal with two separate sources for the accounts, Josephus is clearly himself not exactly sure of the precise course of events.

This matters because it is highly likely that Vitellius's approach to, or brief (three days) residence in, Jerusalem marked a moment when a breakdown in order left Jerusalem in a state of volatile flux as to who was really governing it, and who would be governing it in the future. For the messianic movement, it would have been a time of heightened, even hysterical expectation, a blessed moment of opportunity; for the authorities, a time of crisis as happens when the old gives way to the new. Collaborators might have cried, "We have no king but Caesar," but Caesar was dead (murdered) and there was some doubt about the succession.

In short, the historical record provides us with the best explanation for why Jesus was probably crucified in Jerusalem in March 37 CE, and how that event was linked to the beheading of John the Baptist, most likely in 36 CE.

THE REAL DATE OF JESUS'S CRUCIFIXION

Josephus in *Antiquities* 18, chapter four, recounts the cause of Pontius Pilate's downfall in an account set sometime between late 36 and March 37 CE.

Josephus records how a Samaritan, much given to deception, announced to a multitude that if they assembled on Mount Gerizzim, the Samaritans' holy mountain, he would show them all the "sacred vessels" secreted under it by Moses. Armed crowds gathered at a village called Tirathaba; Pilate's cavalry and infantry appeared, blocking the roads to the holy mountain. Seeing armed men and supposing a rebellion, the soldiers fell on the crowd, slaying some and capturing others. Pilate ordered the fittest of the captured to be killed.

This atrocity may be identical to that reported to have befallen "Galileans" in Luke 13:1–5. According to Luke's report, it was rumored in Jesus's circle that Pilate's victims had "asked for it" on account of sin:

> There were present at that season some that told him of the Galileans, whose blood Pilate had mingled with their sacrifices. And Jesus answering said unto them, "Suppose ye that these Galilaeans were sinners above all Galilaeans, because they suffered such things? I tell you, Nay: but, except ye repent, ye shall all likewise perish."

Superficially, there is the hint that Jesus bore sympathy for the supposed "rebels"; perhaps he knew the facts. However, the statement amounts to saying no more than that those dead Galileans were really no worse than the rest of their countrymen, and if they too refused to "repent" then they too would die in the same manner. One can smell the embers of the Jewish Revolt of 66–73 CE behind this barbed judgment attributed to Jesus. One should not, I think, make too much of the term *Galilaeans* in this context. At the time of the Jewish Revolt, the term *Galilaean* was for Romans practically synonymous with *rebel,* following Judas the Galilean's savagely suppressed rebellion against Quirinius's tax imposition of 6 CE. Besides, Pilate did not govern Galilee; Antipas did, though Pilate sought Antipas's military help in suppressing insurrection, as we shall see. The Samaritan incident may have been incited by Galilean zealots, perhaps persons familiar to Jesus's—or indeed John's—entourage. Josephus's Samaritan "given to deception" sounds very much like the heresiarch Simon Magus of Gitto. Simon's later followers claimed he was so close to John the Baptist that he would have been his successor, but was away at Alexandria at the time of John's execution.

In fact, the Tirathaba atrocity was highly significant. So incensed was the Samaritan senate that its members sent an embassy north to Vitellius in Syria (probably Antioch). They petitioned that contrary to what Vitellius might have heard, no one had gone to Tirathaba to rebel against the Romans. Rather, they went to "escape the violence of Pilate." According to Josephus, Vitellius sent a friend, Marcellus, to "take care of the affairs of Judea" and ordered Pilate to go to Rome "to answer before the emperor to the accusations of the Jews." Josephus then says that Pilate made haste to Rome, "but before he could get to Rome Tiberius was dead." Tiberius died on March 16, 37 CE.

This leaves it rather an open question as to how far Pilate got, or if indeed he actually left Jerusalem. With favorable winds, it took only nine days by sea from Puteoli in Italy to Alexandria, and if Pilate actually did leave Jerusalem and heard about Tiberius's death on the way, it is just as likely that he returned, as it was a practice of Tiberius at his palace at Capri to keep supplicants in such cases locked up before dealing with them, first, to show displeasure at their possible incompetence, and second, to indicate to their accusers that Roman justice was impartial, and that "something was being done," while in the meantime, the tumult that caused the appeal should cease. This was Tiberius's known method, and if Pilate knew anything about Tiberius's likely successor, Gaius "Caligula" (and Caligula's supporter Macro), he had good reason to sit tight, given the fundamentally altered circumstances of an imperial era's end.

When an emperor died, much of the previous emperor's business became void, since so much depended on the emperor's personal will; the new emperor might have very different ideas. If Vitellius ordered Pilate to go to Tiberius, and Tiberius no longer lived, the original order ceased in effect. Like so much else, Pilate's status would be in a kind of limbo until the new emperor established fresh policy. If Caesar had not made a decision to remove Pilate from his prefectship, Pilate was still prefect. Vitellius himself would encounter this fact of imperial life shortly.

There is, furthermore, something fishy about Josephus's account. It shows Vitellius as a reasonable man, guarding against excesses in Roman administration. However, if Vitellius was disposed to calm Samaritan and Judean nerves about Roman intentions, there was a practical reason for it. After all, Pilate had been an effective, dependable prefect who had kept the peace. The reason for Vitellius's reasonableness soon becomes clear. On Tiberius's instructions, Vitellius was preparing to teach Aretas IV a singular lesson in what happened to those who opposed Rome's appointees; a punitive march to Petra was planned. The emperor had demanded Aretas's head. If Antipas could not deliver it, Vitellius would. Vitellius needed Judeans and Samaritans to keep quiet while the job was accomplished. Pilate was probably told to "keep out of the way" for a time, pending Tiberius's "considered judgment" on the matter. But events probably got in the way of the process; Tiberius's death changed everything.

Josephus recounts that after the Samaritan atrocity, Vitellius entered Judea, going up to Jerusalem around Passover time, apparently to assert imperial authority over a restive populus. If this was Passover 37 CE, then the date would be toward the end of March, just about the time news would have arrived announcing the emperor's death, caused, so the Roman mob believed, by the hand of Caligula's ally, Naevius Sutorius Macro, prefect of the Praetorian Guard. These were tense times. Vitellius, "magnificently received," according to Josephus, sought support. In a bid to pacify the population with unaccustomed Roman generosity, Vitellius removed taxes on food bought and sold. He even gave instructions for the high priests's vestments to be removed from the Antonia Tower after years in Roman custody and returned to the priests. Formerly released only with Roman permission for special events, the concession was regarded by Josephus as greatly important to his people. Was this notable concession granted in response to a "We want the vestments!" cry akin to the familiar "We want Barabbas!" mob demand?

Josephus does not mention Vitellius's friend Marcellus, who was supposed to be taking care of affairs in Judea, nor indeed does he tell us specifically why Vitellius made this visit to Jerusalem in person, or why, during it, he also "deprived Joseph, who was also called Caiaphas, of the high priesthood, and appointed Jonathan the son of Ananus, the former high priest, to succeed him." Caiaphas, of course, is the name given in the Gospels to Jesus's principal accuser. One wonders what Caiaphas had done to make him so unpopular as to give Vitellius a means to appease the population by removing him. Josephus's account concludes with the words, "After which, he [Vitellius] took his journey back to Antioch."

In his next chapter, Josephus recounts the battle between Herod Antipas's and Aretas's armies, lost, "the Jews" believed, because Antipas had taken the life of a righteous man: John. Antipas stood under divine judgment.

Vitellius was under orders from Tiberius: *Aretas, dead or alive.*

Josephus's chronology is difficult to fix precisely in relation to the

Samaritan atrocity recounted previously. The sequence of events makes best sense if we see the actual battle between Aretas and Antipas as having taken place *before* the Samaritan episode, since there must be time allowed for Herod to have written to Tiberius about it, for Tiberius to have ordered Vitellius to annihilate Aretas, and for Vitellius to have organized an invasion force properly equipped for the long march south to Petra in Nabataea. Josephus says as much himself with the words, "So Vitellius prepared to make war with Aretas, having with him two legions of armed men; he also took with him all those of light armature, and of the horsemen, which belonged to them, and were drawn out of those kingdoms, which were under the Romans, and made haste for Petra, and came to Ptolemais."

That phrase of Josephus's "make haste" should not be confused with being "hasty" or "hurrying." He is signifying *intention* above all: an outcome. Vitellius "came to Ptolemais." Well, that is not very far from Syrian Antioch, Vitellius's administrative base. Ptolemais, on the coast ten miles west of Herod Antipas's tetrarchy of Galilee, was still in the Roman province of Syria. The army had another two hundred miles to go.

Pilate would have known of the preparations no doubt, and would have been anxious to make sure there would be no resistance to the passage of the legions through his jurisdiction of Judea and Samaria. This could well account for Pilate's anxiety about armed religious Samaritans (or "Galileans," that is, Zealots) gathering near Mount Gerizzim, and also for the uncompromising manner in which he responded to it.

Josephus then recounts that Vitellius's army, having left Ptolemais to make their way through "Judea," the number of images (of the emperor) on the troops' ensigns offended religious sensibilities. Vitellius was persuaded by the people's leaders that to avoid offense, his army should march down the Great Plain. Usually understood as the Plain of Esdraelon, the plain runs just southeast of the Galilee-Samaria border on the Samaritan side. That might make the offended "Judeans" into Galileans, under Herod Antipas's jurisdiction. Alternatively, the issue could have been bound up with the Tirathaba atrocity—possibly a move on Pilate's part to protect Vitellius's flank from possible Zealot sabotage. Indeed, the geography makes most sense if the objection to Vitellius's troops came from *Samaria,* for if the troops were to avoid the heart of that region, they could either march due south down the Plain of Sharon near the coast or head down the Great Plain toward the Decapolis, which though a diversion, would keep the legions out of both Judea and Samaria. Thus, Pilate's atrocity in Samaria makes historical sense as having taken place very shortly before Vitellius's march south to engage with Aretas. The complaint about ensign images could then have come from the Samaritan senate along with demands for justice as regards Pilate's violence at Tirathaba. Vitellius would have been keen to avoid situations, which could threaten his rear supply lines, during his imperial mission to humble Aretas. Pilate's peremptory action in Samaria may have annoyed Vitellius as an inconvenient case of unnecessary "overkill," or, alternatively, secretly pleased him.

This scenario may contribute then to our understanding of why, in the middle of his campaign against Aretas, Vitellius, according to Josephus, along with, most interestingly, "Herod the tetrarch and his friends" went up to Jerusalem "to offer sacrifice to God, an ancient festival of the Jews being then just approaching." As with Josephus's previous account of a possibly earlier visit to Jerusalem, Vitellius was "honorably entertained by the multitude of the Jews." Vitellius apparently stayed "for three days." In that time he "deprived Jonathan of the high priesthood, and gave it to his brother Theophilus." Not explained, the removal of Jonathan was almost certainly a decision to court popularity. It is the only serious difference between the two accounts of Vitellius's visiting Jerusalem. The period, as recounted by Josephus, was marked by a very high turnover of high priests, so great in fact that ex-high priests were still called "high priests" even though there was only one officially accepted as such at any time. This fact has caused much confusion and this discrepancy may be an instance of it.

Josephus now tells us that on the fourth day of this visit to Judea's capital, letters arrived informing Vitellius of the death of Tiberius. Realizing that this highly sensitive news could incite the Jerusalem mob, Vitellius demanded that the "multitude" immediately make a public oath of fidelity to Caius, the new emperor (nicknamed "Caligula" or "Little Boots"). Such an occasion might well have elicited that now fateful cry, "We have no king but Caesar!" (John 19:15) attributed to the multitude on being asked if they cared to save the "King of the Jews" from death.

The presence of Galilee's tetrarch, Herod Antipas, in Jerusalem is recorded in the Gospels only in Luke (23:7–12). The occasion, note, is the *trial of Jesus*. Remarkably, Antipas appears in Luke in the company of his "men of war." Since he was not in his own territory, and was therefore a guest in a territory under Roman jurisdiction, the presence of men of war should strike us as incongruous to the normal run of events. Luke does not explain Antipas's presence in Jerusalem, though Josephus's account offers both evidence and cause for it. According to Luke, Pilate finds it convenient. Hearing that Jesus has allegedly been stirring up the Galileans, Pilate requests Antipas to judge the matter. All of this is curious.

We then hear that Herod is "exceedingly glad" to make Jesus's acquaintance, at last. He asks him many questions and hopes for a miracle. Did he think he was looking at John the Baptist's "angel?" He should have known more about Jesus, for according to Luke (8:3), Herod's own steward, or minister, Chuza had a wife, Joanna, who was funding Jesus's activities! It is especially incongruous if Pilate was in full command at the time, for if he had been, it is hard to think of him giving over legal authority to Herod, or even for being hesitant in judging Jesus one way or another. Admittedly, the chief priests and scribes keep accusing Jesus "vehemently," so much so that Herod himself gives in: "And Herod with his men of war set him at nought, and mocked him, and arrayed him in a gorgeous robe, and sent him again to Pilate" (23:11). For some reason, Luke records that on this day, Herod and Pilate became friends, having long been at enmity. Pilate wants nothing to do with the case and, having assembled the "chief priests and the rulers and the people" (the "rulers" might well have included the Syrian governor and his entourage), Pilate states his intention of releasing Jesus. Herod does not seem to object. Like Pilate perhaps, he too had had enough of the consequences of executing religiously motivated "troublemakers." He was doing his best to earn back political points with his Roman masters after the battle that followed the death of John.

The extreme reluctance of Pilate to execute his will has long been commented on. The main explanation is that the gospel writers wanted Gentile readers to understand that Jesus had not been put to death as a rebel or terrorist by Roman authority, but as a prophet denied by his own people. Crucifixion was reserved for those who challenged Rome's authority; how had the Son of God died from a Roman form of execution? Answer: "the Jews" demanded it with threat of breakdown of order and were prepared to shoulder the responsibility for it.

Incongruities vanish, however, the moment we put these events into the historical and political context of Jerusalem in early 37 CE. Josephus reports that Herod Antipas *accompanied Vitellius* on his march to Petra. Antipas wanted to be seen as the good, dependable tetrarch, the man Rome could rely on: one who could be given Philip's tetrarchy, currently under Vitellius's control, as a reward for exemplary behavior. Pilate's apparent looseness of control makes perfect sense once we see that in 37 CE he was in serious trouble for having allowed his severity to turn into action so provocative that it threatened both fundamental order and Vitellius's campaign against Nabataea. Pilate's situation had not been settled. He was still prefect, but there was a question mark over his future. A politically sensitive decision involving crucifixion of an alleged "Galilean" regarded by followers as exceptionally righteous would have hovered on the razor edge of his competence—especially if the Syrian governor was present, or very near. Pilate was in enough trouble as it was. The likelihood of Pilate retaining his job when the matter was finally settled was low. The Emperor Tiberius's expected successor, Caius "Caligula," was a friend of Herod Agrippa, and Herod Agrippa wanted Judea for himself. Besides, the chief case against Jesus was one of blasphemy, a religious charge; such slippery issues were bound to make a Roman official nervous. Pilate would have been delighted to "wash his hands" of the whole affair.

Now, what if Vitellius was present to observe the proceedings? Here was an opportunity perhaps, to judge for himself what this Pilate was like when confronted by a restive people. Was he as violent and vicious as the Samaritan Senate declared? Was he a liability to Rome? *Bring on the prisoner!* Over to you, prefect! And Pilate does not want to make a judgment. Is he weak? Has his judgment suffered?

The gospel story of a custom that a prisoner should be released at the feast has no evidence to support it. I refer to Jesus's accusers' demand for the release of an alleged criminal or terrorist leader, Barabbas. However, we have seen that when Syria's governor arrived in Jerusalem he was willing to make concessions to popular feeling, including high ranking sackings. Nevertheless, the "release" from custody of the formerly "imprisoned" priestly robes was doubtless a significant enough concession for Roman authority to make; over half a century later, Josephus considered it remarkable. The "Barabbas" story makes little historical sense. Releasing known enemies for no obvious political return would have been ruinous policy. Had the enemies of Jesus—and of John too—in the temple organization been at the occasion in sufficient numbers, and given that they were convinced Jesus was a blasphemer and someone who would create, or who was creating, a serious challenge to their regime, then the call to have the prisoner crucified would have raised Vitellius's eyebrows. People who preferred Caesar to a "King of the Jews" were to be encouraged. Pilate would have listened. Would he be seen as weak, or even unjust, if he accepted the call for the death penalty, or as strong: someone who understood the need of the moment and how to master it—one who could see the essential *Roman interest* of the moment?

As far as Barabbas is concerned, it is worth mentioning as a reasonable speculation that while the name makes no sense as a real

Hebrew name (it means "son of the father"), "Barabbas" might have been an error for the Greek "Brabeus," which means "a judgment," "umpire" or "umpire's decision," as in the games. The cry "We want Barabbas!" then could have been a literary corruption of an original clamor for a deciding judgment in the face of Pilate's unease and political insecurity. Such might explain Pilate's seeking Herod Antipas's opinion. The gospel writers want us to believe it was the baying mob ("the Jews") who secured the decision, but the ultimate "thumbs down" in our historical scenario would most likely have come (perhaps secretly) from the authority of the governor of Syria, and it would have done the Christian cause no good at all if this detail were repeated unequivocally years later, if indeed such was ever known outside of government circles.

If this scenario bears any resemblance to what really happened, we may conclude that Jesus's execution resulted from an expedient complicity of the Syrian governor, Pilate, Jesus's enemies in the temple hierarchy, and, possibly, Herod Antipas. According to Saul of Tarsus, writing years after events *in which he may very well have taken part*, Jesus's condemnation was simply God's will; without the shedding of blood there could be no redemption. Saul, or Paul's theory of vicarious atonement took precedence over any historical quibbles. Mere men were blind instruments of primordial destiny. If the dark spiritual powers governing unredeemed humanity had actually known what they ("the princes of this world") were really doing, and *who* they were condemning, "they would not have crucified the Lord of glory" (1 Corinthians 2:8) for, according to Saul/Paul, the Lord's hanging on wood was the trigger in the snare that trapped them (1 Corinthians 1:23).

It looks very much like Jesus's crucifixion can be understood politically as the result of a disturbed time, a perceived, if temporary breakdown of order within the Roman control of Judea, and a fateful moment, which the messianic party failed to capitalize on, as they may have had cause to hope, and which the Temple Sadducaean Party did their utmost to exploit.

There were new powers, waiting in the wings, to fill the vacuum, ready to see off every living legacy of the Baptist in the new order.

Josephus informs us that once Vitellius had absorbed the news of Tiberius's death, he had no choice but to recall his army from their march to Petra. The reason was that "upon the devolution of the empire upon Caius [Caligula], he [Vitellius] had not the like authority of making this war, which he had before." Tiberius's war order was void. Until further orders, he would have to retire his army to their quarters.

Aretas himself, Josephus reports, had consulted his diviners when he heard of the impending attack on Petra. They had told him that "it was impossible that this army of Vitellius's could enter Petra; for that one of the rulers would die, either he that gave orders for the war, or he that was marching at the other's desire, in order to be subservient to his will, or else he against whom this army is prepared." Like his account of the battle between Aretas and Antipas, Josephus rounds the story off with an oracular prediction and a note of Vitellius's retiring to Antioch.

The dénouement to our story however, is not quite so harmonious. At Tiberius's death, Herodias's brother Herod Agrippa was released from the captivity into which Tiberius had cast him for having been overheard favoring Caligula over himself. Coming to power, Caligula rewarded Agrippa's preference with the gift of his half-uncle Philip's tetrarchy of Trachonitis, Ituraea, and Batanaea. Salome also benefited from the new order. Apart from the "head of the Baptist," Philip's widow also received the hand in marriage of Agrippa's brother, Aristobulus of Chalcis. Aristobulus would eventually become King of Armenia Minor (55–72 CE) and as such would help Nero against the Parthians. As for Antipas, his best-laid plans were now awry; Herodias was incensed.

Agrippa returned to Judea in 39 CE (one Marullus had apparently been prefect since late 37 CE, having replaced either Marcellus or Pilate) to the horror and annoyance of his sister Herodias. She found Agrippa's newfound airs unbearable. Agrippa had once come penniless to her husband, begging support. Anxious lest Agrippa acquire Judea and Samaria, Herodias persuaded Antipas, much against his will, to travel to Rome to make a case for Caligula that he, Antipas, inherit Judea. When the couple saw the emperor in Rome, Caligula was already in receipt of a letter from Agrippa accusing Antipas of making overtures to Artabanus II, King of Parthia, enemy of Rome. When asked about the distribution of his troops, Antipas's answer confirmed Caligula's enflamed suspicions. He exiled Antipas to Lyons, Gaul. Caligula then offered Herodias her husband's tetrarchy. Herodias bravely declared she had married her husband to suffer ill, as well as good, fortune: Herodias's last great moment. Enraged at the rejection, Caligula stripped Herodias of her possessions and sent her off to Gaul with her husband. He then gave Antipas's tetrarchy to Agrippa.

After Caligula's assassination in 41 CE, his successor, Claudius, whom Agrippa had befriended, gave Agrippa official control of Judea and Samaria, making Agrippa a great power in the East and, in Josephus's judgment, a wise one. According to the Acts of the Apostles, Agrippa persecuted the "primitive Christian Church" on account of its opposition to the existing religious order and for believing Jesus was the Messiah and had been resurrected (Acts 12:1*ff.*). According to the version of events in Acts, Agrippa's persecution just missed having the benefit of an extremely able heretic-investigator called Saul. Saul had had a nervous breakdown on the road to Damascus involving a complete overturning of his religious convictions; he realized that to attack Jesus was to attack himself and to pursue Jesus was to pursue himself. In due course a sublimely confident, revived "Paul" (Roman name) would turn his attentions to followers of John the Baptist.

With regard to Damascus, Paul left intriguing details:

> But when it pleased God, who separated me from my mother's womb, and called me by his grace, To reveal his Son in me, that I might preach him among the heathen; immediately I conferred

not with flesh and blood: Neither went I up to Jerusalem to them, which were apostles before me; but I went into Arabia, and returned again unto Damascus.

Then after three years I went up to Jerusalem to see Peter, and abode with him fifteen days. But other of the apostles saw I none, save James the Lord's brother. (Galatians 1:15–19)

In Damascus the governor under Aretas the king kept the city of the Damascenes with a garrison, desirous to apprehend me: And through a window in a basket was I let down by the wall, and escaped his hands. (2 Corinthians 11:32)

Both of these verbatim snippets flatly contradict the account of Saul's conversion and subsequent activities in Acts 9:10–30. Luke has Saul being brought into the Jerusalem assembly practically straightaway. Even the detail about his having been lowered in a basket down the walls of Damascus was, according to Acts, "because the Jews took counsel to kill him" (v. 23). Luke knows nothing of Aretas's governor wanting to get his hands on Saul. Was, I wonder, Aretas trying to get his own back on someone who (perhaps working for Herod Antipas) had opposed John the Baptist, the righteous man who had tried to save Aretas's daughter from the dishonor of divorce?

Aretas IV had taken control of Damascus, formerly a city of the Decapolis, in Syria, during the war of 36–37 CE. If credit is given to Luke's account in Acts, Saul must have been stuffed with boundless confidence to think he could walk into Damascus, armed only with paper authority from Jerusalem's religious authorities, to arrest and bind men and women and drag them back to Jerusalem. Luke seems unaware of the political realities. Why would Aretas's governor in Damascus allow synagogue leaders in his city to accede to letters from Jerusalem's high priest, involving the loss of citizens' liberties? The cities of the Decapolis prided themselves on being free cities. If Damascus was less free under Aretas, it was certainly not in the high priest's jurisdiction. Given the recent bitter conflict, Damascus would hardly have been a welcoming place for an agent of Herodian and Sadducean control. However, neither Paul's own accounts, nor those of Acts make it precisely clear *who* he was working for when he, the most zealous, most uncompromising, and deadliest persecutor among Jesus's enemies "wasted" the "church of God" (Galatians 1:13). The point made in Acts that Saul went to the high priest for letters to give to synagogues outside of Judea does not tell us *who* he represented, or who provided the muscle. In 39–40 CE, he could have been Herod Agrippa's agent. Agrippa was now tetrarch of Philip's old territory, some twenty miles south of Damascus.

In Acts, Saul simply *appears.* He is a young man holding the coats of those stoning the "first Christian martyr," called Stephen (which means "crown"). However, it is impossible to take Acts as reliable history, though there is history behind it, and historical personages appearing in it, as in the Gospels.

For those wondering why we have gone beyond the beheading of John the Baptist (if only by a few years), it is to try to understand the source of the long-running polemic against John the Baptist, his baptism, and spiritual status, so to establish whether or not Christian tradition has represented John accurately. There can be little doubt that the source of the anti-John polemic has been treated very generously indeed, even though he first appears as a destroyer of almost everything John and Jesus had established:

> But I certify you, brethren, that the gospel, which was preached of me, is not after man. For I neither received it of man, neither was I taught it, but by the revelation of Jesus Christ. For ye have heard of my conversation in time past in the Jews' religion, how that beyond measure I persecuted the church of God, and wasted it: And profited in the Jews' religion above many my equals in mine own nation, being more exceedingly zealous of the traditions of my fathers. (Galatians 1:12–14)

Saul admits to having been thoroughly vicious in his treatment of the church. He offers no apology; he did what he believed right, indeed could pride himself on his extra-extraordinary zeal. He got more out of the Jews' religion than almost anybody. But he had decided to change tack. Or rather, it had been decided for him; he had found Christ not in anybody's teaching; he had found the Son of God in himself.

Since Aretas, whose governor was in control of Damascus when Paul "saw the light," died in 40 CE, Saul's change of direction in life must have occurred between 37 and 40. At a reasonable outside, we might date it to 39 CE, though it could have been 38. In 39 CE Agrippa returned to Judea from Rome, the year in which Antipas and Herodias left Galilee and Perea never to return. Josephus gives us very little information as to what was happening in Judea between late 37 and 39; perhaps he just could not find anything to say about it. He was himself a baby and toddler at the time.

It is reasonable to suppose that the people who pushed for Jesus's execution were the same as those who opposed his followers in Jerusalem and elsewhere thereafter, when they had the chance. Unless Saul had an equally startling conversion to the cause of "threatenings and slaughter" (Acts 9:1) as he experienced on the road to Damascus, he was likely to have been party to the arrest and crucifixion of Jesus: a rather staggering thought, but not without merit.

Now that we have a historically realistic date for the crucifixion, and for the execution of John, and have been able to put these events within their political context as far as we can, we see that Saul was not, as popularly imagined, a kind of second generation *arriviste* into the "Christian story" but a man of the time, a player, albeit a shady one, until he "came out of the shadows," as it were, in the late 30s and early 40s. But did we ever *really* know who "Paul" was? And if Saul's violent activities now bring us closer to the crucifixion, would it be baseless to suspect the presence of Saul's hand in the arrest and execution of John the Baptist as well?

Saul/Paul never detailed the extent of his intimidations and slaughters: no names, no detail, no apology. For him, it was all a kind of inner struggle; Paul was never anything less than right about everything. If he was humble, as he admitted, it was for a purpose; if he was a fool, then likewise. Wisdom baffles brains; and if he had no brains, why are you reading this? And if Saul condemned to death in the name of God, then was it not right? Paul, after all, was never in a moment's doubt that without the shedding of blood, there could be no salvation. Jesus had to die. John, we may suppose, likewise. It was God's will.

If Saul had *that* much blood on his hands, and if a spiritual awakening did finally, and suddenly, dawn on his angry-young-man consciousness, is it any wonder he collapsed in a neurotic heap of catastrophic psychic self-recrimination, hearing "a voice": "Saul, Saul, *why* are you pursuing me?"

Oh, you did not know the Greek verb *diōko* is just as well translated as *"pursue,"* as "persecute?" It is a subtle difference, but rather significant, is it not?

Why are you pursuing me?

Was it a voice crying in Paul's wilderness?

Chapter 7

JOHN AND JESUS
Comrades in a Secret Plan

WHAT PICTURE of John the Baptist would we enjoy in the Gospels if John had been released by Herod Antipas, instead of being executed? Would we even have any Gospels? What would have happened to the main story?

The orthodox view of John the Baptist requires John to bow out just in time for Jesus to take center stage. The "herald" scenario only works in terms of *Jesus* being the one heralded *if* Jesus can be shown as the one who comes "after" John. Otherwise, we must assume that the "one" who was coming after was someone or something different. As we have seen, the biblical prophecies employed by the evangelists strongly suggest that the way was being prepared for the Lord God to come to his people. That the chosen mode of coming meant that the coming one turned out *not* to be the "Lord God" directly, but the "Son" to be followed by the Holy Spirit or "Paraclete" appears to be the conclusion of Jesus's followers, not John. How John himself might have seen the figure of the messiah is still an open question. The New Covenanters, and popular zeal, required a messiah who would lead a holy war to a swift victory over the "Sons of Darkness."

If John was the herald, Jesus the one to "come after," then the herald scenario required John's death—and pretty quickly, too. If this were a novel, one might ask, "Why has the author killed off the hero"—or, arguably, one of the two leading characters—"so soon?" Why does Luke go to the trouble of giving us such a big buildup for John, an entire birth narrative involving parents and miracles (1:5–80), if John is simply going to back offstage, out of the limelight? Since John did not, as far as we can tell, "hand himself over" to Antipas and beg for execution—*I'd rather die than hang around and spoil Jesus's chances!*—we must presume that the killing of John was traumatic for his followers. According to Josephus, Judeans regarded John's death as a catastrophe that so displeased God that it caused another catastrophe (for Antipas at least): his army's defeat by King Aretas's forces. The public, according to Josephus, believed that *God was displeased* with Antipas for killing John. You will not find this thought in the New Testament.

However, even internal gospel evidence, if "evidence" is the right word, appeals against this simplistic scenario, that is, the "he [Jesus] must increase and I [John] must decrease" narrative (John 3:30). Both Matthew (11:2–6) and Luke (7:18–23) relate an intriguing story wherein John's disciples come to Jesus to ask him, "Are you he who is to come, or shall we look for another?" In Matthew, John's disciples receive their instructions from a John who is actually *in custody* at the time. Luke has nothing to say about this; Luke never treads into the John-imprisonment stories. The real function of these *pericopes,* or story and saying fragments about John's enquiries concerning Jesus, remains unclear. The Gospels begin more or less with John announcing the coming one and baptizing Jesus; why should he then order his disciples to undertake a fact-finding mission? John has, allegedly, already declared Jesus to be the Lamb of God (the Messiah). Are the story fragments intended to "rub it in" or are they based on historic fact? Much depends on how they are read. Given the custodial setting for John, for example, I should be inclined to take the enquiries as being, in their historical context, rather indignant: *Who do you think you are? Are you now saying you are the one we've been watching out for? Just what are you, Jesus? The moment I'm arrested I hear you're doing all these things—baptizing and leading the crowds. Should my followers now follow you?* Even if John was not in prison when enquiries might have been made, there is still the unmistakable impression of a *rival* program, or of someone trying, unexpectedly, to assert himself in the absence of the "leader." Besides, if John was "out" (as Luke's account might suggest), why send disciples at all; why not just ask Jesus directly?

Luke and Matthew simply take the setting as the opportunity to make it plain as day to all comers that Jesus is the Messiah. Indeed, Jesus's answer to John's question is simply to demonstrate messiahship. In Luke, Jesus actually cures diseases, removes plagues, exorcises evil spirits, and restores sight to the blind "in that hour." Amazing. He then asks the messengers to add this display of wonders to his already staggering aggregate of cleansing of lepers, making the deaf hear, preaching good news to the poor, and raising up the dead. That should convince John! Jesus adds at the end, "And blessed is he who takes no offense at me." Surely, Jesus seems to imply, surely the great John is not thinking of joining those who find this revelation threatening. Surely he, John, would not take offense. It would appear that Jesus thinks offense *has* been taken—by John!

The gospel texts suggest John and his disciples have been on the "watch," looking out for the signs of the coming kingdom, and for the Messiah in particular. That would explain the part about, *Are you the coming one? Or should we look somewhere else?* Jesus speaks through his acts: *Cease looking, I'm here. Yes, it's me. Rest assured.* The idea seems to be very similar to Luke's account of Simeon in the Temple, waiting for the Lord (2:25*ff.*). Having seen the child Jesus, Simeon can now "depart in peace," for his eyes have seen his salvation. The same message seems to be going out to John: *It's all right; you can go now.*

Why would John be convinced by Jesus's sixty-minute demonstration?

Among the Dead Sea Scrolls, dated by Geza Vermes to the very early first century CE, is a *Messianic Apocalypse* (4Q521). This text actually lists the signs of the messianic kingdom, signs to be perceived by the righteous. The signs are: the recognition of the pious, the calling of the righteous by name, the renewal of the Lord's poor and faithful by his spirit, the glorification of the pious on "the throne of the eternal kingdom," the liberation of captives, the restoration of sight to the blind, the straightening of the bent, the doing of glorious things never seen before, the healing of the wounded, the leading of the uprooted, the feeding of the hungry, the giving of good news to the poor, and, *take note,* the revival of the dead, when "the Life-giver will raise the dead of his people." Jesus's operation, as demonstrated to John's followers, ticks practically every box. Why then, one might ask, would Jesus not release the captive John? Again, we can hardly be unmoved at the coincidence of Dead Sea Scroll New Covenanter-cherished material with the historical background to accounts of John the Baptist.

Disturbingly, the accounts of John's messengers' visit to Jesus in Matthew and Luke are concluded by what appears to be a somewhat premature obituary for John: glowing, all-glowing, no doubt, but with caveats. Having demonstrated his own status, Jesus now generously sums up John's career while setting him in his place, albeit rather confusingly. If there is any historical actuality behind the words, they would seem to be more appropriate for reflection after John's death:

> And as they departed, Jesus began to say unto the multitudes concerning John, What went ye out into the wilderness to see? A reed shaken with the wind?
>
> But what went ye out for to see? A man clothed in soft raiment? Behold, they that wear soft clothing are in kings' houses.
>
> But what went ye out for to see? A prophet? Yea, I say unto you, and more than a prophet. For this is he, of whom it is written, Behold, I send my messenger before thy face, which shall prepare

thy way before thee. Verily I say unto you, Among them that are born of women there hath not risen a greater than John the Baptist: notwithstanding he that is least in the kingdom of heaven is greater than he.

And from the days of John the Baptist until now the kingdom of heaven suffereth violence, and the violent take it by force. For all the prophets and the law prophesied until John. And if ye will receive it, this is Elias [Elijah], which was for to come. He that hath ears to hear, let him hear.

But whereunto shall I liken this generation? It is like unto children sitting in the markets, and calling unto their fellows, And saying, We have piped unto you, and ye have not danced; we have mourned unto you, and ye have not lamented. For John came neither eating nor drinking, and they say, He hath a devil. The Son of man came eating and drinking, and they say, Behold a man gluttonous, and a winebibber, a friend of publicans and sinners. But wisdom is justified of her children. (Matthew 11:7–19)

This summing up of John is a very mixed bag of sources, and its meaning is not clear. John as "a reed shaken with the wind" appears very poetic; we shall examine the idea in due course. The business about the man in a soft garment is far from obvious. John Fenton, the late English commentator on Matthew and one of my tutors at Oxford, believed Jesus was making a kind of exaggerated joke, on the lines of, "Did you think you were going to see someone fancily dressed, an important person, an aristocrat?" This idea seems to come out of Luke who, I think, misunderstands Matthew completely and adds the following to the note about those wearing soft raiment being in kings' houses: "Behold," Luke's Jesus says, "those who are gorgeously apparelled and live in luxury are in kings' courts" (Luke 7:25). Luke seems to think John would be the last person to wear a "soft garment" (the Greek word for "soft" even has the hint of femininity about it). But a soft garment does not necessarily equate with gorgeous apparel; Luke has missed the point here, I think. Furthermore, the parallel rhetorical idea—of the multitude's expectations being "wrong" on this and two other counts—does not hold in Jesus's three questions to them. The multitude's thoughts about John are not wrong, just *inadequate:* John *is* a reed shaken by the wind; he *is* a prophet; he *did,* I am sure, wear a soft garment. (Camel hair and leather would not be seen as "soft," but rough, by the way.)

Taken within the Gospels' context of Jesus talking about John to the multitude, Jesus is talking about John's *dignity.* John stands in the desert. He is a prophet and *more than* a prophet. He is Elijah, and that, together with everything else, makes him the greatest man who was ever born of woman (Jesus was also born of woman).

John is the messenger sent to prepare the way for the Lord. *So,* he wore a soft garment. Those in soft garments are found in kings' houses. There is a multiple implication here, played out on a pun. The play is on the words *kings* and *houses.* Those wearing soft garments in kings' houses are the *king's servants;* make no mistake. The "king" here is *the Lord,* and John is his servant, and is therefore dressed as a servant: dress fit for a king and fit for the glory of the King's House. Second, *the* house of the king (the Lord) is the Temple. John then is wearing the clothing of the Lord's servant *in the Temple* (the Temple that has become a wilderness, *for the "husbandmen" of the Temple/Vineyard have failed*—see Mark 12:1–9). This "soft garment" would then equate with the white linen of a *priest.* John is a prophet and a priest.

It should be borne in mind here that when the Gospels appeared, the Judean temple system had been destroyed. Who would want to know that Jesus and his associates were associated with the priesthood of the *actual* Temple that, Gentiles believed, God had condemned? Paul had said that the body of the baptized Christian was the temple of the Lord. The idea of priesthood is underplayed in the Gospels except, notably, where issues of birth and background come into play.

My tutor also missed this point and wrote in his commentary that John could not have been the kind of rich, aristocratic type, attending regal courts. He was in prison. Nothing "soft" about that! Well, Macherus might appear from gospel narratives to be a prison, and it may well have had something like a dungeon, but it was *not* a prison; it was a palace, as modern archaeology has adequately shown. It was a "home from home" for Phasaelis, remember: a resort. In short, it was a king's house, and if there is any historical actuality behind these sayings attributed to Jesus, they simply tell the truth. John is in soft raiment in a *king's house*. Macherus is a king's house, so the implied pun exists to pose a subsidiary question: which Lord does John *serve*? He is of course the "guest" of Antipas's political will, but John is not the king's servant; he is God's.

We then get some confused passages. The first is on the lines of "the first shall be last, and the last shall be first" motif. Those who are present for the revealing of the true messiah, the "first fruits of repentance," are first in line, compared to those who in the past prophesied the coming one. Primacy is apparently for those who receive the Spirit at the end-time. He who is the smallest in the kingdom of heaven is greater than he (John). Why? This sounds like a late theological afterthought, lest anyone think John is more important than, well, Jesus. Jesus tells all who have ears to hear that John *now* belongs to the era of the "the prophets and the law." Now Jesus has come, that era is apparently over, "fulfilled"; it's an all-new show from now on. John is the greatest prophet but he is apparently missing something. He is not today's man. This sounds a trifle triumphalistic, like Paul on the alleged inadequacy of John's baptism again.

The time-sense of the passage now goes haywire. Suddenly, John the Baptist is past history: "From the days of John the Baptist until now the kingdom of heaven has suffered violence, and the violent take it by force." This might be applied to the arrest of John, though we do not know if John was taken by force. The feeling and sense seem to refer to the time of, and after, Jesus's crucifixion, when his followers were pursued unto death.

John is now declared to be Elijah, but the force of this is dramatically lessened, since the time of the prophets is already done, we are told. He has prepared the way; now, let that be an end of it. The script is writing John out altogether. By verse 19, John is definitively past history: "For John came neither eating nor drinking, and they say, "He hath a devil." *Who* says John has a demon? We have not heard that one; that's supposed to be what Jesus's enemies say of *him.* Anyhow, the force of the parallel between John and the "Son of man" who came "eating and drinking" to be condemned for impure company is simply to pump up Jesus. John lived according to the laws of righteousness, and he is a "demon," *I* live in the new freedom of the Holy Spirit (Paul's idea of it anyway), and I'm condemned also. The force is simple: if you had believed the prophets (including John, the *last* of them), you would have believed me. But *you* (who is "Jesus" supposed to be addressing here?) did not believe them either; you (the Jews) rejected them. On this count, John is already dead. And as far as the Gospels are concerned, he is. John's death goes without saying, you might say.

Somewhere under all this must be some real history.

Now perhaps you see more clearly why I asked the question at the beginning of this chapter: *What would have happened if John had been freed by Antipas and had reentered circulation?* Today it appears that John *had* to die to make way for Jesus. His demise was simply a *fait accompli.* But is this a misinterpretation? Have the demands of a Christocentric theology overtaken completely the history of John's true relations with Jesus?

What says the evidence?

Well, the evidence of course has long been cooked up to present the narrative we have been examining. One would hardly expect it to testify against itself. But it does. The Gospels are full of curious details that rather give away the intentions of the writers. The Gospels, note, were not composed so that they could be placed next to one another in a bigger book we call the Bible. They were individual treatises, and subject to editing from copyists. It was a long time before believers had the benefit of seeing them "all" together. That was not how they were intended to be seen, or heard. So the composers and compilers of the writings did not think their painstaking needlework would be unpicked by scholars or anyone else. We may expect that they expected their labors to be gratefully received, not analyzed.

In many respects the writers appear to have been eager not to write propaganda as such, but to tell as much as could be woven together of what was available to them. They tried to find a place for their sources and doctrinal priorities in a fairly well-established narrative framework, though many caveats might be attached to that process. We have seen how essential historical and political contexts are "missing," and we may doubt if they were ever "there" in the first place. There was no point looking backward. The only thing that really mattered before the message was preached to the Gentiles was Jesus: the rest was, well, *history,* and that only mattered insofar as the story of how Jesus came to be called the Lord required it.

We may suspect that part of the confusion evinced in the previous account of John the Baptist had something to do with what was probably a source for it, except that the source would not do, as it were, what it was "supposed" to do. That is, the source in question did not relegate John the Baptist sufficiently. It did not follow company policy. Not only that, it suggested a far more profound link between John and Jesus than Matthew and Luke might have liked.

JOHN AS SON OF MAN

The source in question is Mark 9:9–13. It is a passage that Luke is not interested in; he thinks he has dealt with John the Baptist sufficiently in the previous account. Matthew alters it to pull it more into line with his narrative. Hear Mark:

And as they [Peter, James, and John] came down from the mountain, he [Jesus] charged them that they should tell no man what things they had seen, till the Son of man were risen from the dead. And they kept that saying with themselves, questioning one with another, what the rising from the dead should mean. And they asked him, saying, "Why say the scribes that Elias [Elijah] must first come?" And he answered and told them, "Elias verily cometh first, and restoreth all things; and how it is written of the Son of man, that he must suffer many things, and be set at nought.

"But I say unto you, That Elias is indeed come, and they have done unto him whatsoever they listed, as it is written of him."

And when he came to his disciples, he saw a great multitude about them, and the scribes questioning with them.

Mark clearly includes John/Elijah under the destiny allotted to the "Son of man": that he must suffer and be set at nought. Matthew (17:9–13) has noticed the inference that Jesus speaks of John in terms of the suffering of the "Son of man" and is upset by it, as far as we can tell, for he changes the text to distinguish between Jesus and John. "Likewise also shall the Son of man suffer of them":

But I say unto you, "That Elias is come already, and they knew him not, but have done unto him whatsoever they listed. Likewise shall also the Son of man suffer of them." Then the disciples understood that he spake unto them of John the Baptist.

Luke wants nothing to do with this saying: it is far too ambiguous for his narrative. However, and most tellingly, he includes the "set at nought" destiny in his unique account of Herod Antipas's interrogation of Jesus in 23:11: "And Herod with his men of war set him at nought." *They* set Jesus at nought, but Luke appears to have got his idea of setting the "Son of man" at nought from Mark, where it is plainly John/Elijah/Son of man who has been set at nought.

What is even more interesting is that Luke goes along with the narrative that precedes these sayings of Jesus, but cuts away from the concluding sayings, which we have above. And what is the preceding narrative? It is the story of the Transfiguration. Now, there is a curious relationship between the story of the Transfiguration and the earlier summing up about John that followed the story of John's disciples coming to ask whether Jesus was the one expected. That account, as we noted, was in Matthew and Luke, but not in Mark. The nearest thing to that discussion in Mark is the pericope above that concludes the transfiguration story.

One might be forgiven for suspecting that the discussion, apparently about John, where Jesus asks "the multitude" what they went into the wilderness to see, a reed in the wind, a prophet, and one in soft raiment, originally appeared *in the context of the Transfiguration.*

THE REED, THE PROPHET, THE MAN IN FINE RAIMENT

In the story of the Transfiguration, Peter, John, and James are taken up a "high mountain" where, according to Mark, Jesus's garments "became glistening, intensely white, as no fuller on earth could bleach them" (9:3). Three chosen disciples then see what they believe to be Moses and Elijah talking to Jesus. Awestruck, Peter concludes that a booth be erected for each figure of this radiant triumvirate.

It is clear why Mark follows this account with a discussion of John the Baptist and Elijah, and about the Son of man rising from the dead. At least it looks like it ought to be clear. But as we have seen, Luke shies right away from this discussion; Matthew tinkers with it.

What Mark's Gospel has to say about John and Elijah is said in terms of a shared communion of Jesus with Moses and Elijah. Mark says very little else about John. One wonders if there was once a discussion attached to the transfiguration narrative on the lines of, "What went ye up the mountain to see? A reed shaken by the wind? A man clothed in soft raiment? And a prophet?" The three descriptions might originally have stood for three men who each could be properly described as a "Son of man," these three being Moses, the reed shaken by the wind; Jesus, dressed in soft garments;and Elijah, the prophet. Understood this way, Jesus's three famous questions, intriguingly applied to John, work very well.

What, you may ask, has Moses got to do with the reed shaken in the wind?

Much.

The "Red Sea" of Exodus through which Moses took the Children of Israel to freedom was actually the *Yam Suph* or *Reed Sea* (mistranslated in the Greek version of Exodus). And *suph,* the Hebrew for "reeds," also can be punned with *suphah,* meaning "storm," and *soph,* meaning end. The storm in the reeds was Pharaoh's nemesis, or as Exodus 15:10 has it, "Thou didst blow with thy wind, the sea covered them [the Egyptian army]: they sank as lead in the mighty waters." The crossing of the Reed Sea is the archetypal salvation-event of Israelite history. A "reed shaken in the wind" is, then, a superb condensation of the entire miracle, with added connotations of Moses (John?) alone in the wilderness, of his famous staff of power, and so on.

We may even find here a double recognition of *John's* spiritual nature. John is not only the culmination of the prophets (Elijah) but also of the Law (Moses). John, like Moses, is a kind of "ferryman," seeing the Children out of bondage in sin (Egypt) to the Promised Land beyond (salvation). If we recall the reference in John (1:28) to *Bethabara* "beyond Jordan," where John baptized, we may see that John, like Moses, conducts the Children of Israel through the waters via a crossing point or ford. John as Moses is also the psychopomp who leads the faithful into the "fiery" wilderness for purification and—who knows?—to the revelation of a new Law.

If the "reed shaken in the wind" and "the prophet" (Elijah) are both in a sense John, then who is the man in "soft raiment?" In the transfiguration story, the chosen disciples envision a man in soft raiment. It was apparently Jesus, in garments whiter than no earthly fuller could bleach them. Were these the garments to be found in kings' houses? Then the allusion may be to the holy mansions of God and the garments of angels. But again, do we not sense a link with the spiritual identity of John also? It is as though the identities of Moses, Elijah, John, and Jesus are fused in a state of heightened vision of their meta-real, transcendent being as "Son of man."

And the *prophet*? Elijah, that is, John, and John is therefore *more than a prophet*.

Why is John more than a prophet? He prepares the way of the Lord: he makes the path straight.

Now we may bring in Mark's conclusion to the transfiguration narrative. There we find John's true greatness: "Elias [Elijah] verily cometh first, and restoreth all things; and how it is written of the Son of man, that he must suffer many things, and be set at nought. But I say unto you, That Elias is indeed come, and they have done unto him whatsoever they listed, as it is written of him" (Mark 9:9–12).

Elijah has indeed come! See John, see Elijah!

John should have been easily recognizable as Elijah, for John did exactly what Elijah did. What did Elijah do? Elijah went to King Ahab and condemned the sinfulness of his marriage to Jezebel (1 Kings 18:7*ff.*) and condemned Ahab's sinfulness for respecting foreign gods who had no power. This John did too, to the face of Herod Antipas, calling shame on Antipas's marriage to Herodias. This John did, with stupendous moral courage. Even old King Ahab's lines could have been written for Herod Antipas:

> And it came to pass, when Ahab saw Elijah, that Ahab said unto him, *Art thou he that troubleth Israel?* And he [Elijah] answered, I have not troubled Israel; but thou, and thy father's house, in that ye have forsaken the commandments of the LORD, and thou hast followed Baalim [foreign gods]. (1 Kings 18:17–18)

John troubled Israel, in all the right ways. He did what was to be expected of a Son of man.

And what is a Son of man?

The gospel writers are never exactly sure, to be sure. They know it is a title Jesus used. It sounds like "Son of God" and in places becomes interchangeable with it. There are not many today who can offer a clear explanation of it. Some Jewish scholars are inclined to say the Christian tradition simply makes too much of it, and that it just means "man," as you might say: a "son of Adam," as C. S. Lewis uses the term in his Narnia books. So when the Lord addresses the prophet Ezekiel (2:1) as "Son of man," he just means "O man!" That may arguably have been the case as to the first usage of the term, but it is clear that by the time of John the Baptist, this term had acquired a thoroughbred pedigree of prophetic and messianic meaning:

> And he said [a voice that addresses Ezekiel] unto me, Son of man, stand upon thy feet, and I will speak unto thee. (Ezekiel 2:1)

This exhortation comes after Ezekiel, sometime in the 550s BCE, enjoyed the privilege of witnessing the *glory* of the Lord. He had seen "the likeness as the appearance of a man above upon it" [the divine throne in the vision]. *Man* is made in the image of God. And, at the blazing heart of the Glory, the image of God is seen by Ezekiel to be like a man, but like no man ever seen.

Following this vision, Ezekiel is addressed as "Son of man," as if *initiated* or rendered reborn by the vision: the son, fruit, or child of the vision of the divine Man, the image at the heart of God's Glory: the manifest reflection of God's limitless light. Those few vouchsafed the vision—the restoration of the being made in the image of God—constituted an elite; little wonder then that the astonished Cephas, true to his nickname, reacted to the vision by wanting to build memorials to mark a place where eternity touched time and a new spiritual exodus was born.

Long after Ezekiel's vision, the phrase "Son of man" became a staple of apocalyptic and revelatory writings. Four centuries later, for example, the book of Daniel, well known and much quoted from in the time of John and Jesus, used the term to mark a chosen prophet:

> Therefore, thou son of man, prophesy against Gog, and say, Thus saith the Lord GOD; Behold I am against thee, O Gog, the chief prince of Meshech and Tubal. (Daniel 39:1)

Apocalyptic writings impacted hugely on John and Jesus's era, and a new brand of apocalyptic came into being during the latter half of the first century CE: Christian apocalyptic ("apocalyptic" describes writings that reveal what has formerly been hidden). Christian apocalyptic was sometimes added on to Jewish revelatory works, as in the case of the "Ethiopic" Book of Enoch, though at what date precisely is unknown. In the Christian apocalyptic "Book Two" added to Enoch (chapters 37–72) we find the "Son of man" as a complete heavenly figure in his own right.

Confusion over the meaning of the "Son of man" engendered by Jesus's use of the term in the Gospels seems to have led to a mistaken conflation of the title with the *original image itself* in the divine Glory seen by Ezekiel. That is to say, the divine image *became* the "Son of Man," and the "Son of Man" was then used to stand for the Messiah in heaven, as we see here in passages from the later Ethiopic Book of Enoch:

> And it came to pass after this that his name [Enoch's] during his lifetime was raised aloft to that Son of Man and to the Lord of Spirits from amongst those who dwell on the earth. And he was raised aloft on the chariots of the spirit and his name vanished among them. . . . And it came to pass after this that my spirit was translated. And it ascended into the heavens: And I saw the holy sons of God. They were stepping on flames of fire: their garments were white [and their raiment]. And their faces shone like snow. . . . And he [the angel]

came to me and greeted me with His voice, and said unto me: "This is the Son of Man who is born unto righteousness; And righteousness abides over him, And the righteousness of the Head of Days forsakes him not." (Book of Enoch 70:1–2; 71:1, 14)

The original Book of Enoch was a hot writing in the first century CE, and a fairly recent one too. Several versions were found among the Dead Sea Scrolls, and their contents accord with Josephus's point that the Essenes valued books of angels. These Aramaic versions do not contain "Book Two" with the "Son of Man" figure. This rather confirms the point that the "Son of Man" as a heavenly figure, at least in the Book of Enoch, is a Christian development. The Gospels then stand midway in the development of the figure.

The Jesus of Mark 9 appears to have used the term for one who had seen the Glory and would have to suffer as a result. The "suffering" of the Son of man derives from linking the title "Son of man" to the prophet Isaiah's idea (eighth century BCE) that the special prophet picked by God to serve him would be set at nought by the "sons of men" who would not see the special man for what he really was. In the end, however, the Son of man would be exalted:

> For he shall grow up before him as a tender plant, and as a root out of a dry ground: he hath no form nor comeliness; and when we shall see him, there is no beauty that we should desire him.
>
> He is despised and rejected of men; a man of sorrows, and acquainted with grief: and we hid as it were our faces from him; he was despised, and we esteemed him not.
>
> Surely he hath borne our griefs, and carried our sorrows: yet we did esteem him stricken, smitten of God, and afflicted. But he was wounded for our transgressions, he was bruised for our iniquities: the chastisement of our peace was upon him; and with his stripes we are healed.
>
> All we like sheep have gone astray; we have turned every one

to his own way; and the LORD hath laid on him the iniquity of us all. He was oppressed, and he was afflicted, yet he opened not his mouth: he is brought as a lamb to the slaughter, and as a sheep before her shearers is dumb, so he openeth not his mouth.

He was taken from prison and from judgment: and who shall declare his generation? For he was cut off out of the land of the living: for the transgression of my people was he stricken. And he made his grave with the wicked and with the rich in his death; because he had done no violence, neither was any deceit in his mouth.

Yet it pleased the LORD to bruise him; he hath put him to grief: when thou shalt make his soul an offering for sin, he shall see his seed, he shall prolong his days, and the pleasure of the LORD shall prosper in his hand. He shall see of the travail of his soul, and shall be satisfied: by his knowledge shall my righteous servant justify many; for he shall bear their iniquities.

Therefore will I divide him a portion with the great, and he shall divide the spoil with the strong; because he hath poured out his soul unto death: and he was numbered with the transgressors; and he bare the sin of many, and made intercession for the transgressors. (Isaiah 53:2–12)

While we may be familiar with parts of this text in relation to prophecy applied to Jesus, we should realize that this text was already familiar to John and to Jesus, and if they applied it at all to their own destinies, they may certainly have applied it *to each other,* for all Isaiah was doing was describing the destiny of God's chosen men for all time. It was in the interests of later commentators to set John and Jesus apart. This anxiety we have seen demonstrated very clearly over Mark's conclusion to the transfiguration story.

Now perhaps we can see that the three men envisioned at the "Transfiguration" constituted a holy elect. In this company, the "inner three" disciples were privileged to see the "real Jesus," a transfigured, radiant being: the being the sons of men cannot see. Each in this elect communion was a "Son of man," for a "Son of man" is one who has seen the Glory of the Lord. Moses had ascended the mount in Sinai to receive the commandments; he saw the Glory of the Lord (Exodus 24:17). Elijah was called to witness God's appearance at Horeb where, through earthquake, wind, and fire, Elijah finally heard the "still small voice" (1 Kings 19:12). And Elijah also was taken up in a "fiery chariot" to the very mansions of the Lord.

And Jesus, in the transfiguration story at least, is presented *as* the Glory of the Lord, intimately linked, I think, to the spiritual being of John.

The late Gilles Quispel, one of the world's leading scholars of the Gnostic Gospels, used to say that the vision of the "Divine Man," or (in Greek), "Anthrōpos," was the "stock vision" of the Gnostic, the one who *knew*, the one who had made the link that bound the essence of Man to the essence of God.

Such speculations were as frightening a business for the religious authorities of the first century CE as they are for religious authorities today. No orthodox authority likes to confuse the established distinction between Man and God, and yet has that not been the precise theological difficulty of the history of Christianity? Is Jesus Man of Son, or Son of Man? And what is Man?

In the key quotation from Mark 9, it is clear that Jesus knows that John, as a Son of man, is in this world destined to "suffer many things" and be "counted as nought," that is to say, he will not be recognized for what he is, for what he is is not valued by those in control. He, the Son of man, has authority, the only authority, but he is set at nought. Therefore, God is set at nought. Therefore, there will be judgment. And in that judgment shall the Son of man, the one who has stood up, stood firm, stood straight, stood for the truth, stood like a reed in the wind of the Spirit, he, the Son of man, is raised among the dead.

That is why, coming down from the mountain, the conversation of Jesus and the "inner three" concerns the rising, or resurrection, and its relation to the Son of man's destiny, which they do not understand:

> And as they came down from the mountain, he [Jesus] charged
> them that they should tell no man what things they had seen, till
> the Son of man were risen from the dead. And they kept that saying
> with themselves, questioning one with another, what the rising from
> the dead should mean. (Mark 9:9–10)

The dialogue then proceeds to the question of Elijah's coming, something the scribes insist on as a preamble to, presumably, a general resurrection. Jesus seems to correct this view, saying that Elijah has come indeed and "restoreth all things" and that "they have done unto him [Elijah-John-Son of man] whatsoever they listed, as it is written of him." (v. 13) A feeling definitely lingers here that a prophetic quote has been edited out, either by Mark or a later copyist concerned that Elijah/John's destiny suddenly appears too similar to that reserved for Jesus. The quote, which might have begun with the words "as it is written," would almost certainly have been from Isaiah 53, as above.

What does Jesus mean when he says that Elijah must first restore all things, as well as "suffer many things, and be set at nought?" Elijah/John's restoring all things refers to the trials of Elijah in chapters 18 and 19 of 1 Kings where Elijah's zeal for restoring the Lord's desecrated altars is linked directly to the suffering of the prophets:

> And he [Elijah] said, I have been very jealous for the LORD God of
> hosts: for the children of Israel have forsaken thy covenant, thrown
> down thine altars, and slain thy prophets with the sword; and I, even
> I only, am left; and they seek my life, to take it away. (1 Kings 19:10)

For destroying her priests of Baalim, Ahab's wife Jezebel determined to kill Elijah, as Herodias would, in Mark, set out to kill John, for revealing her shame. In 1 Kings 18:30–31, Elijah, undeterred by thought of consequences, restores the altar of the Lord:

And Elijah said unto all the people, Come near unto me. And all the people came near unto him. And he repaired the altar of the LORD that was broken down. And Elijah took twelve stones, according to the number of the tribes of the sons of Jacob, unto whom the word of the LORD came, saying, Israel shall be thy name: And with the stones he built an altar in the name of the LORD.

If we take this account as an allegory, we might be forgiven for thinking that the calling of the "twelve," the *stones* for the new, restored temple of Israel, is the work not, as we usually think, of Jesus, but of Elijah/John. But then, Elijah was a Son of man, as was John, as was Jesus, as was Moses, and what *one* did, so did the others.

Behind Mark's references, we see a Jesus who has looked at that story of Elijah restoring the altar and observed that Elijah only rebuilt the altar as a prelude to calling God to work his fire on the bullock of sacrifice, which fire then consumed the sacrificial bullock, and the water that surrounded the altar, and the stones of which the altar was built. And it would seem to me that Jesus has also thought of the image of the one who lies down on the altar, who for love of God is sacrificed. If Jesus understood the deeper meaning of the story of Elijah, its inner meaning, and how it related to the ancient prophecies of the servant who suffers and is set at nought, and of the Son of man who is granted the vision of the Glory, then we may be sure that John understood these things too, and, we may even say, showed Jesus the way. But this was not as "herald" in the orthodox sense but as master of ceremonies, brother-guide, psychopomp, exemplar. While we can see that this likely historical actuality was not acceptable to the post-Pauline gloss that we find in the mainstream treatment of the Gospels, it nonetheless has survived in fragments, with one of which we have been dealing. It is not the only one. Look again, for example, at Mark 11:27–33, a pericope that appears in Matthew and Luke as well:

And they come again to Jerusalem: and as he was walking in the temple, there come to him the chief priests, and the scribes, and the elders, And say unto him, By what authority doest thou these things? and who gave thee this authority to do these things?

And Jesus answered and said unto them, "I will also ask of you one question, and answer me, and I will tell you by what authority I do these things.

"The baptism of John, was it from heaven, or of men? answer me."

And they reasoned with themselves, saying, "If we shall say, 'From heaven'; he will say, 'Why then did ye not believe him?' But if we shall say, 'Of men' they feared the people: for all men counted John, that he was a prophet indeed."

And they answered and said unto Jesus, "We cannot tell." And Jesus answering saith unto them, "Neither do I tell you by what authority I do these things.

John's baptism was "from heaven." *From heaven,* mark you, not just "of [earthly] water"! According to this story, John's authority was Jesus's authority.

Now perhaps we can see that John and Jesus were not originally, or in their own minds even, "before and after," but were united, comrades in a higher prophetic and secret visionary struggle to save Israel—and the world—from spiritual catastrophe.

JOHN AND JESUS

How could we have missed it?

It was because we were not asking the right questions. We have never been encouraged to.

Most of Luke's first chapter's eighty verses are devoted to a colorful account of John the Baptist's birth and of his relations with Jesus and with Jesus's parents. We never obtain anything like this level of information about any other figure's birth in the whole of Christian

scripture, save Jesus himself. Luke gives us an intricate divine plan
unfolded with six-month staggered births and angelic visitations to
all parents concerned. The obvious intertwining of the two boys' destinies was not lost on the great Renaissance artists inspired by Jesus's
and John's infancy. The saintly toddlers are seen playing together;
their mothers are friends. Angels watch over them.

At the end of Luke's account of John's birth, Zacharias sings a great
song about his new son. The son's ordained purpose is nothing less than
to "give light to them that sit in darkness and in the shadow of death, to
guide our feet into the way of peace" (1:79). Then, after all that, John's
next thirty-six years or so are summed up in a few words: "And the
child grew, and waxed strong in spirit, and was in the deserts till the day
of his shewing unto Israel."

After all the stories of John's birth, we might have expected more.
Could it be that Luke's source was utterly ignorant of John's education and maturity, or might it have been that what John was or
was not doing "in the deserts" or elsewhere was either not consistent
with, or was not of service to the rest of Luke's account? Certainly
the next time John appears in Luke's text, during the fifteenth year
of the reign of the Emperor Tiberius, he is a fully fledged master of
his destiny. Given that John was probably born in 7 BCE, he would
have been about thirty-six years old when in 29 CE, if Luke's information is reliable in this instance, John received his call to preach
repentance.

As we have noticed before, Luke's account of Jesus's baptism is
curiously removed from the person of John. Luke mentions John was
imprisoned for confronting Herod with the evil of his deeds, and
then says that "when all the people were baptized, it came to pass
that Jesus also being baptized . . ." (3:21). There is no conversation
between John and Jesus, no declaration by John that Jesus is, well,
anything; there is silence, as though John was not there. There is no
direct recognition of Jesus by John, as we find in the other Gospels. If
it were not for the testimony of the other Gospels, we should think at

this point that John was in prison, and that Jesus was perhaps baptized by one or some of John's followers in John's absence. It is odd. And it goes even further than the other three Gospels' unlikely suggestion that John, apparently never having seen Jesus before in his life, was suddenly confronted by the very one he had allegedly prophesied would come "after." In Luke, John and Jesus do not even *communicate*. The reason may be, as discussed earlier, that Luke, being a "Paul man," does not want the coming of the Holy Spirit on Jesus to be linked to John's baptismal agency. Nevertheless, the impression seems to be that Luke feels uncomfortable with the idea that John and Jesus had any real personal connection in adulthood *at all*. Luke simply removes the possibility by two literary devices. He piles in a big chunk of stories between his account of the birth of John and his appearance as a Baptist, and he intercuts his account of John's baptizing and Jesus's being baptized with a pericope about John's imprisonment. Clearly, an uncomfortable fact is being obscured.

How, even if there is only the merest granule of historical fact in Luke's elaborate John and Jesus birth stories, could the two men *not* have known one another, or recognized each other, after thirty-six years in the same country, sharing, as far as we can tell, practically identical interests? And, what is more, why does Jesus himself only appear as a man at the time John is baptizing, that is, when John appears—not *after* John appears, note, but *when* John appears? Jesus almost comes out from behind John's back.

Two of Jesus's disciples are John's, the Gospel of John tells us, and one of them, Andrew, recruits his brother Simon (renamed "stone" in Aramaic: Cephas = Greek *Petros*), who is described in John 1:42 as "the son of John," which the King James version of the Bible shortens to "Jona," indicating discomfort at what the translators must otherwise have felt would provide cause for confusion (or undesirable enlightenment). Notwithstanding, John's Gospel says that Cephas was the *son of John,* which could mean much or nothing, since John was a common enough name. It was not uncommon in the ancient world for a master to call a close disciple "my son," since the master took a paternal role over the one under instruction.

Whatever all this might mean, common sense strongly mitigates against the gospel picture of John up and running with a complete operation of repentance-baptism-preaching activities, backed by a devoted following, if Josephus is to be credited, and Jesus just turning up, getting baptized, then poaching a few of John's closest followers, and then, apparently, dropping them for a while until emerging from the wilderness "temptation," or, better, initiation.

This picture does not add up, historically speaking. It is theological propaganda.

Let us return to our original question. What would have happened if Antipas had released John? Since the removal of John is clearly, in the gospel presentation, the point at which a Jesus-led operation commences, then we must suppose that Jesus would have found it difficult, to say the least, to run a rival or "continuity" operation. Jesus's first message was, "Repent ye for the kingdom of heaven is at hand." This was John's message, and if John had been there to provide it, what would Jesus have had to do? The entire conundrum dissolves, however, the moment we accept that Jesus and John were entwined in the same fundamental operation, an operation whose progress was suddenly and severely interrupted by John's arrest, so adding urgency and a heightened sense of danger and destiny to Jesus's activities. If the dating we discussed in chapter 6 is accurate, Jesus's own fuse was also short. Sooner or later, the authorities were either going to be toppled, or they would catch up with him.

Is Luke's account of John's and Jesus's birth historical? Evidence supporting Luke's narrative is fragmentary, but what exists supports the reasonable conclusion that Jesus's family milieu was, like John's, of the priestly class. Luke 1:3–25 describes John's father, Zechariah (*Zacharias* in Greek), as a priest "of the division of Abijah." John's mother, Elizabeth, was "of the daughters of Aaron." This means her father was a priest. Aaron's male descendants inherited priestly authority and could supervise temple sacrifices.

Zechariah and Elizabeth lived, according to Luke, in a city of Judea "in the hill country." We may think in terms of priestly *dachas* in the country, and we may also think of priests being associated with "wilderness camps" such as are described in the Dead Sea Scrolls "Community Rule" and *Damascus Document*.

Luke 1:36 says that Mary, Jesus's mother, was a "kinswoman" (Greek *syngenis*) of Elizabeth; she is also called a "handmaid to the Lord." "Handmaid" is a translation of the Greek *doulē*. It means a female slave, one sold into the service of God; the temple owned her. It was not unusual for virgin daughters of pious parents with temple links to be "dedicated" to temple service. Temple priests could find their wives from the ranks of the dedicated Temple slave girls. Note the ordinances for priests in Ezekiel 44:22:

> Neither shall they [priests in the Temple] take for their wives a widow, nor her that is put away: but they shall take virgins of the seed of the house of Israel, or a widow that had a priest before.

Once the girls had "known" a man, their freedom from slavery to the temple organization would be redeemed; they would then be rededicated to their husbands.

Temple services were dominated by twenty-four groups of priests. Each group served twice a year for a week at a time. As there were so many priests, lots were drawn for morning and evening sacrifices. The most coveted lot permitted the winner to burn incense in the Temple. The rising fumes signified the people's prayers rising to God. It was supposed to be performed but once in a priest's lifetime. Since many never got the opportunity, the story Luke tells of Zechariah's special day packs punch. This was the height of Zechariah's life as a priest, and he could look forward to crowning it by making a special blessing for the people. But according to Luke, when Zechariah emerged, he found himself struck dumb. He had witnessed God's messenger, Gabriel.

Luke had some authentic knowledge of temple management. Zechariah's belonging to the priestly "division of Abijah" is based on fact. Abijah means "my father is Yahweh." Fragmentary manuscripts from the Dead Sea Scrolls dated some time in the late first century BCE include details of the six-year rotation of priestly courses, all of the divisions under the biblical names given in 1 Chronicles 24:10. These were written within decades of the time when Luke's account of a priest of the Abijah division should be set.

Luke's source-knowledge of the temple system may even extend to a hidden riddle. According to the account in Chronicles, composed about 300 BCE, Abijah was descended from Eleazar, the son of Aaron, a chief of one of the twenty-four orders into which the priesthood was divided by David. Abijah received the eighth lot. The ninth lot went to *Jeshuah*. Jeshuah is of course the name we know better as Jesus, meaning "God is salvation." So, the choice of Abijah in Luke's text may have involved the idea that a new, spectacular course of priesthood was about to follow: that of Jesus, the next child born in Luke. That is to say, a cataclysmically new priestly order was about to happen.

A priestly background to John's and Jesus's families makes a great deal of historical sense. It seems likely that John was separated for priesthood, not at the end but the beginning of his spiritual career. The same may be said of Jesus. Jesus's days of youth are absent from the Gospels, but for Luke's accounts of Jesus being brought to the Temple: first, to offer sacrifices attendant on his mother's purification and second, a "caravan" trip to the Temple for his bar mitzvah (ca. 6 CE). We then have the charming story of Jesus astounding the wise men in the Temple. If they had been truly amazed, they would doubtless have marked him out for priestly training.

Support for the shared priestly background of Jesus's and John's families comes from two second-century CE sources: first, the

Protoevangelium of James (ca. 140–175 CE), and second, the account of Jewish Christian historian Hegesippus (ca. 165–175 CE), extracts from which Eusebius included in his *Ecclesiastical History* (ca. 300 CE). These sources and the historical background to Jesus's family are dealt with thoroughly in my book *The Missing Family of Jesus*.

The *Protoevangelium of James* is an account of the birth, family, and marriage of the Virgin Mary. It presents Mary's mother, sometimes called Hannah, as being married to a priest, Joachim or Yonakhir (depending on which version of the text one reads); they die when Mary is twelve, whereafter she joins seven other virgins entrusted to the care of an elderly priest called Zadok and his wife, Sham'i. Sham'i, Mary's stepmother, dies when Mary is fourteen.

The *Protoevangelium* presents Zacharias, father of John the Baptist, as the high priest. Zacharias is advised to seek the Lord's guidance regarding Mary's getting married now that her stepmother has died and she is an adolescent. He enters the holy of holies. According to the Syriac version of the Gospel, an angel bids him assemble a meeting of men belonging to the royal house of David. One of them is Joseph. A temple dove alights on Joseph's rod, then his head. Joseph is considered right in any case, for he and Mary were "each the child of the other's uncle." Joseph objects because he is old, and his wife is already the mother of sons and daughters. His wife's name is given as Mary; her sons were Jacob (James) and Jose (Joseph). In the Syriac, this other Mary seems to be alive, but in the Greek he is a widower, while his second son is Samuel, sometimes corrected to Joses or to Simon. This apocryphal gospel does not say that Joseph was himself a priest, but he is bound up with the society that surrounds and serves the Temple, and Mary's father is shown to be a priest. Joseph lives in Bethlehem, and both he and his wife-to-be, Mary, are descendants of King David, from which tree the Messiah was prophesied to be born.

Hegesippus's account of James, the brother of the Lord, who was murdered in 62 CE by connivance of the High Priest Ananus, makes it clear that Jesus's brother was certainly a priest and wore the linen of a priest and served in the Temple, being one of the poorer priests, who throughout the period were dominated and bullied by the pro-Herodian Sadducee party:

> James, the Lord's brother, succeeded to the government of the Church, with the apostles. He has been called the Just by all men, from the days of the Lord down to the present time. For many bore the name of James; but this one was holy from his mother's womb. He drank no wine or other intoxicating liquor, nor did he eat flesh; no razor came upon his head; he did not anoint himself with oil, nor make use of the bath. He alone was permitted to enter the sanctuary: for he did not wear any woollen garment, but fine linen only. And alone he used to go into the temple: and he used to be found kneeling and praying, begging forgiveness for the people, so that the skin of his knees became horny like that of a camel's, by reason of his constantly bending the knee in adoration to God, and begging forgiveness for the people. Therefore, in consequence of his pre-eminent justice, he was called the Just, and Oblias, which signifies in Greek "Rampart of the people and righteousness," as the prophets declare concerning him. (ca. 170 CE, Hegesippus, *Commentaries on the Acts of the Church*, Book 5; paraphrased in Eusebius, *Ecclesiastical History*, Book II, 23)

The picture of two men, John and Jesus, growing up with intimate knowledge of the life of the Temple in Jerusalem lacks nothing in plausibility. The awful circumstances that surrounded the Temple after Herod the Great's death in 4 BCE would have been sufficient, one would have thought, to turn any learned and sensitive young person into profound opposition to the ruling elite, an elite that was mashing up the spiritual traditions of the Jewish people in an effort to gain more power and remain on the right side of Roman government.

When Archelaus (Antipas's brother) became Ethnarch of Judea after his father Herod's death, a conflict with the priests and Torah scholars of the Temple led to a conflagration that darkened the Temple's precincts with charred wood and the blood of Jews slaughtered by foreign troops. The young men had erected tents in the temple courts and had demonstrated for righteousness and the restoration of ancient religious customs, customs such as not having the high priesthood imposed by foreigners, as the Herodians were perceived to be. Under the Herodians, the temple system became a byword for corruption. Young Mary the slave girl would have known all about it, intimately.

According to Matthew, when Joseph brought his family back from exile in Egypt after persecution by Archelaus's father, he had hoped to return to his Judean homeland, but on hearing that Archelaus had attained ascendancy due to a late change in Herod's will, Joseph opted to remove his family to Galilee. He must have had a better appreciation of Herod Antipas's capacity to respect the traditions of a righteous people. This, after all, was long before Antipas met Herodias and embarked on a course that would see him exiled to Gaul for trying to please his wife. Joseph was also, we may suppose, trying to protect the remains of the Davidic dynasty. Herod had had all the genealogical records of the Jewish aristocracy destroyed, that is, where they were housed in places he could get at them, so that none could challenge his right to rule on genealogical grounds. Herod had married into the once-ruling Hasmonaean dynasty and that was deemed sufficient claim. Who would dare challenge it?

Joseph doubtless kept his genealogy secret. Where did he go to in Galilee? The Gospels think a city called "Nazareth," but as we shall see in the next chapter, this is probably an error. Joseph is described in Mark as a *tektōn,* an architect or builder. Priests built the Temple. Joseph may have made an enclave for his family, or it is possible that he and his family joined one. "Natseret" can mean a consecrated place, or "Keeper-land" or "Watcher-land." He may have established his own "Nazareth," a place set apart: a holy place.

In such an enterprise, he and his family may have drawn on the experiences and literature of descendants of the New Covenanters who had made a covenant in the wilderness region of Damascus, northeast from Galilee. They had established a severe rule of messianic-inspired righteousness, directly opposed to the corruption and religious division that preceded Pompey's conquest of Jerusalem and possibly the corruption of the system that followed Herod the Great's accession to the throne of Judea in 37 BCE.

Ideas we have found associated with John, at least, suggest something of a revival, if not continuity, of many aspects of the fervor for spiritual righteousness to be found in the sectarian documents of the Dead Sea Scrolls. It is impossible to ignore such ideas as can be found in the following extract from the "Community Rule," discovered at Qumran and since translated by Scrolls expert Geza Vermes. Here we find, from an authentic first-century-BCE source, key priorities that makes sense of Jesus's and Johns's consistent interest, first, in the wilderness, and second, in the making of a new, holy community, to prepare the path for the coming of God's salvation:

In the Council of the Community there shall be twelve men and three Priests, perfectly versed in all that is revealed of the Law, whose works shall be truth, righteousness, justice, loving-kindness, and humility. They shall preserve the faith in the Land with steadfastness and meekness and shall atone for sin by the practice of justice and by suffering the sorrows of affliction. They shall walk with all men according to the standard of truth and the rule of the time.

When these are in Israel, the Council of the Community shall be established in truth. It shall be an Everlasting plantation, a house of holiness for Israel, an Assembly of Supreme Holiness for Aaron. They shall be witnesses to the truth at the Judgment, and shall be the elect of Goodwill who shall atone for the Land and pay to the wicked their reward. It shall be that tried wall, that *precious cornerstone,* whose foundations shall neither rock nor sway in their place [Isaiah 28:16]. It shall be a Most Holy Dwelling for Aaron, with everlasting knowledge of the Covenant of justice, and shall offer up sweet fragrance. It shall be a House of Perfection and Truth in Israel that they may establish a Covenant according to the everlasting precepts. And they shall be an agreeable offering, atoning for the land and determining the judgment of wickedness and there shall be no more iniquity. When they have been confirmed for two years in perfection of way in the Foundation of the Community, they shall be set apart as holy within the Council of the men of the Community. And the Interpreter shall not conceal from them, out of fear of the spirit of apostasy, any of those things hidden from Israel, which have been discovered by him.

And when these become members of the Community in Israel according to all these rules they shall separate from the habitation of unjust men and shall go into the wilderness to prepare there the way of Him; as it is written, *Prepare in the wilderness the way of . . . make straight in the desert a path for our God* [Isaiah 40:3] This (path) is the study of the Law, which He commanded by the hand of Moses, that they may do according to all that has been revealed from age to age, and as the prophets have revealed by His Holy Spirit. (The "Community Rule" VIII:1–15; *The Complete Dead Sea Scrolls in English*, p. 109; italics added)

Most notable here are of course the references to a council of twelve men and three priests (Jesus, John [the Baptist?], and James?) and, startlingly, the "Community Rule" interpretation of the key prophecy of Isaiah 40:3 used to announce John the Baptist's part in the Gospels. Here, the way of God is prepared by members going into the wilderness and studying the Law. Certainly we have very vivid accounts of John and Jesus at some time going into the wilderness as part of their training, but here a group or community activity is definitely asserted. Our understanding of John's and Jesus's wilderness sojourns are presented to us primarily as solo excursions, though this may be a conception subject to interpretation. John, after all, is said to have been joined by multitudes, and Jesus, when he enters the wilderness after baptism and walks straight into a personal crisis of great magnitude (the "Temptations") around the time of John's arrest, is ministered to by "angels," which might originally have meant simply purified members of a religious community.

Trying to compare "Christian doctrines," as may be found in the Gospels, with the strict legalism of the New Covenanters is a fairly fruitless task in some respects. It has led Robert Eisenman to create a powerful, but unproven hypothesis of a swords-drawn division between New Covenanter proto-"Jewish-Christians" (represented by the "Zadokite" James the "brother of the Lord"—where "Lord" is understood not as a person but a concept of salvation) and the "Herodian" Paul with a salvation based on release from the Law and the embrace of spiritual universalism protected by Roman order as God's instrument.

Jesus and John did not have to belong to the so-called Qumran sect! And in the absence of evidence that they did, we may content ourselves with the thought that as young men they would have had the opportunity to explore a number of clamoring alternatives to the corrupt life of the urban priesthood in Jerusalem. There can be no doubt that John and Jesus shared with the New Covenanters a profound critique of the temple system of their day, finding themselves in difficulties with both religious and civil powers as a consequence: difficulties that cost them their lives. That they were opposed by some aspects of conservative religious interest is well known. It is also highly likely that they were opposed by more radical interests over questions of interpretation of the specific demands of righteousness, and of the men's role in establishing righteousness. There were doubtless conflicting variants in the world of Jewish messianic expectation in the early first century that could, if needs be, rub along in a common crisis. The Gospels give us at least one named Zealot in Jesus's "twelve," but the picture as we have it is a mixed and in many ways an indefinite one.

Where we can get on to firmer ground is in examining the ideas that may be associated directly with Jesus and John, based on the fragmentary evidence available.

It is time to examine the *great prophecies* that so powerfully motivated the two men. There, I think, we shall find a distinct viewpoint to be found neither in the Dead Sea Scrolls, nor anywhere else: a secret plan.

Chapter Eight

THE GREAT PROPHECIES

> *But what think ye? A certain man had two sons; and he came to the first, and said, Son, go work today in my vineyard. He answered and said, "I will not": but afterward he repented, and went. And he came to the second, and said likewise. And he answered and said, "I go, sir": and went not.*
>
> *Whether of them twain did the will of his father? They [the chief priests and elders of the Temple] say unto him, "The first." Jesus saith unto them, "Verily I say unto you, That the publicans and the harlots go into the kingdom of God before you. For John came unto you in the way of righteousness, and ye believed him not: but the publicans and the harlots believed him: and ye, when ye had seen it, repented not afterward, that ye might believe him."*
>
> (MATTHEW 21:28–32)

A JUDGMENT can be a good thing or a bad thing. Outside of a court, after a long trial, we are accustomed to see tears, bitterness, pain, and recrimination, or else joy, vindication of hope, even ecstasy and decorum's abandonment at the verdict. The verdict is the same for good or ill.

193

The fundamental message preserved of John is *repentance and imminent judgment.* Judgment would divide the sheep from the goats. Judgment would reveal the reality: who was open to God and who was not. For some this judgment would be a glorious message of salvation, freedom, hope, and triumph; for those who failed to repent of their injustices and hypocrisies, who put faith in their own "securities," it was something to be feared. Fear engenders two primary responses: ridicule and violence. John and Jesus would incur both: they would be set at nought and killed, their followers likewise.

John's voice of judgment was aimed at everyone, but, as far as we can tell, it was particularly focused on the leading parties of the temple hierarchy, the Pharisees and the Sadducees. They were the bad shepherds who led the people into dangers, whose blind warring among themselves had opened Holy Israel up to foreign invasion, desecration, shame, and poverty. These groups, said John, constituted a "generation of vipers." They bruised all Israel's heel with their biting. They crippled her, preventing her from walking the straight path. The chief priests and elders put their hope in their past, their faith in their position, but "now also the axe is laid into the root of the trees" (Matthew 3:10). The whole rotten tree was being uprooted. They were chaff; they were heading for the fire. One is coming, cried John, "Whose fan is in his hand, and he will thoroughly purge his floor, and gather his wheat into the garner; but he will burn up the chaff with unquenchable fire" (3:12).

John declares the harvest open: a mighty joy for some, a hell for others.

Note the reference to the "purging of the floor," and recall how the first Temple was built on the site of an ancient threshing floor. The background to John's prophecy is of course the "messenger prophecy" from Malachi: "The Lord whom ye seek, shall suddenly come to his temple, even the messenger of the covenant, whom ye delight in: behold, he shall come, saith the LORD of hosts. But who may abide the day of his coming? And who shall stand when he appeareth? For he is like a refiner's fire, and like fuller's soap" (Malachi 3:1–2).

We shall see that the idea of "standing," remaining upright in the face of the coming blaze of fire and water, wind and quake, will open up another dimension, a spiritual dimension, to all the imagery of crackling flame and stormy, elemental destruction.

We should be clear in our minds that it was not all doom and gloom. John would hardly be remembered if he was simply another depressing prophet harping on about the end of the world. There is another dimension to these supervivid images of harrowing and harvest. For example, Matthew uses the Greek word *ptuon* for the winnowing fan that will rend the grain from the chaff. This word can mean the large basket from which the threshed corn was raised into the air for the wind (breath, or spirit?) to separate the good from the waste, or it could mean a simple wooden pitchfork (the origin of the demonic trident used to prong sinners into the fires of hell in medieval pictures, by the way). Be that as it may, the winnowing fan played a highly significant role in religious festivals of harvest, of both wheat and wine, in the Near East. The fan was a sacred object in its own right.

The sacred *liknon,* or winnowing fan, the noun of the verb *likmaō* ("I winnow"), was the word employed for the winnowing fan sacred to Dionysus, the Roman Bacchus. It was carried on the head in procession and filled, note, with *first fruits* and sacrificial utensils. Dionysian ceremonies linked the idea of fruits and of sacrifice. Analogous ideas were expressed in the Temple ceremony at the Feast of Weeks, though, unsurprisingly, without the Bacchic revels, liberties, excess of wine, and ecstasies familiar to pagan celebrants of the god's mysteries.

The winnowing fan was also the "cradle" for the birth of Bacchus; Greek poets used the word *liknon* to denote a "cradle." We note the ideas of birth and rebirth central to the harvest. We may also note the parallel idea of the famous dismemberment of Dionysus by the Titans, his subsequent rebirth, with the beheading of the Baptist: the initiator whose sacrifice is given powerful meaning within the appointed destiny of the Son of man. Leonardo da Vinci's visual linkage of John the Baptist and Bacchus was not without mythological root.

The judgment initiated by John carried a promise, a promise of new wine:

> And it shall come to pass in that day, that the mountains shall drop
> down new wine and the hills shall flow with milk, and all the rivers
> of Judah shall flow with waters, and a fountain shall come forth of
> the house of the LORD, and shall water the valley of Shittim [acacia
> trees; possibly Abel-Shittim in Perea]. (Joel 3:18)

We saw in the last chapter how the New Covenanters interpreted unto themselves Isaiah's famous prophecy of the precious cornerstone laid in Zion that initiates purification:

> Therefore thus saith the Lord GOD, Behold, I lay in Zion for a
> foundation a stone, a tried stone, a precious corner stone, a sure
> foundation: he that believeth shall not make haste. Judgment also
> will I lay to the line, and righteousness to the plummet: and the hail
> shall sweep away the refuge of lies, and the waters shall overflow the
> hiding place. (Isaiah 28:16–17)

The New Covenanters' "Community Rule" took this prophecy to refer to their "Council of the Community," which would be "an Everlasting plantation, a house of holiness for Israel, an Assembly of Supreme Holiness for Aaron." Their Assembly would witness "to the truth at the Judgment," executing judgment on the wicked according to the exact measure of righteousness: "It shall be that tried wall, that *precious cornerstone,* whose foundations shall neither rock nor sway in their place." The Covenanters were inspired by the rigidity of the stone, its solemn, legal, calibrated perfection: a stone of the righteous, if not the self-righteous.

According to Matthew (21:42–44), Jesus, addressing the chief priests and elders in the Temple, looked into the prehistory, as it were, of this "precious cornerstone." He found it in Psalm 118:22–23. There it transpires that the "precious cornerstone" had first been *rejected*—by the *builders*! (Remember Jesus is put *in the Temple* with the chief priests when he says this: the new temple built by priests and masons under Herod the Great's orders.)

> Jesus saith unto them, "Did ye never read in the scriptures? The stone, which the builders rejected, the same is become the head of the corner: this is the Lord's doing, and it is marvelous in our eyes?" [Psalm 1:18]. "Therefore say I unto you, the kingdom of God shall be taken from you, and given to a nation bringing forth the fruits thereof. And whosoever shall fall on this stone shall be broken: but on whomsoever it shall fall, he shall be winnowed."

Now, *who is it that has been rejected?*

The parable preceding this saying in Matthew refers to servants (prophets) being sent by "a certain householder" (the LORD) to collect the first fruits of the harvest from his vineyard (the Temple) with its Tower (the Antonia Tower used by Roman soldiers). The servants are rejected, stoned, beaten up, and killed by the husbandmen (chief priests and elders). Finally, the "householder" who has planted the vineyard, sends his son and heir to collect the fruits. The husbandmen "caught him, and cast him out of the vineyard, and slew him." Jesus then asks what the lord of the vineyard should do when he comes back to his plantation. The priests admit he will "miserably destroy" the wicked husbandmen and let it out to other husbandmen happy to pay the first fruits. Then Jesus brings in the quote from Psalm 118 about the rejected stone.

Naturally, Christian exegesis takes the "rejected one" who has become the cornerstone as being the "son" (Son of God) of the preceding parable. However, while *we* know the gospel story that the priests will very soon be plotting to destroy Jesus (the "son"), such an idea was not obvious at the time. At the time, if indeed the dialogue ever took place, or wherever it took place, the figure who would have been uppermost in the men's minds would have been *John the Baptist,* and they would have seen the attack on the "wicked husbandmen" as straight revenge, or righteous justice, for a killing, which Josephus informs us was regarded by the people as what caused the defeat of Herod Antipas's army by the Nabataeans. Jesus seems to know that John's death was not all the doing of the king, but that John had offended the temple management too. This would certainly be consistent with John's speech recorded in Matthew from Malachi, which speaks of the purging of the Temple, so that it may offer first fruits acceptable to God.

We may then note the charming and amusing saying that rounds off the disquisition, where Jesus appears to link the "rejected stone" idea with the mighty stone "cut without hands" that brought down a veritable empire in Daniel 2:34*ff.* Jesus says that he who trips on the stone, that is to say, he who *does not see it,* or is indifferent to it, or even attacks (falls on) the stone will be smashed to smithereens by it, whereas he on whom the mysterious stone falls will be winnowed (*likmēsei*). "Ground to powder" is a weak translation. The verb's root is the same as that of the sacred *liknon,* the sacred winnowing fan. One would naturally expect the stone that falls (from heaven) to break the unfortunate's head to pieces. Expect the unexpected, implies Jesus.

When the stone comes from above, it winnows he on whom it falls. That is to say, the stone "judges," it divides, or, better, refines, purifies, and purges he on whom it falls. It is, in a sense, the true "philosopher's stone": it brings the gold forth from the *massa confusa,* the darkness.

Lesson: do not ignore the rejected stone. Do not reject the rejected.

Certainly, with hindsight, the saying may refer to Jesus, but it really refers to the rejected "Son of man" in general, the one who is *always coming* with the winnowing fan. In the context of Jesus's dispute with the chief priests and elders, it refers to John. John is the rejected stone who now stands at the foundation of the new Temple: a "marvelous thing" in the eyes of those who see it. The stone from heaven is also the sparking stone that sets the process of purification into action. The *fire* comes from the stone. So the stone is also the Holy Spirit that comes from heaven, the breath, or wind, of God that shakes the reeds. It is the stone cast out of the Temple, without which the Temple must fall. It is the stone of he who has never sinned.

On this message, on this stone, Jesus and John stood together.

THE NAZARENES

During the 40s and 50s, according to Acts, Jesus's followers were known as the "sect of the Nazarenes" by enemies in Jerusalem (Acts 24:5). The name has never been adequately explained. It is either taken to mean followers of "Jesus of Nazareth" or to be in some way linked to the Nazarite vow taken by pious Jews. What is striking, for our purposes, is that to this day, the Mandaeans, an Iraqi baptizing sect of great antiquity who hold John the Baptist in very high esteem, call their priests "Nasuraiah," Arabic for "Nazarenes," while one Mandaean text, as we shall see, dismisses Jesus as "Christ the Roman." If, as seems likely, the name "Nazarene" links followers of both John and Jesus, we had better explore what "Nazarene" means.

First, we can dispense with the idea that "Nazarene" refers to a "city" in Galilee, as Matthew refers to Nazareth (2:23). There is no substantial archaeology in modern Nazareth from before the second century CE. There may have been a rough wooden settlement or camp, devoid of stone foundations (certainly no "city"), but anyhow, the place-name "Nazareth" is unknown both to Josephus, who knew Gaililee intimately, and to Jewish scripture, making it likely that Jesus was linked to Nazareth either because of a mistaken understanding of what "Jesus the Nazarene" originally meant, or due to ignorance of what "Nazareth" or "*a* Nazareth" may originally have meant. Moreover, Matthew's reference to a "city" of Nazareth (2:23) is, on examination, introduced to show only the fulfillment of an unknown prophecy: "He shall be called a Nazarene [*Nazōraios*]," which, whatever else it might indicate, definitely does not indicate a place.

The nearest text to this prophecy in Matthew is, "He shall be called a Nazarite unto God" (Judges 13:2–5), uttered by an angel of the Lord prophesying the birth of Samson in a story curiously similar to the annunciation of Mary the mother of Jesus. Samson would "deliver Israel"—from the Philistines. When we think of Samson's long hair, we may find a "hairy Elijah" connection, and thus link him to John. And of course Samson was one of the great *judges* who brought down the foreigners' heathen temple with the power of God. Matthew would appear to have found the similarity of "Nazarene" to "Nazarite" satisfying enough; the subtleties are lost in the Greek. Anyhow, if the book of Judges is the source for Matthew's fulfillment text, then it is a clear reference not to a place, but to the Nazarite vow. The vow, detailed in Numbers 6:1–21, required fasting and visits to the Temple for prayer. Its performance would necessitate leaving Galilee for Jerusalem; the Nazarite must go to the "door of the tabernacle of the congregation."

Nazarite, from the Hebrew *nezer,* spelled with a Hebrew letter *zayin* or "z," means "consecrated," "separated," "dedicated," as well as "crown" and even "hair." It applies to someone dedicated to holiness to God. The high priest's miter was called a nezer, and on it were inscribed the words "Holy to God." Taking the Nazarite vow made an individual "Holy to God" for the vow's duration.

More intriguingly, and more pertinent to the case, in my judgment, the word *Nazorean* may stem from the Hebrew verb "to keep" (as in keeping the Law) and, above all, "to watch," suggesting, prosaically, a hill lookout, or watchtower: prosaic in the first instance, but which upon closer inspection opens the required missing link to the Nazarene. The Hebrew נצרים NATZARIM from *natzar* (or natsar) means "watchers." It occurs, significantly, in Jeremiah 4:16–17:

Make ye mention to the nations; behold, publish against Jerusalem, that watchers come from a far country, and give out their voice against the cities of Judah. As keepers of a field are they against her round about; because she has been rebellious against me, saith the LORD.

The Watchers (*natzarim*) come from beyond the cities of Judea to publish or proclaim the judgment. They "give out their voice" against those who have fled from the path of God. They are "keepers," "keepers of a field." Now recall Jesus's parable delivered in the Temple about how God's vineyard will be let to new keepers or "husbandmen," because the old, corrupt field hands killed God's prophets. Soon we shall discover what is meant by the "far country" from which the Watchers come.

The imperative "Watch!" is powerfully expressed in Mark's apocalyptic thirteenth chapter. It opens with a judgment concerning the corrupt Temple:

And as he went out of the temple, one of his disciples saith unto him, Master, see what manner of stones and what buildings are here! And Jesus answering said unto him, "Seest thou these great buildings? there shall not be left one stone upon another, that shall not be thrown down."

This Samson-like declaration ("thrown down") launches a chapter full of classic eschatological imagery, much of which is taken from the book of Daniel, including the "Son of man" coming on the "clouds of power." Mark 13 concludes with an extraordinary command-parable in which the imperative "Watch!" is repeated no less than four times:

Take ye heed, watch and pray: for ye know not when the time is. For the Son of man is as a man taking a far journey, who left his house, and gave authority to his servants, and to every man his work, and commanded the porter to watch. Watch ye therefore: for ye know not when the master of the house cometh, at even, or at midnight, or at the cockcrowing, or in the morning: Lest coming suddenly he find you sleeping. And what I say unto you I say unto all, Watch.

He is coming, and who will *stand* when he comes? If you wanted a name for this movement, look no further: welcome to the harvest of the *Watchers!* The Greek "Nazōraiōn" (Acts 24:5), *Nazarenes,* is thus revealed as a Greek transliteration of the Hebrew *Natzarim.* The "Natzarim" publish the judgment; they keep God's commandments, and they watch, watch, watch!

When we join the respective meanings of the words *keeper* and *watcher,* we produce, in English, the word *guardian,* and that may be the best sense for us to understand the nature of the original, authentic movement of John and Jesus. They were the Guardians, the Watchers. They loved their country and wished to restore it to true, spiritual Godliness.

The Greek imperative "Watch!" comes from the verb *grēgoreō* (the origin of the name "Gregory"), which means, as well as "I am watchful" or "alert," "I am *awake*" (as in the night). The true guardian, like the true prophet, stands, endures, remains to the end, is awake, watches: a perceiver, a man of light in the darkness, someone you can trust, someone who *stands,* like a reed in the breath of God.

The disciples, the guardians, fell asleep in Gethsemane; that was Jesus's agony. They failed to see they were in Paradise. Paradise means a garden, where the story of Man's fall began, and where it could end.

In modern Hebrew, the Galilean city of "Nazareth" is called *Natseret* (with a *tzaddi*). The Hebrew word for *land* or *earth,* especially dry land, even desert or scrub, is *aretz* or *arets.* Coupled with the idea of the *Natsarim* we might, in "Nazareth," be looking at the remains of a compound word for "keeper-land" or "watcher-land." If Jesus's father Joseph built an enclosure for *Natzarim,* it would be an apposite name for a place for those who watched and waited for the fulfillment of

God's secret plan, keeping faith with God's commandments, removed from the wickedness of the state. There is even an archaeological link between a later settlement on the site and the old Jerusalem priesthood.

A third- or fourth-century CE Hebrew inscription of Galilean towns and villages, discovered in Caesarea in 1962, revealed where a priestly (*kohanim*) family of the Hapizzez, the eighteenth of the twenty-four priestly courses, settled. This was presumably after the priests, and indeed all Jews, were expelled from Jerusalem by the Emperor Hadrian after 135 CE. The inscription reveals a priestly residence, spelled with the Hebrew tzaddi. The priestly house was at Natzareth, a name possibly derived from a distant time when the sons of Joseph and their friends, the Nazarenes/Natzarim could have looked down from those heights to the Plain of Megiddo (Armageddon) and further south, where the sun was most cruel, beyond Samaria to Ephraim and Judah.

THE FOUNT OF LIVING WATERS AND THE HIDDEN CORRUPTERS OF EARTH

One of those Natzarim was, I believe, Jesus's brother Judas. Judas is the best candidate for the authorship of what Christian Bibles call "The General Epistle of Jude." *Jude*, the deliberately shortened form of *Judas* provided an English translation for reasons fairly obvious. Judas was too well known as the "traitor," so, seeing the name "Jude," most people never guess that the Greek original is absolutely stark in attributing the letter to *JUDAS*, "the slave of Jesus Christ, and brother of James" (1:1).

Jesus's brothers names, according to Mark, were Judas, James (Jacob), Joseph, and Simon (Mark 6:3). James and Cephas ("son of John"), the "pillars," led the Nazarenes after Jesus was crucified. We know little of brother Judas, except, intriguingly, that his grandsons were interrogated by the Emperor Domitian (81–96 CE) at the end of the first century. Judas's grandsons were interrogated as members of the politically suspect House of David (Eusebius, *Ecclesiastical History,* Book III, 19–20). This "Judas the Obscure" was the probable author of the last little letter of the New Testament.

The letter shows Judas's indebtedness to the prophecies of Enoch and that work's author's evident familiarity with the esoteric tradition of the *evil* Watchers: archenemies of Jeremiah's keeper-Natzarim. Following the Book of Enoch, Judas defined these hidden sowers of wicked seed as "angels, which kept not their first estate, but left their own habitation, he hath reserved in everlasting chains under darkness unto the judgment of the great day" (Judas, v. 6).

Here we come to what is probably the secret and hidden aspect of the judgment that John and Jesus proclaimed. While all men and women must turn to God for their salvation, the *primal* culprits behind the corruption of the creation (the *creation,* note, not just the Temple) were the wicked, rebellious angels who quit heaven out of lust for the daughters of men and brought forbidden knowledge to the spiritually immature. This theory involved an esoteric interpretation of Genesis 6:1–4. Genesis describes the birth of the Nephilim, usually translated as "giants," but with a Hebrew root word suggesting "fallen." Judas holds fast to the Enochian prophecy that the Lord will come to execute judgment on all those who have permitted themselves, through ill will and self-will, to become infected by the primal wickedness:

> And Enoch also, the seventh from Adam, prophesied of these, saying, Behold, the Lord cometh with ten thousands of his saints, To execute judgment upon all, and to convince all that are ungodly among them of all their ungodly deeds, which they have ungodly committed, and of all their hard speeches, which ungodly sinners have spoken against him. (Judas, vv. 14–15)

So we see that in the early first century, the term "the watchers" (*natzarim*) had a specific esoteric meaning as well as an exoteric, prophetic meaning. The Book of Enoch brings the exoteric and the esoteric together. Familiar to the Essenes, to the New Covenanters or "Qumran sect," the Book of Enoch provides essential rationale and mythology for the Nazarene message. Dated (in parts) ca. 100 BCE–70 CE, Enoch, like the letter of Judas, is seldom read today, possibly because it has practically nothing to say to the Pauline Christian. That is a pity, for both works have much to say about the authentic worldview of Jesus and his close comrades.

Enoch's "Watchers" are the angels of God, imagined or manifest as stars, lights in the darkness, looking down on us, guarding, guiding, and keeping us. Enoch is called to proclaim judgment on the evil and rebellious Watchers, who have too long been tolerated by the "Father of Lights." They are to be bound to Earth as punishment, joined forever to unrepentant humankind. The Father of Lights declares to Enoch, "And whosoever shall be condemned and destroyed will from thenceforth be bound together with them [the evil Watchers] to the end of all generations." Judgment is coming:

> And destroy all the spirits of the reprobate, and the children of the Watchers, because they have wronged mankind. Destroy all wrong from the face of the earth, and let every evil work come to an end: and let the *plant* of righteousness and truth appear: and it shall prove a blessing: the works of righteousness and truth appear: and it shall prove a blessing: the works of righteousness and truth shall be planted in truth and joy for evermore. And then shall all the righteous escape, and shall live until they beget thousands of children, And all the days of their youth and their old age shall they complete in peace. (Enoch 11:15*ff.*, my italics)

We are told in chapter 12 of the book that before the end, "Enoch was hidden. . . . And his activities had to do with the Watchers, and his days were with the holy ones." Enoch was about his Father's business, as his descendant Jesus was (Luke 3:37):

And I, Enoch, was blessing the Lord of majesty and the King of the ages, and lo! the Watchers called me—Enoch the scribe—and said to me: "Enoch, the scribe of righteousness, go, declare, to the Watchers of the heaven who have left the high heaven, the holy eternal place, and have defiled themselves with women, and have done as the children of earth do, and have taken unto themselves wives: "Ye have wrought great destruction on the earth . . ." (Enoch 12:3*ff.*)

Apart from drawing on the *Nephilim* (giant) myth in Genesis 6, key parts of the Book of Enoch appear as a kind of *midrash* or expansion on Jeremiah 4:15–17, where the word *natzarim* appears in the Hebrew original:

For a voice declareth from Dan, and publish affliction from Mount Ephraim. Make ye mention to the nations; behold, publish against Jerusalem, that watchers [natzarim] come from a far country, and give out their voice against the cities of Judah. As keepers of a field, are they against her round about, because she hath been rebellious against me, saith the Lord.

Enoch takes up Jeremiah's declaration from Dan. In doing so, Enoch gives Dan great significance in the apocalyptic itinerary, significance not lost, I believe, on the Nazarenes/Natzarim. It is from *Dan*, in the far north, that Enoch will publish the judgment on those "rebellious" against the Lord: "And I went off and sat down at the waters of Dan, in the land of Dan, to the south of the west of Hermon: I read their [the Watchers'] petition till I fell asleep." (Enoch 13:7*ff.*) The petition came from Azazel, prince of the fallen Watchers. It begged Enoch to intercede with the Lord of Spirits against the Watchers' coming judgment. Azazel may be identified with the "prince of this world" or "Satan," whose dramatic fall Jesus famously envisioned (Luke 10:18; John 12:31). Interestingly, the name Azazel probably derives originally from the Hebrew "scapegoat" (from the Hebrew stem "azel" = "remove";

see Leviticus 16:8–10), loaded with the people's sin at Yom Kippur and sent out of the city into the wilderness to be cast from a mountain. Readers of deep cross-symbolism may grasp the significance of this.

It is a pity that Dan's significance to Jeremiah and Enoch has been lost to the Christian tradition. However, when we restore that significance, we see at once how closely the Nazarenes/Natzarim followed the esoteric itinerary of judgment, even though long obscured to second-generation Christian commentators and their descendants.

This is the Dan that Jesus will visit, the Dan renamed and Romanized by Herod Antipas's half-brother Philip as *Caesarea Philippi.* This is the place chosen by Jesus to ask the question, "Whom do men say that I am?" to which question he would receive the telling answers: "John the Baptist: but some say, Elias [Elijah]; and others, One of the prophets." And this is the place where Cephas declares Jesus to be the Messiah (Mark 8:27*ff.*), where Jesus speaks of the "Son of man" only to be rebuked physically, that is *attacked,* by an enraged Cephas for saying the Son of man must be rejected and killed—the unbearable opposite of everything Cephas has hoped for. He, Cephas, after all, was Jesus's *protector.* Jesus sees evil spirit working through Cephas and casts this "Satan" (or evil Watcher) aside: "Get thee behind me, Satan: for thou savorest not the things that be of God, but the things that be of men." The defeat of the fallen Watchers, bound to them that do evil, requires a reversal of the world's expectation: the Messiah must die; *he* must be the scapegoat! But Jesus insists his disciples keep what they might grasp of this disturbing mystery secret:

> And he charged them that they should tell no man of him. And he
> began to teach them, that the Son of man must suffer many things,
> and be rejected of the elders, and of the chief priests, and scribes,
> and be killed, and after three days rise again. (Mark 8:30–31)

Jesus could hardly have chosen a more potent or significant place than Dan to speak openly, if discreetly, to his fellow "natzarim" of the mysterious means by which the prince of this world and his evil Watchers would confront their judgment and lasting incarceration.

Today, Caesarea Philippi is a ruin among ruins. Raised by Philip the Tetrarch in 3 BCE, the grand construction was adjacent to the springs of Paneas (Josephus called Philip's city "Caesarea Paneas") where Philip's father Herod the Great had built a marble temple in honor of his patron Caesar Augustus. The Natzarim would have seen it: the crumbs of the dog served back to its master. They would also have seen an elaborate *temenos,* or sanctuary, to the god Pan, the god of shepherds, of victory (for he puts "pan-ic" in his enemies), whose name means "the All." Paneas came from Pan.

Sacred since time immemorial, the springs of Paneas attracted pagan devotions that would have been observed by the Natzarim, and we must presume that John the Baptist would have come to Paneas also. How could he not? For in his day, a giant spring used to gush from a limestone cave whence the waters wove their way down to the Huela marshes, thence southward. According to Josephus, this mighty spring was held to be the source of nothing less than the living waters of the holy River Jordan: "Now the fountains of Jordan rise at the roots of this cavity outwardly; and, as some think, this is the utmost origin of Jordan" (*Wars* 1:21:3). How could a prophet not be deeply moved at the poetry and spiritual atmosphere of such a place, close to the source of the purest water that rose within the body of the holy Mount Hermon?

Today, visitors to what is now called Baneas can still see a Roman bridge that passes by the springs. It supports the old road to Damascus. Perhaps Saul stopped at Paneas during his pursuit of the Nazarenes. Perhaps coming to the source proved too much for him. The sun, reflected on all of that meaningful water, would have been pretty blinding. And perhaps Paneas impacted on the New Covenanters also. The Qumran *Damascus Document* (ca. 70 BCE) announces a new covenant between the "remnant" of Israel and the God of righteousness "in the land of Damascus." Damascus is about twenty miles northeast of Paneas by direct road:

> None of the men who enter the New Covenant in the land of Damascus, and who again betray it and depart from *the fountain of living waters,* shall be reckoned with the Council of the people or inscribed in its Book from the day of the gathering in of the Teacher of the Community until the coming of the Messiah out of Aaron and Israel. [my italics]

While the document's reference to the "fountain of living waters" seems largely symbolic of the purity of the Law, it would make sense to see its visual analogue as the Jordan's gushing spring at Paneas, where Enoch slept before declaring the judgment against the wicked Watchers.

Enoch reveals what had formerly been kept secret: that behind the sin of humankind is a cosmic drama, played out between the Lord of Spirits and rebel angels who have possessed much of humankind and played them like sleeping puppets. According to Enoch, the "evil spirits on earth" derive from the evil Watchers. Understanding this background helps us to grasp the significance of Jesus's exorcism operation, his casting out of devils. Jesus knows whom they serve and he knows he has authority, and therefore power, to banish them. We may recall the case of the famous lunatic of Gadara, whose disgruntled devils hop into the Gadarene swine only to hurl themselves suicidally from a cliff like so many fanatics. In John's Gospel, "Satan" is the "prince of this world" whose legion of spirits the *Natzarim* will cast out (John 12:31; 14:30; 16:11). The enemies of God are *spiritual* enemies. Swords will not destroy them. The world needs the divine power of messianic exorcism: "deliver us from evil," not phalanxes of self-righteous "holy warriors" breaking the commandment not to kill.

STANDING THE TRIAL

Along with the esoteric judgment comes an esoteric salvation, for how else could the "Son of man" himself, whoever he may be, withstand the spiritual tremor of divine judgment?

The Son of man is the one to whom God has revealed his glory. *What is within the divine glory?* Answer: the divine image: *Man,* the first idea of Adam, Man as he reflects the mind of God. This heavenly figure—the Coming One on the brink of actualization—John has, I venture, seen. And insofar as Jesus has seen it, he too is a Son of man who reflects the divine Adam in the image of God. And he knows how the blind eyes of the world will treat the Son of man: he must undergo the trial, the test, the cutting, the threshing, the winnowing.

What is he made of?

What will *stand the trial*? We may recall the "tried wall," the "precious cornerstone" of the New Covenanter's "Community Rule." We may reflect that Jesus gave a new name to "son of John" Simon. Jesus called him *cephas,* a stone. After the crucifixion, James, the brother of Jesus, was called a "bulwark" or wall, a protector of the righteous. And Jesus was of course familiar with Isaiah 28: "I lay in Zion for a foundation a stone, a tried stone, a precious corner stone, a sure foundation. . . . And when the waters shall overflow the hiding place" the foundation will remain.

Foundation, cornerstone, stone, wall, bulwark, pillar: all images of standing, of permanence, of certain protection. We find an analogous confidence in God's power in Qumran Thanksgiving Hymn No 11:

> *I thank thee, O Lord,*
> *For Thou art as a fortified wall to me,*
> *And as an iron bar against all destroyers.*
> *Thou hast set my foot upon rock. . . .*
> *That I may walk in the way of eternity*
> *And in the paths, which Thou hast chosen. . . .*

So when the awful day came when John was removed from his comrades and followers, how were they to understand the calamity? In Mark's telling of the Transfiguration and Jesus's subsequent reflections on John, Elijah, and the suffering and rising from the dead of the Son of man (9:9–13), Jesus appears to go deeply into himself to consider his own destiny. He sees John's death, I think, as a sign. He tells his incredulous followers that the Son of man must die and be raised on the third day; they do not understand him.

Had they not listened to the voice of the prophets? There was a whole world of prophecy for comfort and guidance in the wilderness, such as had sustained John in his own trials with the will of Herod Antipas, and the powers visible and invisible behind that high personage who would die uncelebrated, unnoticed, and unrecorded, in Gaul. John knew the prophesied fate of the righteous, he who stood, who endured to the end, who stayed awake, who kept faith. It was written in the prophet Isaiah 26:1–4:

> In that day shall this song be sung in the land of Judah; We have a strong city; salvation will God appoint for walls and bulwarks. Open ye the gates, that the righteous nation, which keepeth the truth, may enter in. Thou wilt keep him in perfect peace, whose mind is stayed on thee: because he trusteth in thee. Trust ye in the LORD for ever: for in the LORD JAHVEH is everlasting strength: For he bringeth down them that dwell on high; the lofty city, he layeth it low; even to the ground; he bringeth it even to the dust.

As for John's enemies: "They are dead, they shall not live; they are deceased, they shall not rise: therefore hast thou visited and destroyed them, and made all their memory to perish" (Isaiah 26:14).

We now come close to the heart of the mystery of righteous suffering: the good death of the zaddik, the pious, the righteous. The whole point about being a "Watcher-keeper," a Guardian of the Vineyard, centers on the absolute conviction that the prophets foretold the very time the Watchers would be watching. *Now* is the time for the fulfillment of the words of Isaiah, Daniel, Enoch, Zechariah, Malachi, Joel, Jeremiah, Ezekiel, Moses, and Elijah. The word was being made flesh. What had been visionary was becoming reality. The hour had come; very little time remained to accomplish the work of the hour in the watch of the night.

Isaiah had spoken of those who had been, and who would be, struck down by the wicked. They would emerge victorious from the alembic of judgment and trial, not only unharmed, but remade:

> Thy dead men shall live, *together with my dead body shall they arise*. Awake and sing, ye that dwell in dust: for thy dew is the dew of herbs, and the earth shall cast out the dead. (Isaiah 26:19; my italics)

The Earth itself will not hold the righteous, and when the Day of the Lord comes, the Earth herself will live again: "He shall cause them that come of Jacob to take root: Israel shall blossom and bud, and fill the face of the world with fruit" (27:6).

Isaiah seems to speak of John and those responsible for his death. Those bereft now will have the comfort of knowing in the future that they will be able to look back and see how God has stayed his hand from hurting the righteous, even when it looked as though the good had been slain. God smites only those who have smitten "him": the righteous servant. The slaughter that men do, impressive though it is, may be overturned by God; indeed, the slaughter of the wicked is as nothing to the *absolute* slaughter God reserves for those who kill his own:

> Hath he [the Lord] smitten him, as he smote those that smote him? Or is he slain according to the slaughter of them that are slain by him? (Isaiah 27:7)

Jesus doubtless understood this prophecy as a clear message for the ultimate vindication of the zaddik. Before his death, John doubtless knew it too; he was ready for the trial. And Jesus knew that those who slew John, and who slew the prophets, and who, holding fast to evil, would soon slay him, were already, dead men.

But John . . . *John would rise again!*

Chapter 9

THE THIRD DAY

And suddenly, when they had looked round about, they
saw no man any more, save Jesus only with themselves.
And as they came down from the mountain, he charged
them that they should tell no man what things they had
seen, till the Son of man were risen from the dead.

(MARK 9:8–9)

WE HAVE SEEN that John and Jesus enjoyed intimacy with the
spirit of the great prophets. They had fully absorbed the spiritual promise and transformative message of God's transcendent care for those
who looked beyond appearances to heavenly things. The righteous man
would be raised from among the dead; though he appeared fallen, God's
Holy Spirit, his living breath of life, would ensure that he would stand,
vindicated in the ultimate fulfillment of God's purposes for creation.

First, the warning had to be given. As the prophet Ezekiel knew in
the sixth century BCE, standing amid the "alien corn" of Babylon, this
necessitated the Son of man being separated from his fellows as well
as his carnal self, and being entrusted with the awesome responsibility
of warning the people of what was to come, the unwanted herald of
reality:

Son of man, I have made thee a watchman unto the house of Israel: therefore hear the word at my mouth, and give them warning from me. (Ezekiel 3:17)

There was a price to be paid, both for the "Watchmen" who gave the warning (the Natzarim) and those who heeded it. Those who heed the warning do not receive an "automatic pass," any more than an insurance scheme can prevent the damage. Indeed, the penitent might suddenly find the world a distinctly *less* comfortable place than hitherto; they might be called to witness, summoned to the test and slain for righteousness's sake. The forgiven are not to complain that they "did the right thing" and "all they got for it" was misery and degradation: the perennial cry of self-loving depression. They must bear the brunt because they can. The same is so for the "Son of man." The world may judge them dead and finished. They may appear forgotten. Their flesh may rot, their bones dry out, but the terrible love of God would be vindicated, and the Son of man who knows, with it. John and Jesus knew Ezekiel's stunning vision of how the "hand of the Lord" took "Son of man" Ezekiel, the most eloquent prophet, to the valley of dry bones, a wilderness of the forlorn remains of the faithful:

The hand of the LORD was upon me, and carried me out in the spirit of the LORD, and set me down in the midst of the valley, which was full of bones, And caused me to pass by them round about: and, behold, there were very many in the open valley; and, lo, they were very dry.

And he said unto me, Son of man, can these bones live? And I answered, O Lord GOD, thou knowest. Again he said unto me, Prophesy upon these bones, and say unto them, O ye dry bones, hear the word of the LORD. Thus saith the Lord GOD unto these bones; Behold, I will cause breath to enter into you, and ye shall live: And I will lay sinews upon you, and will bring up flesh upon you, and cover you with skin, and put breath in you, and ye shall live; and ye shall know that I am the LORD.

So I prophesied as I was commanded: and as I prophesied, there was a noise, and behold a shaking, and the bones came together, bone to his bone. And when I beheld, lo, the sinews and the flesh came up upon them, and the skin covered them above: but there was no breath in them.

Then said he unto me, Prophesy unto the wind, prophesy, son of man, and say to the wind, Thus saith the Lord GOD; Come from the four winds, O breath, and breathe upon these slain, that they may live. So I prophesied as he commanded me, and the breath came into them, and they lived, and stood up upon their feet, an exceeding great army.

Then he said unto me, Son of man, these bones are the whole house of Israel: behold, they say, Our bones are dried, and our hope is lost: we are cut off for our parts. Therefore prophesy and say unto them, Thus saith the Lord GOD; Behold, O my people, I will open your graves, and cause you to come up out of your graves, and bring you into the land of Israel. And ye shall know that I am the LORD, when I have opened your graves, O my people, and brought you up out of your graves, And shall put my spirit in you, and ye shall live, and I shall place you in your own land: then shall ye know that I the LORD have spoken it, and performed it, saith the LORD. (Ezekiel 37:1–14)

The miraculous "raising from the dead" was not an invention or discovery of the Christian Church. It was foretold by the Hebrew prophets as a symbol (the raising from the grave of hopelessness), and it was, if we are to believe the accounts of Elijah in 1 Kings, and of Jesus in the Gospels, *performed,* as the most sublime gift of divine compassion: the widow's son, Jairus's daughter, Lazarus. Raising the dead was always understood as an absolutely divine *sign,* calling on the hidden powers of life, unseen, secreted in the creation (the four winds). God is the life *in* the life of creation. As John the Baptist declared, God can raise men from stones:

The Son of man is delivered into the hands of men, and they shall kill him; and after that he is killed, he shall rise the third day. (Mark 9:31)

I have always wondered what the "third day" could possibly refer to. It cannot, to my mind, have been so banal an idea as that suggested in the "Sunday school" picture of the Son of man's body being tucked up in the tomb on Friday night, to rise before dawn on Sunday morning (Matthew 21:1). That is *not* three days by any clear computation.

Or is it? Those keen to find the Bible literally "true" (accurate) on this point argue for a Thursday morning Passover crucifixion (14 Nisan), taken as a "Preparation Day" for the next day's *Friday* "Sabbath" or special holy rest day for the Feast of Unleavened Bread (15 Nisan), followed by the "ordinary" end-of-Jewish-week Sabbath (Saturday), followed by the first day of the week (Sunday) and the Feast of First Fruits at the Temple (first Sunday after Passover). Bearing in mind the old Hebrew system of beginning the new day from sunset, rather than midnight (as we do), you could then conceivably arrive at three nights and three days: Thursday, Friday (starting at sunset Thursday), and Saturday, so long as the first day is counted from the time of Jesus's death. This interpretation, while possible, does not accord with a straightforward reading of the gospel record, where there is no mention of two consecutive Sabbaths. Furthermore, it is based on astronomical lunar observations made on the assumption that Jesus was crucified in 33 CE, which is not our information. It is, above all, an interpretation designed to fulfill to the letter Matthew 12:40, which, at first sight, *appears,* with hindsight and the weight of two thousand years of tradition, to refer to Jesus being dead and in the tomb:

For as Jonas was three days and three nights in the whale's belly; so shall the Son of man be three days and three nights in the heart of the earth.

This saying announces what Jesus calls the "sign of Jonas," which is the bitter fruit he offers the unrepentant. He refers to Jonah being swallowed by the whale as a prelude to Jonah's finally accepting he must declare God's judgment to the sinners of Nineveh. Jesus says that the men of Nineveh would "rise in judgment with this generation" and condemn it, because they, the men of Nineveh, repented when Jonah warned them, while the wicked of "this generation" do not. The wicked have ignored the appeal of John the Baptist. They ignored the Son of man. They strove to silence the voice of judgment crying in the wilderness.

The verb used by Matthew for the men of Nineveh rising in judgment is precisely that used for rising from the dead, for resurrection (*anastēsontai*). Jesus presents the startling image of the penitent rising from the dead to condemn the unrepentant of Jesus's generation.

What Jesus actually meant by being in the "heart of the earth" for three days and three nights is not as obvious as one might think, any more than his referring to the "third day." What would we put in the "heart of the earth?"

A seed.

Joseph of Arimathea's tomb was carved into rock; the Greek *gēs* for "earth" would tend to mean soil. The idea of planting is there. The Son of man will, apparently, be planted, as a prelude to the resurrection of the martyrs and the judgment of the sinners. Or has he been "planted"—a reed shaken in the wind—already?

As regards that overfamiliar explanation of the "third day" referring to "Easter Sunday," we may naturally ask, "The third day of *what*?" Being in the tomb? That does not necessarily work and is banal. Why should the Friday crucifixion be counted as a "first day," anyhow? "First day" of what? The Gospels indicate the day before the Sabbath as the day of "Preparation" (14 Nisan) when the lambs were slaughtered for Passover: the day of offering. But, it must be said, this is all after-the-horse-has-bolted *interpretation*. Moreover, what was significant about the "second day," the Sabbath, according to the Gospels?

Nothing, apparently. Are we to think the third day meant the "third day in the tomb?" We are now going round in circles. Jesus's body was not *in* the tomb, according to the gospel story, for three days. According to Matthew, the women arrived at the tomb *before* the dawning of the first day of the week (Sunday) to be told by a fabulous angel that Jesus had *already risen.* Matthew does not follow the idea of the "Sunday" having begun at the sunset of Saturday: "In the end of the Sabbath, as it began to dawn toward the first day of the week, came Mary Magdalene and the other women to see the sepulchre" (28:1).

How could Jesus *know* the precise circumstances of what would happen when he was arrested? And if, providentially, he did, well, what can you say? If he was *that* confident, that well informed of revival after the nightmare of crucifixion, there would be only *process:* no self-offering in faith, no agony in the garden, no "take this cup away from me," no "My God, my God, why hast thou forsaken me?"—the cry that made onlookers believe he was calling for Elijah (John?) to come and save him. If Jesus was authoritatively certain of rising from the dead three days after death, he would have entered the Passover events with the conceit of a mentally prepared radical with a bomb strapped to his chest, or the obliviousness to doom of the Gadarene swine, possessed. If rising from the dead was, as it were, *automatic,* or even, as an extreme possibility "preplanned" (that is, he was not actually dead), such an event would carry very little *meaning,* except to the theological system-maker.

For a real man, or woman, for a truly loving, good person, the final step of such a journey as the Gospels describe would be simply terrible: letting go forever, not of a bad dream that one wished was over, an act of despair, but the willing offering of all that one had, all that one loved, all that one was. It meant being judged as a condemned sinner when one knew one was innocent, spotless. *All that a man hath will he give for his life* (Job 2:4). Death is the King of Terrors when fully contemplated. Some have looked to death itself to remove the fear: "let it all be over, then the pain will end and the fear cease." But death is death, and the tomb slams shut.

Whatever we may believe happened to Jesus's body after crucifixion, we are still left with the question of what he meant by "the third day."

I think there is more to this "third day" idea than arithmetic. I do not think the expression originally referred to the "Easter itinerary." The disciples "understood not that saying [about the third day], and were afraid to ask him" (Mark 9:32). Only with hindsight perhaps, and poor arithmetic, could they say afterward, "Oh, *that's* what the third day meant!" They were not privy to the meaning of the "third day."

I suspect both John and Jesus knew precisely what it meant.

Clearly the phrase "the third day" got attached very early on to the familiar (perhaps too familiar) story of the resurrection, and rightly, we are at liberty to believe, or not. But what did the phrase "the third day" *originally* mean? What did Jesus mean by it when he uttered it, if he uttered it? For it ought to be plain to the meanest intelligence that if there is any reality to the saying, he cannot have been referring, in his own mind, to the story of Joseph of Arimathea's tomb and the events of what we call "Easter Sunday," named generously after the pagan goddess Eostre, linked to the radiant dawn and celebrated at a Spring Equinox festivity in Anglo-Saxon Northumbria.

In fact, the phrase "the third day" makes perfect sense within the circle of prophecies familiar to John and his relative.

SECRET ISRAEL

Remember this? *And the evening and the morning of the third day* . . . The third day.

On the third day of creation in *Genesis,* God made the plants to yield fruit, and the seed that carries in itself its seed:

And God said, "Let the earth bring forth grass, the herb yielding seed, and the fruit tree yielding fruit after his kind, whose seed is in itself, upon the earth": and it was so. And the earth brought forth grass, and herb yielding seed after his kind, and the tree yielding fruit, whose seed was in itself, after his kind: and God saw that it was good. And the evening and the morning were the third day. (Genesis 1:11–13)

This is the work of the third day. These are the first fruits of pure creation, and they are acceptable to God; God saw that they were good, pristine. And every plant had its seed within itself, so that it might go into the heart of the Earth and rise again as its creator willed. The epiphany of life on Earth chimes right in with Isaiah's prophecy of God's Day of new creation, once the darkness is banished:

In that day sing ye unto her, A vineyard of red wine. I the LORD do keep it: I will water it every moment: lest any hurt it, I will keep it night and day. . . . He shall cause them that come of Jacob to take root: Israel shall blossom and bud, and fill the face of the world with fruit. (Isaiah 27:2, 6)

The *end* of the just man is like the beginning of life. The work undone by Man's disobedience, his fall, is remade. Creation is restored, and the just man and God are reconciled. On the third day, the fruit, the seed of Adam, shall be raised.

The background to this interpretation becomes clearer when we recall to mind the Book of Enoch. Enoch revealed to Jesus's generation that humankind had been corrupted by evil angels, evil "Watchers," stellar beings, rebellious "sons of God" who came to Earth and took the daughters of men. By quitting heaven and descending to Earth, the Watchers had explicitly transgressed God's work of the first and second days: the creation of the light and the fundamental division of the heavens from the Earth. The evil Watchers had trespassed across their ordained boundary and brought spiritual havoc to the work of creation. The work of the *new* third day then is the restoration of the original seed of life: wine will flow. Its symbol and requirement was the spiritual glorification and revelation of the Son of man: his "rising on the third day."

On this understanding, it appears that Jesus and John led a secret movement, under the skin of Israel, a spiritual underground, a hidden Israel, a true Israel, a faithful Israel, a band of perceivers, watchers, guardians, dedicated to galvanizing the *eschaton,* the end-time. Their task involved exorcising the world of evil powers. God would bind the powers and raise the martyrs. This was an esoteric, spiritual struggle. Spiritual things are spiritually discerned, and without the Spirit, neither John's nor Jesus's followers could understand the true dimensions of the operation. This plan to rebuild the work of creation, the "temple" built in three days, was not something for the ears of kings and Roman governors: the kingdom envisioned was not of *their* world; it was a spiritual mission, the work of brother builders: the Natzarim who stood awake as the world slept.

What they were really about, and the level on which they were operating, was not such as would alert either worldly historians or journalists.

When the Son of man stands the test of "fire," of Spirit, the third day is reenacted, creation's corruption by evil spiritual powers is overturned, and the New Day begins: the new Creation, the New Man raised from the alembic of Test, vindicated in the "judgment." He stands on the original square of creation, the divine cornerstone.

Now, what of the Son of man being three days and three nights in the *heart of the Earth*? This is without doubt an esoteric concept, very much in tune with the third day and the "raising." The solution rather stares one in the face. "And God called the dry land Earth; and the gathering together of the waters called he Seas: and God saw that it was good" (Genesis 1:10).

That was on the third day. God made the *Earth*. Then, three days and three nights later:

And God said, "Let us make man in our image, after our likeness: and let them have dominion over the fish of the sea, and over the fowl of the air, and over the cattle, and over all the earth, and over every creeping thing that creepeth upon the earth." (v. 26)

What was Adam made of? His very name was identical with it: ". . . for out of it [earth] wast thou taken: for dust thou art and unto dust shalt thou return" (Genesis 3:19). The Hebrew for "Earth" is "Adama." A Son of man is a Son of Earth. When God made Earth, the idea of Man, the seed of Man, of Adam, was there, living, buried in the "heart of the Earth" for three days and three nights.

Today we might say that all the essential elements of the genome have existed since the creation of the Earth. Though Man did not appear at once, he was in the heart, in the mind of Earth, *in potentia:* Man's coming was the fulfillment of that potential. On the third day of the end-time—*please understand that this is all symbolic language*—the story of the creation's corruption is, as it were, reversed. So *shall* the Son of man be in the heart of the Earth for three days and three nights. The perfect Adam redeems the sons of Adam, though "buried," that is, killed by those in the grip of the evil Watchers; his sojourn lasts only until the completion of the new creation when he emerges from the Earth, this world, as the *first fruit,* with seed in himself to make new sons of God.

We have of course ample assurance that Jesus used the image of the sowing of the seed in the earth by the "Sower" (God) as his most universal and well-known parable: men are like plants. Some get burnt up, some get choked by bad company or thoughts, some yet grow to ripeness and are cut for harvest. The Messiah was called the "Branch," born of Jesse's "stump": he too would have to be harvested, lest there be no Bread of Life, and the soul of the world go hungry.

And what do we find? The *third day* of Passover, 16 Nisan, was the *Feast of First Fruits,* when the sheaf of new barley, cut, was waved by the priest over the golden altar:

And the LORD spake unto Moses, saying, Speak unto the children of Israel, and say unto them, When ye be come into the land, which I give unto you, and shall reap the harvest thereof, then ye shall bring a sheaf of the first fruits of your harvest unto the priest: And he shall wave the sheaf before the LORD, to be accepted for you: on the morrow after the sabbath the priest shall wave it. And ye shall offer that day when ye wave the sheaf and the lamb without blemish of the first year for a burnt offering unto the LORD. (Leviticus 23:9–12)

The Son of man emerges pure from the Earth on the third day: a perfect offering to God, a perfect offering from God. First fruit: humanity reborn. "Now in the place where he was crucified there was a garden; and in the garden a new sepulchre, wherein was never man yet laid" (John 19:41).

Paradise was restored by the new fruit of the new tree in the Garden, and Jesus appeared to Mary Magdalene as a gardener (John 20:15).

Chapter Ten

A REED SHAKEN
IN THE WIND

NOW THAT WE HAVE GLIMPSED the mysterious heart of John and Jesus's physical and spiritual operation, undertaken, it should be recognized, in the most trying circumstances imaginable, we may ask the question, Was the operation a success? Obviously, an answer to that question depends on the point of view of the person asking it.

What were the *aims* of the operation, as far as we can tell?

Certainly, there was felt an overwhelming obligation to fulfill prophecy, not out of conceit, but from a sincere conviction and profound realization that the prophecies' time of fulfillment had actually come: all the signs were there, and the Watchers could see them, and they acted. The *purpose* was, literally, to make a way for God, to galvanize the fulfillment of God's will for Israel and humankind; knowledge of how long this would take to complete was not in the gift of the men and women who set the train in motion.

What were arguably the most spiritually meaningful events of 37 CE passed unnoticed and unrecorded by the world at large, the world of power and pomp: the world of illusions. In retrospect, the stories of these events present us precisely with the *first fruits,* not the ultimate banquet. Though it may be argued that the symbolic harvest has begun, we are far from any historic feast. The spiritual and physical rebirth of creation, and the revelation of Man in his actualized fullness, we may suppose to be a project of practically inconceivable scope, from the perspective of the human earthly lifespan, and from the time process in general. A very long-term project indeed! Some might call it evolution, of a kind, but with a *purpose,* a spiritual evolution unlike the purely naturalistic or materialist evolution that dominates much of contemporary thought.

In the short term, and in spite of all the odds, we can, with hindsight, see that the principal target-aims of John and Jesus's operation were achieved, and spectacularly so. By the end of the century, the Herodian family had ceased to exist. Herod the Great's temple was obliterated in 70 CE. The Sadducees were "history." The bickering and rioting in the Temple was over. The old Temple priestly organization was gone, and an esoteric form of Judaism was well on its way to exploding its fruits, madness, wisdom, anarchy, and glory into the non-Jewish world where, after extreme compromise to exoteric practice, power, and politics, it appeared to conquer the spiritual life of the larger part of the empire, and even to outlive "the greatest power on Earth" beyond all expectation. It was called "Christianity": a religion that claims to follow Jesus, and whose members succeed in avoiding that uncomfortable path as much as possible.

For all the catalogue of catastrophes that may be laid at the door of the dominant Christian Churches, the inner "door" to authentic spiritual transformation, the call to the highest, the gospel of forgiveness and love, the faith in justice and truth, the cultivation of esoteric knowledge, the ancient call to the good, the true, and the beautiful, the vision of spiritual liberty, all have somehow survived, if only just, and thoroughly battered, the attacks of their enemies, among whom we must frequently include those who have claimed the mantle of "Christian authority." From the social and political perspective, then, and from the point of view of the realist, the operation has been a tremendous, if qualified, "success."

However, while we have seen the shoots, we are very far indeed from seeing the actualization of the flower, or anything like it. Visions have abounded, of course, but visions planted in this world are like the dreams of holidays to come; they seldom match up. Christian triumphalism is misplaced. The *purpose* of Christianity, for example, cannot be "Christianity." John the Baptist was not a Christian, nor was Jesus. However, if we understand the "end" of the world properly to mean the *purpose* and intended fulfillment of the fruitful part of the world, we can look forward to many divine "days" yet before the potential released to a hostile world in the first century actually *cooks*, not a bread merely good enough to eat in the event of hunger, but the bread of life itself.

In terms of the supracosmic operation, the permanent defeat of the "evil angels," one is inclined to wonder if Enoch did not sleep too long at Dan before making his proclamation of judgment on Azazel and his rebel legions! On closer inspection, though, we find that the Enochian prophecy looked to the binding of the wicked *on Earth* to the rebellious powers, not the annihilation of spiritual powers *in toto*, however deviant. The *promise* is that for those who are prepared to endure and follow in the path made straight by John, then the ongoing test of judgment will be bearable, and the powers of evil will no longer dominate the soul; nothing less than *transfiguration* would count as ultimate success on this road, and we see little sign of it, but perhaps we seek in the wrong place. In this sense, the rebellious powers' kingdom is under check; notice has been served, as it were, and those who embrace its servitude find themselves brought to book in due course, one way or another. The "thousand-year *reich*" lasted a little over a decade, and though it saw the ruin of all it inherited, the cost was great.

Since the time of John the Baptist's call, a great part of the world has been aware of living in the "last times," but when we consider the "three days and three nights" it took to bring forth Adam from the heart of the earth in the divine scheme, and the many billions of years it took to constitute the optimistically named *Homo sapiens* in the human and terrestrial scale, we might realize that there is a long, long way to go! If we confine our assessment to the world of time, we are really far closer to John and his wilderness than we might think. Those expecting the Son of man to appear on the "clouds of power" in the foreseeable future obviously have never seen the Son of man. Such persons are like people standing at an imaginary bus stop, waiting for a bus that is not going to come. They could really use their precious time in this world doing something more wholesome and practically useful than manipulating dates, numbers, and calendars. They think they carry comfort to the "saved," but they simply distract and slow down the march of the "great army of God." Salvation may be urgent, but the world's end is not. That is the view of the best spiritual minds I have found on the subject, and I daresay, it is one that will annoy those who have not looked deeply *enough* into the question. Sometimes the world is like a dull or painful play; we can hardly wait for it to end.

For those who demand "signs," the Natzarim offer the "sign of Jonah." If you had truly repented, you would have been waiting not for the end, but the beginning.

PROBLEM PAUL

As we have been discussing, the churches have been their own worst enemies all too frequently, standing in their own way. This is regrettable but seems inevitable. How else otherwise could we account for the fact that the source of the greatest denigration to the person and reputation of John the Baptist has been the very person who punctured the Judaic skin of the message of the Natzarim and threw it headfirst into the marketplace of the Gentiles whose spiritual governors, Jews believed, were fallen angels? Saul, the pursuer of the Nazoraeans, became Paul the converter of the Gentiles: a fantastic irony that almost has the whiff of some paradoxical providence about it.

However one looks at it, Paul opposed the baptism of John. The time has come to examine whether his reasons for doing so do honor or disservice to the man Jesus, whom Paul claimed had been "revealed in him," described as unsurpassed by the greatest men ever born of woman, a statement that must certainly be taken to mean that Saul, their younger contemporary, for all his genius, was probably inferior to the man whose baptism he denigrated. For make no mistake about it, the chief problem the gospel writers had when writing about the magisterial figure of John was the widespread view abroad in Christian churches by the last quarter of the first century that John was somehow deficient, a man whose role had to be "decreased" so that Jesus's glory might be "increased."

The circumstances of Paul's run-in with the church of John are related, in tantalizingly fragmentary form, by Paul's disciple Luke in the eighteenth and nineteenth chapters of the Acts of the Apostles, a very late work (ca. 90–110 CE):

> After these things Paul departed from Athens, and came to Corinth;
> And found a certain Jew named Aquila, born in Pontus, lately come
> from Italy with his wife Priscilla (because that Claudius had com-
> manded all Jews to depart from Rome), and came unto them. And
> because he was of the same craft, he abode with them, and wrought:
> for by their occupation they were tentmakers. (18:1–3)

Paul stayed a "good while" in Corinth making tents and preaching before taking Aquila and Priscilla with him to Syria, thence to Ephesus, where he left them:

> And a certain Jew named Apollos, born at Alexandria, an eloquent
> man, and mighty in the scriptures, came to Ephesus. This man was
> instructed in the way of the Lord; and being fervent in the spirit, he
> spake and taught diligently the things of the Lord, knowing only
> the baptism of John. (18:24–25)

Apollos spoke boldly in Ephesus's synagogue. Hearing him, Aquila and Priscilla took Apollos aside and, as Acts puts it, "expounded unto him the way of God more perfectly." From this account, Apollos appears to have been fully co-opted into the Pauline camp, for when Apollos decides to go preaching in Achaia, in the northwest of the Greek Peloponnese peninsula, the Corinthian brethren endorse Apollos's mission by requesting that the "disciples" there receive him. A mighty preacher in Achaia, Apollos "convinced the Jews and that publicly, shewing by the scriptures that Jesus was Christ" (18:28). According to Acts, Paul returned to Ephesus some time later while Apollos was at work in Corinth:

> And it came to pass, that, while Apollos was at Corinth, Paul having passed through the upper coasts came to Ephesus: and finding certain disciples, He said unto them, Have ye received the Holy Ghost since ye believed? And they said unto him, "We have not so much as heard whether there be any Holy Ghost. And he said unto them, Unto what then were ye baptized?" And they said, "Unto John's baptism." Then said Paul, "John verily baptized with the baptism of repentance, saying unto the people, that they should believe on him, which should come after him, that is, on Christ Jesus." When they heard this, they were baptized in the name of the Lord Jesus. And when Paul had laid his hands upon them, the Holy Ghost came on them; and they spake with tongues, and prophesied. And all the men were about twelve. (19:1–7)

You will have observed how in this account Paul's insistence that John told his followers to believe "on him, which should come after him," is followed by Paul's explaining who that "him" was: "Christ Jesus."

Close comparison of Luke's late account with Paul's contemporary deliberations in his first letter to Corinthian converts shows a more nuanced, more troubled picture of Paul's relations with John's church and with "John's baptism." Luke has oversimplified what must have been a complex and fascinating encounter. Sadly, we are not privy to what, if anything, passed between Apollos, the Alexandrian Jew with the golden tongue who knew the "way of the Lord," and Paul, apostle of "Christ Jesus" to the Gentiles.

Luke's picture consists of Paul, with Aquila and Priscilla's help, easily waiving aside John's baptism in favor of Paul's baptism of the Holy Ghost and of fire. Aquila and Priscilla put Apollos straight on the issue, and Paul straightens out what appear to have been Apollos's Ephesian converts to the "way of the Lord," while Apollos himself is away in Corinth, preaching.

Paul's first letter to the Corinthians presents a different picture; Paul is in a jam over a question of his authority. Written from Ephesus, on the west coast of modern Turkey, some hundred and eighty miles from Corinth by sea, the letter is dated to ca. 53–57 CE. If we take into account Luke's reference to Aquila and Priscilla's "late" expulsion from Rome, the low end of that date spectrum is to be preferred since the Emperor Claudius died in 54 CE. Roman historian Suetonius's *Life of Claudius* (25.4), records, "As the Jews were making constant disturbances at the instigation of Chrestus, he expelled them from Rome." Messianic ructions of some kind may be assumed. Jewish communities were plainly in a state of anticipatory excitement. Paul and Apollos doubtless capitalized on this, even if they were not themselves among the causes of it.

First Corinthians weaves a delicate dance around the issue of Apollos. Paul does not go out of his way to offend but wants it understood that *his* is the point of view to observe: he speaks not for himself, he insists, but for the highest interest, God. Once that is accepted, Paul is magnanimous; he even asserts that baptism was not what he was called to do. It is not really his "thing," as if leaving that function generously to his opponents. He has *higher things* to impart. From this high point, Paul sets himself to appear frankly astonished that anyone should be so mundane as to talk of the "baptism of Apollos" or "the baptism of Paul"—or even of Cephas or Christ, for that matter.

It should be borne in mind that Paul, in the first four chapters of his letter, is fighting on several fronts, not against John's baptism alone, but also against the Gentiles-should-be-circumcised-to-be-saved Jewish messianic interest from which his synagogue opposition comes. This "interest community" appears to have proclaimed a blend of uncompromising New Covenanter-style beliefs (as we find in the Dead Sea Scrolls "Community Rule" and *Damascus Document*) with the slightly more conciliatory Jesus-oriented, mercy, righteousness, and good works stance of James, the brother of the Lord. Paul hopes everyone called to the Messiah will find harmonious reconciliation through his, Paul's, meek presence; otherwise the conflicting Corinthians can expect "the rod" (4:21).

Paul's disciple Chloe has warned him of conflict and acrimony in Corinth. Some say, "I am of Paul"; others, "I of Apollos," others, "I of Cephas" or "I of Christ" (1:12). Paul then jokes that none were baptized in *his* (Paul's) name; they were baptized in Jesus's name (presumably), so why the division? "I thank God that I baptized none of you, but Crispus and Gaius; Lest any should say that I had baptized in mine own name. And I baptized also the household of Stephanas: besides, I know not whether I baptized any other" (vv. 14–16). Paul then says he is not really responsible for baptism: "For Christ sent me not to baptize, but to preach the gospel" (v. 17). And what Paul has to preach to the worthy is the ancient mystery, "the hidden wisdom," the (Nazoraean) mystery of the means by which the "princes of this world" are confounded. Paul is almost certainly referring by inference to the evil angels who have dominated the nations and corrupted the world, whose work has been undone by the suffering and death of the Son of man: "But we speak the wisdom of God in a mystery, even the hidden wisdom, which God ordained before the world unto our glory: Which none of the princes of this world knew: for had they known it, they would not have crucified the Lord of glory" (2:7–8).

Crucifying the Lord of Glory was the evil Watchers biggest mistake (*theirs*, not the Romans, apparently). Those who *thought* they were "doing it" did not, as Luke's Jesus asserts, "know what they were doing"; Jesus forgave them (Luke 23:34). The wicked Watchers—whom Paul calls the "princes of this world"—were really pulling the strings, but while they had stolen much divine knowledge, they were not privy to God's ultimate plan to save his creation, to redeem it from its fall. Paul, by declaring openly the defeat of the dark powers to the Gentiles, over whom those fallen angels had exercised invisible control throughout history, the grip of the Watchers over the converted Gentile soul was broken; they experienced the Holy Spirit and could stand the Test. These Gentiles were the children of God's ancient covenants with Noah, and with Abraham; they were not party to the covenant with Moses and so did not, Paul insisted, stand under condemnation of Moses's law, but under the revived, essential law: love God; love one another.

According to Paul, his manifest opposition was simply a gaggle of men puffed up with their own knowledge. Their knowledge, he declares, must be earthly since Paul's is heavenly, and if it were recognized as such, there would be no contention among men over baptisms or anything else: "But the natural man receiveth not the things of the Spirit of God: for they are foolishness unto him: neither can he know them, because they are spiritually discerned" (2:14). Paul then apologizes for only acquainting the brethren with a *form* of the mystery, one appropriate for their carnal, natural, and, frankly, superficial Gentile minds. Should they doubt their carnality, their unfitness for the "meat" of spiritual instruction, they should think about their behavior: "For ye are yet carnal: for whereas there is among you envying, and strife, and divisions, are ye not carnal, and walk as men? For while one saith, I am of Paul; and another, I am of Apollos; are ye not carnal? Who then is Paul, and who is Apollos, but ministers by whom ye believed, even as the Lord gave to every man?" (3:3–5).

Paul now demonstrates himself well up on New Covenanter-style language concerning the plantation of righteousness that is the council of God's Law, as well as being a creative adept with Nazoraean vineyard, building, and temple imagery. He employs a cunning pun that both praises and undermines Apollos simultaneously with all the skill of a Mark Antony coming not to praise Caesar but to bury him:

I have planted, Apollos watered; but God gave the increase. So then neither is he that planteth any thing, neither he that watereth; but God that giveth the increase. Now he that planteth and he that watereth are one: and every man shall receive his own reward according to his own labor. For we are laborers together with God: ye are God's husbandry, ye are God's building.

According to the grace of God, which is given unto me, as a wise master builder, I have laid the foundation, and another buildeth thereon. But let every man take heed how he buildeth thereupon. For other foundation can no man lay than that is laid, which is Jesus Christ. (3:6–11)

Professor Robert Eisenman has suggested in his pioneering, controversial book *James the Brother of Jesus* that Paul was responding to the goad of the New Covenanters' "Community Rule." That Rule declared the "Council of the Community" (a council of twelve, *note,* with three priests) "shall be an Everlasting Plantation, a House of Holiness for Israel. . . . It shall be that tried wall, that precious cornerstone, whose foundations shall neither rock nor sway in their place [Isaiah 28:26], It shall be a Most Holy Dwelling for Aaron . . . a House of Perfection and Truth in Israel. . . ." Full members of the "Community in Israel . . . shall separate from the habitation of unjust men and shall go into the wilderness to prepare there the way of Him; as it is written, Prepare in the wilderness the way of [the Lord], make straight in the desert a path for our God [Isaiah. 40:3]. This path is the study of the Law, which he commanded by the hand of Moses . . . and as the prophets have revealed by His Holy Spirit." Those who follow the rule are "the men of perfect holiness."

Paul says the foundation of the everlasting house or spiritual temple is the Christ, Jesus. The New Covenanters maintained it was the council of men of perfect holiness. Paul wanted a doctrine for the Gentiles; the New Covenanters a doctrine for a select Israel.

Paul vehemently opposed the strictly *legal* interpretation of these symbolic images, while being at pains to display his knowledge of them, by cleverly reinterpreting and thus recreating them. In his second letter to the Corinthians, for example, Paul interprets the "everlasting building" metaphor as an image for the spiritual body of the holy, that body that transcends and will survive the body of Earth. In doing so he alludes to the supernatural stone "cut without hands" in Daniel 2:34:

> For we know that if our earthly house of this tabernacle were dissolved, we have a building of God, an house not made with hands, eternal in the heavens. For in this we groan, earnestly desiring to be clothed upon with our house, which is from heaven. . . . (2 Cornithians 5:1–2)

Ironically, Mason Brother Robert Samber, commenting on the St. John the Baptist Feast, which took place on June 24, 1723, in London, compared its gluttonous excess—demolishing a "mountain of venison"—unfavorably to what he asserted was the primary ancient commission of Free Masons, namely, to build the perfected house of the spirit, made "without hands."

Nearly seventeen hundred years before Brother Samber's poignant observation, Paul employed both masons' and allied agricultural images to demolish dependence on what he considered the merely human ministry of Apollos and the watery baptism of John. Paul, the self-proclaimed wise "master-mason," the architect, had not stumbled on the Stone, like his enemies who failed to discern correctly its character; he, Paul, had picked it up and built with it, or planted it in the earth, on the correct foundation or "plantation": "*I have planted, Apollos watered; but God gave the increase.*" Apollos's "watering" is obviously a euphemism for John's baptism, and Paul is saying, well, it is useful, so long as we bear in mind *who did the planting,* and who is responsible for the increase or fruitfulness: God.

Note the word *increase* here, for it seems to belong to the same family of ideas that would make the Gospel of John's John declare that he would have to decrease so that Jesus could increase. Indeed, the line may have come from reflecting on Paul's words; they clearly head from, and in, this direction.

Feeling himself on top of the argument, Paul is now in a conciliatory mood. In fact, he says kindly, the planter and waterer are really worth about the same in God's scheme, and they can expect comparable wages, performance-related, that is. By denigrating himself, he denigrates Apollos to laborer status. This is Paul's habitual rhetorical method; he will be as the "filth of the world" if it gets the message across, and he does not mind very much who he brings down there with him. Their lowliness is their exaltation, for the things of God are despised in the world. So it is all right that "another" has built on the foundation he made, since the real foundation is Jesus Christ, whoever had a hand, or did not have a hand, in it. Men as mere men are not that important; their world of values is going to end soon anyway:

> Therefore let no man glory in men. For all things are yours; Whether Paul, or Apollos, or Cephas, or the world, or life, or death, or things present, or things to come; all are yours; And ye are Christ's; and Christ is God's. (3:21–23)

Nevertheless, Paul remains adamant that the Corinthians still see *him*, Paul, as more important than any "mere instructor" in God's mysteries. He is their *father*:

> For though ye have ten thousand instructors in Christ, yet have ye not many fathers: for in Christ Jesus I have begotten you through the gospel. Wherefore I beseech you, be ye followers of me. (4:15–16)

Furthermore, as their "father," Paul is in touch with the great high mysteries of God that, as far as everybody else is concerned, shall be brought to light from darkness only at the time "the Lord come" (4:5).

In the meantime, he has "in a figure [that is, he has 'adapted' them; *metaschēmatizō* = I change the appearance, or transfer by a fiction] transferred to myself and to Apollos for your sakes; that ye might learn in us not to think of men above that which is written, that no one of you be puffed up for one against another" (4:6). Here Paul almost posits himself and Apollos as an apostolic pair, but he is attributing any wisdom Apollos might display not only to God *through him,* but that, if I read this correctly, Apollos does not know the mysteries as they are eternally, only a *form* of them suited to his capacities and those of the Corinthians. It is a difficult passage; one almost feels Paul is claiming a relationship to Apollos that really is not there, for otherwise, why would he not just say, "Apollos and I have spoken and agreed"? Paul is gainsaying, and he is doing it in a series of veiled threats already referred to in chapter 3 of the letter. The coming judgment is going to reveal the true mysteries, in the light of the fire that will bring life for some, destruction for others. The Corinthians had better watch out!

This idea of coming judgment, of fire, allows Paul to reach for what he is sure is his killer argument against the "baptism of John" and those who claim to be "of Apollos." There is a subtle shift in emphasis, but it is powerful.

"*What* is builded," says Paul, "no matter *who* may claim to have built it, will be tried *in the fire*" (my italics). Paul claims the "baptism of fire" *he* administers is a critical step beyond John's—and Apollos's— "watering." This cross-symbolic link of fire and of water, which the holy building—or plantation—must withstand is very revealing, not only of Paul's thinking and argumentative method, but of the precise mechanism through which we can see whether Paul has, or has not, misunderstood or deliberately distorted the authentic position of John the Baptist.

First, Paul uses almost exactly the framework of coming harvest fire closely associated, in the Gospels (*viz:* Matthew 3:10), with John the Baptist:

Now if any man build upon this foundation gold, silver, precious stones, wood, hay, stubble; Every man's work shall be made manifest: for the day shall declare it, because it shall be revealed by fire; and the fire shall try every man's work of what sort it is. If any man's work abide, which he hath built thereupon, he shall receive a reward. If any man's work shall be burned, he shall suffer loss: but he himself shall be saved; yet so as by fire. (1 Corinthians 3:12–15)

The fire will not, however, annihilate the "temple of God": "Know ye not that ye are the temple of God, and that the Spirit of God dwelleth in you? If any man defiles the temple of God, him shall God destroy; for the temple of God is holy, which temple ye are" (3:16–17). One can almost hear the heavy sighs of relief from Paul's, doubtless shaken, audience. That heartening passage of blessed relief from the imminent Trial is, of course, predicated on having received the Holy Spirit: the baptism of fire that sustains the soul through the fire of judgment. Paul seems to be saying, *Forget who administered it. Is your baptism good enough? Is it up to the task? Your instructor won't be able to help you when the time comes. Are you making the right decision? Do you want love, or the rod?*

Even though Paul's chief claim in his "first" letter to the Corinthians is that he is not a baptizer, but the preacher of the hidden mysteries and wisdom of God, in a form appropriate to "children," he is nonetheless the one who works in the Spirit of the Son who can awaken even the Gentiles to God's holy spirit. He, Paul, had the baptism of "fire"; this, evidently, was not a water baptism. According to Luke's account it involved the laying on of hands. The fire or holy spirit "baptism" was both destroyer of chaff and quickener of righteous spirit: a kind of winnowing.

THE PILLARS OF ENOCH

I hope to demonstrate that Paul's subtle, condescending, but highly effective polemic against John's baptism is based on an ancient Hebrew tradition, the tradition of two judgments, and on an ancient Hebrew legend concerning what could be built to stand the tremor of the two judgments. This tradition, at some unknown time, became embedded into the ancient lore of freemasons, that is, master masons of freestone. Given Paul's borrowed and inherited usage of Hebrew masons' lore we should not be altogether surprised. Prophets, priests, and masons were bound together in the codex of Jewish history: after all, much of the prophetic voice was expended on matters pertaining to "heathen pillars," the Temple, and the state-sponsored "bulwarks" that would, or would not, make Israel secure. The psalms, along with Hebrew wisdom literature, echo with grand thoughts of the divine architect who built the universe with wisdom.

Paul's contemporary, Josephus, was well aware of the legend. He related it in his first book of *Antiquities of the Jews* (2:3):

> Now Adam, who was the first man, and made out of the earth, (for our discourse must now be about him,) after Abel was slain, and Cain fled away, on account of his murder, was solicitous for posterity, and had a vehement desire of children, he being two hundred and thirty years old; after which time he lived other seven hundred, and then died. He had indeed many other children, but Seth in particular. As for the rest, it would be tedious to name them; I will therefore only endeavor to give an account of those that proceeded from Seth. Now this Seth, when he was brought up, and came to those years in which he could discern what was good, became a virtuous man; and as he was himself of an excellent character, so did he leave children behind him who imitated his virtues. All these proved to be of good dispositions. They also inhabited the same country without dissensions, and in a happy condition, without any misfortunes falling upon them, till they died.
>
> They also were the inventors of that peculiar sort of wisdom, which is concerned with the heavenly bodies, and their order. And that their inventions might not be lost before they were sufficiently

known, upon Adam's prediction that the world was to be destroyed at one time by the force of fire, and at another time by the violence and quantity of water, they made two pillars, the one of brick, the other of stone: they inscribed their discoveries on them both, that in case the pillar of brick should be destroyed by the flood, the pillar of stone might remain, and exhibit those discoveries to mankind; and also inform them that there was another pillar of brick erected by them. Now this remains in the land of Siriad to this day.

This legend of the twin pillars, erected for the judgments of water and of fire is, I believe, at the root of Paul's critique of John's baptism. Paul's statements about what you can build on the foundation he has laid make it plain. Paul is sarcastic about raising fancy things, gold and silver and precious jewels, on the foundations. This refers to Daniel's prophecy of the smashed Babylonian image, obliterated and transformed by the stone cut "without hands." Paul adds "stubble" and "hay" and "wood" to that built with "feet of clay." Stubble is burnt by fire at the harvest. Stubble was also sought for the making of bricks by the Hebrews in Egypt; from it they gathered straw to reinforce the clay (Exodus 5:4–12). Paul's reference to "hay" is even more sarcastic, since hay is even less substantial than straw! The judgment of water on such watery substances (clay, stubble, hay, etc.) would make short work of it. If you want to withstand fire, however, you need stone. Paul is making a subtle comparison of himself with Apollos. *Who do you trust? What pillar are you going to lean on or cling to "when the chips are down"?*

Paul was well aware of the idea of the leaders of the church being called "pillars," supports, and flanks to the door of holiness and salvation. It may be recalled that the Dead Sea Scrolls "Community Rule" called for a council of twelve ruled by three priests. Together they would stand as the House of Holiness for Israel. According to Acts, those John-followers on whom Paul laid his hands at Ephesus were numbered "about twelve." Had Apollos set up a "holy council" there?

Paul is, as ever, vitriolic about church leadership that does not include him. In his letter to the Galatians (2:9), he describes his troubled negotiations with the Jerusalem leadership over his contention that he, Paul, preach to the uncircumcised: "And when James, Cephas, and John, who *seemed to be pillars,* perceived the grace that was given unto me . . ." That sarcastic phrase "seemed to be pillars" is absolutely loaded, and could be translated as "those so-called pillars." Paul was "underwhelmed" by the men chosen by Jesus.

Paul has an idea of two stages of judgment, and of salvation. First the water, the child's diet of "milk," then the "meat" that can stand a thorough roasting; that is what he has to offer: the higher diet, the real bread. Paul can see no point telling the Greeks of Corinth about Jewish legends of Sethian pillars; those that knew, would know.

Perhaps Paul had visited the pillars referred to by Josephus in Syria. Josephus himself was about sixteen at the time Paul, according to Acts, took Aquila and Priscilla to Syria, before leaving them at Ephesus. In fact, the Greek historian Herodotus (ca. 484–425 BCE) wrote about the pillars of Egyptian King Sesostris in Syria, and this may explain how Josephus knew that Seth's pillars still stood in Syria, his having mistaken Sesostris for Seth. Herodotus had seen the pillars: "The pillars, which Sesostris king of Egypt set up in the various countries, are for the most part no longer to be seen extant; but in Syria Palestine I myself saw them existing with the inscription upon them, which I have mentioned and the emblem" (*History,* 106).

It is possible that the building trade was the source for Paul's knowledge of the two pillars that would survive judgments of water and of fire. At the time of John, according to Josephus, eighteen thousand masons and allied trades were employed in Jerusalem after the burning of temple precincts that took place shortly after Herod the Great's death in 4 BCE. Herod's sons erected a number of classically constructed cities across Syria-Palestine. There were masons all over the place. Galilee did not look like Arizona: more like a building site.

Jesus called Simon "son of John," "a stone," and his brother James was known as the "bulwark" (a defensive wall). And we note that these two men had, by the time Paul encountered them, become known to the Nazoraean assembly as the "pillars," along with one called John.

The Sethian pillars were not simply designed to withstand fire and water; they also encoded the secrets of science discovered by Adam's brainchild, Seth. Paul obviously saw himself privy to the higher knowledge that came not from men, but from God and his Son. Had he not seen what Seth had seen? Paul's mythological background was almost what we would recognize as something like "science fiction."

The legend of the Sethian pillars lies, I think, behind both Paul's criticism of the John tradition and James the brother of the Lord's convictions about the necessity of the Jewish Law. *Can the pillars' building withstand the final test?* Paul asks. Maybe of *water*, but can they match Paul's baptism of *fire*, of Holy Spirit, that has made converts of Gentiles where the Law had repelled them? "I have planted, Apollos watered; but God gave the increase," declares Paul.

It is perhaps odd how these images coincide with Luke's account of Paul's dealings with the Jew Aquila of Pontus and his wife, Priscilla, kicked out of Italy by the Emperor Claudius. Luke's account of Paul's meeting the couple records how their relationship was cemented in the coincidence that both Paul and Aquila were "of the same craft" (Greek: *homotechnon*). They were tentmakers. One wonders if Paul and Aquila got some of their ideas from craft legends, perhaps even a craft society of free . . . *tentmakers?* Not as strange an idea as you might think, for according to the late medieval freemasons' "Charges," now known as the *Cooke Manuscript* (ca. 1420 CE), Enoch's descendant Jabal was the "father" not only of tentmaking (Genesis 4:20), but father of *masonry* as well, for it is written, "The elder son, Jabal, he was the first man that also found geometry and Masonry, and he made houses. . . ." Jabal was the "father of men dwelling in tents, that is, dwelling houses. And he was Cain's master mason and governor of all his works, when he made the city of Enoch. . . ."

This *Cooke Manuscript,* incidentally, was presented to the Grand Lodge of London by Grand Master George Payne on St. John the Baptist's Day 1721, and its contents, you could say, were . . . *absorbed.* Two years later, in 1723, Anderson's *Constitutions* demonstrates knowledge of the "pillars of Seth" referred to by Josephus, while making the point that the "old masons" always called them the Pillars of Enoch. According to Genesis, Enoch, Seth's great-great-great-grandson (Genesis 5:18), was not only the name of the first city ever built (4:17), but Enoch himself never died. Like Elijah, he was assumed to heaven (5:24). If you were building a heavenly city, you would want Enoch on your side.

Enoch was the name by which "Thrice Great" Hermes was sometimes known to medieval Muslim scholars, working from Sabian writings. There may be a reason for the old masons' discretion. For while, according to the *Cooke Manuscript,* it was Jabal who made the two pillars, one of latera (brick) and one of marble to withstand water and fire judgments, to preserve the knowledge of the ancient masters, the *Sloane Manuscript* of 1646 (British Library No. 3848) tells us that it was Hermenes son of Cush who *discovered* the two pillars.

Hermenes, we are told, was afterward called "Hermes, the father of wise men." Thrice Great Hermes is of course an ancient patron of medieval freemasonry, as well as of that gnostic "Hermetic philosophy" dear to Sabian writers, the Florentine Neoplatonic Renaissance, and midwife to modern science's birth. Hermes was the "psychopomp," or soul's guide, of science. In Hermetic Tractate No. 4 we find the story of the "herald" who brought a mixing bowl of divine *mind* (nous) from heaven to which humanity was called to be baptized.

It was the pillars of Seth or Enoch, *not* those of Jachin and Boaz at the porch of Solomon's destroyed temple that held the significance for the old freemasons who emerged in history with written "Charges" in the late Middle Ages.

If Paul grasped the significance of the antediluvian pillars of Seth, there is no reason why John and Jesus, whose father was apparently a technician, may not also have been inspired to think of what kind of structure, what kind of man, could survive the coming fire. Then we might see the symbolism of the *water baptism* as the *first stage* of preparation for the coming fire, the preliminary "judgment" if you will. Josephus tells us that John's baptism was for the washing of the body after repentance.

As we shall see in chapter 11, the last surviving, authentic, and original baptizing sect, the Mandaeans of Iraq, who took, and to this day take, John the Baptist as their great prophet, not only baptize the living, but also wash the dead ritually, in preparation for translation through a purgatorial journey of the soul. It can hardly be insignificant for this discussion that, according to the Mandaeans, the body of John the Baptist could not be *burnt by fire.*

It becomes clear that in his eagerness to establish his own vision of salvation, Paul mixed his metaphors to suit himself. In doing so, he denigrated the baptism of John from his day to ours. Wanting the "fire" to stand both for the judgment *and* the holy spirit "hand baptism," he *effectively* turned the hand baptism *into* the coming of the Holy Spirit—that which would come "after" John's baptism. He turned John against himself. Mixing the fire metaphors, Paul confused his laying on of hands with the primary image embodying the final judgment itself, while he *simultaneously* asserted that only *his* passing on of the "Holy Spirit" could protect the soul from the conflagration to come. Paul did this to establish his own apostolate as the supreme authority of salvation. Anyone who differed was to be "accursed," rejected, held as unclean, utterly condemned, damned:

> But though we, or an angel from heaven, preach any other gospel unto you than that which we have preached unto you, let him be accursed. As we said before, so say I now again, "If any man preach any other gospel unto you than that ye have received, let him be accursed." (Galatians 1:8–9)

On this basis, John was cursed already, since John did not preach Paul's Gospel. Paul completely misrepresented John. John did not mix his "fire" metaphors. John saw the fire as taking care of the chaff that had been separated by the winnowing action of the Son of man. The holy spirit of righteousness and piety, *that* was what made the man stand in the wilderness. The one built on such a firm foundation would stand upright, square, we might say, a pillar able to survive the coming harvest conflagration.

Long before Paul's dramatic conversion, if that is what it was, it was John who had declared the coming of the fire. John was fully aware of the prophecies concerning the pious, righteous one, the one who could stand the coming of the Lord God. And how can we doubt that John was aware and awake to the idea that *standing* was symbolically equivalent to building upward with divine stones: a building that would, in Daniel's prophecy (2:31–35), stand the presence of the smiting stone that struck the Babylonian image with feet of clay, and of iron, and "became like the chaff of the summer threshing floors"? This, I dare say, is the primitive essence of symbolic Freemasonry, though the Craft has long forgotten it.

John's "winnowing" is both the judgment and the spiritual salvation; only the chaff is burnt thereafter. It is clear to us now that John and Jesus saw clearly that the holy building was the righteous man in whom the spirit of the divine law had *become* heart and will, as Isaiah, Jeremiah, and Ezekiel prophesied, and who could therefore withstand not only the judgment as God poured his spirit on him, but also the threats and murderousness of the unrighteous.

Paul's tone in general, though often wise, always clever, displays, I think, what we should now call a marked neurotic insecurity, hardly surprising in one who had judged so many, and so many to death, yet who forbade any to judge him (1 Corinthians 2:15; 4:3–4). Paul's famous "thorn in the flesh" may have derived from complicity in the executions of either or both John and Jesus; such would explain much.

Wilier than a serpent, Paul's first letter to the Corinthians piles on argument after argument, line after line, to say the simplest thing, always keeping himself in the central picture, save that if you move Paul out for a second, or he moves out for our benefit, you are compelled by his will to see Christ or God behind him. Resistance, he wants you to believe, is useless. Reject me; reject *all*. This kind of anxious insecurity is, I think, the abiding psychological mark of Paul's writings and is detectable, in my experience, in many of those who have immersed themselves in the Pauline worldview: a scriptural quote for every occasion, defensive, quick to anger, judgmental, utterly convinced in the face of contradiction, threatening, haunted by the world's end, never letting a point drop, overbearing, obsessed with defending the meanest grain of precious "truth," materialistic, profoundly intolerant of those that disagree, suppressed-aggressive, perpetually nervous at God's imminent displeasure: all that and much else too, and never simply *holy,* never simply *good,* seldom *kind* without scriptural backup and justification, and seldom, if ever, sensitive to, or respectful of, spiritual beauty. The thoroughly Pauline type knows everything there is to know about salvation. They come, as it were, to the gates of heaven with their own guidebook. Many have fallen under Paul's brand of the "fear of God," so impersonal, so intense, so demeaning, so self-righteous. Accept all Paul or reject him, and reject all. He wanted to be, and was convinced he was, Jesus's No. 1, and for many, he succeeded. For many, Paul's interpretation *is* Christianity; arguably, he invented it. The Catholic and Orthodox Churches are built on Paul. The man was a genius.

Paul's critique of John's baptism, his supplanting of the Nazoraean vision, his consigning of John to the past, his speaking for Jesus, have not only seeped unchecked into the landscape of Christian scripture, but have led to innumerable problems for Christians over the meaning and application of key doctrines and practices. How often have we heard about a distinction between "real" versus "nominal" Christians? How long the debate between "sprinkling" of water at infant baptism and the claims of the scripture-laden "born-again" for full hydroimmersion? The confusion stems from Paul. The results of Paul's confusion of meaning concerning what is actually meant by "holy spirit," "judgment," "baptism," and "rebirth" are to be found wherever Christianity is preached. Innumerable sects differ over just these very things, and the children inherit the disorder, the pain, the confusion.

Paul introduced the conflict over what is meant by a "spiritual gift" because he confused the fruits of the final judgment with his laying-on of hands. Strange phenomena became the proof of "rebirth"; for some, psychic ecstasies of babbling "prophecy" and "speaking in tongues" became signs of having been already "resurrected." Spiritual benefits such as a refined sense of justice and peace and mercy and a sober and reasonable hope seemed dull compared to strange, mostly temporary, phenomena. Others went further, claiming, like Paul, they had penetrated the veil of matter altogether and had become equal to the angels; they were the "pneumatics," the "spirituals," superior to everyone. So-called "charismatics" (the "gifted") claim superiority to the merely "nominal" faith of quiet and pious persons living their own holy life without thumping, clapping, twanging, and wailing as if the entire world should be a gospel choir and salvation the prize for one moral decision made under the duress of threat of imminent judgment and the insidious accusation of personal responsibility for the crucifixion.

I dare say Paul tried to rein in the extremists, but it was he who had let the cat out of the bag, against the better judgment of the "seeming pillars" for whom he had so little respect.

Paul is a problem, no doubt, and his first victim, perhaps literally as well as figuratively, was John the Baptist, a greater man than he, if Jesus's testimony is to be believed.

And yet . . . one cannot help but admire him.

Chapter Eleven

ST. JOHN'S MEN
TODAY

THERE ARE IN THE WORLD two principal groups of people for whom John the Baptist has significant spiritual meaning, though in the case of Freemasons, I should say a group for whom John *ought* to have spiritual meaning; Masons have mostly forgotten why they were once "St. John's men." The second group is more remarkable: the Mandaeans. Known as "Sabians" among Iraqi and Iranian Muslims, the Mandaeans trace their history back through Israel to Egypt, and beyond to Adam, their first great prophet. John the Baptist is revered as their *last* great prophet. Mandaeans build tributaries called "Jordans" off the Tigris where they conduct baptismal initiation rites to this day. You can see them on the Internet.

The word *Mandaean* means "Knower" or "Gnostic." When first encountered by Jesuit missionaries in 1559, the Jesuits called them "John Christians," but Mandaeans have a very different story to tell of the significance of John the Baptist. They have a book titled *The Book of John the Baptizer*. They say John received his wisdom from the divine "Life" and from "Primal MAN" who is "LIGHT." In other words, they understand John, like Enoch, is a "Son of man"—one whose eyes have beheld the Light and looked within it.

Of John the Baptist, the Mandaeans say, "Fire cannot burn him."

Whether or not Mandaeans had any contact with medieval masons working in Syria for the knightly orders that flourished in the Crusades is unknown. As we discussed earlier in this book, John was the patron saint of many religious institutions, including, notably, the Knights Hospitaller. John's significance as the Lord of Midsummer, the fruit, if you will, of harvest sacrifice, must explain his main attraction to mason guilds, religious confraternities, and the common people. John was linked to life and life eternal.

There is, however, another tradition about John and the medieval period that sticks up stubbornly, refusing to settle. Once allowed into the mind, the idea never quite goes away, regardless of strong rational impulses for dismissing it. I refer of course to the mystery of Baphomet, an image, a head, alleged to have been revered by Knights Templar during interrogations of Templars that took place after Philip the Fair of France seized the Order in 1307.

BAPHOMET

If you ask a Mason today why Freemasonry enjoys a "John the Baptist" connection, he might well say it is because many Masons believe that in some way they derive from Templars. Pressed, he might mention something about a head "worshipped" by Templars, held by enemies as heretical, but really harmless. This is not the place to enter into the historicity of such ideas; they are, anyway, components of fringe-Masonic mythology, which contains much "Johannite" material. Somehow, John has become linked to the "head" or *caput mortuum* (death head) touched by some Templars with the waist cords of their dress in the thirteenth century. The late (after 1725) Masonic 3rd Degree ceremony does deal with facing death and emerging, raised, from the threat of the "King of Terrors," but any idea of a link to a thirteenth-century figure called "Baphomet" seems hopelessly strained.

Templar interrogation records reveal that the head, which may have had two or three faces, was respected as a source of fertility and germination. There is obviously a link here with the idea of the "Lord of Midsummer" and the summer solstice. While some scholars reckon the word *Baphomet* was simply a corruption of "Mahomet" and employed to accuse Templars of apostasy to the Islamic faith, esoteric scholarship has tended to focus on the possibility of the name's being derived from the Greek words *baphē mēthra,* that is, the baptism of "mithra." Mithraism was a cult very popular with Roman soldiers, involving degrees of initiation. The Roman cult was probably derived from Iranian traditions of a redeemer called Mithra. In the Roman cult, Mithra slays a bull, drawing from it the promise of life, and everlasting life. Mithra (Roman form "Mithras") was seen as sharing a banquet with the god of the Sun: *Sol.* This is all very suggestive of course.

When Thomas More wrote his famous *Utopia* (1516), he resolved religious dissension by inventing a country where everyone worshipped the source of universal life. The deity was known to Utopians as Mithra.

A figure called Mithra also figures prominently in the Gnostic Manichaean religion, which flourished in the East in late antiquity; St. Augustine was a Manichee "hearer" until hearing of the "Word made flesh." As in the Enochian speculation, trouble in the Manichaean universe stems from the mixture of higher and lower realities, the realms respectively of light and of darkness, a crossing of the boundaries, in which events the Primal Man, called Ohrmazd in the Iranian form of the religion, is temporarily captured by *Hylē,* that is, matter. In response to this holding back of the encroachments of darkness, the king of light sends a being described as "the beloved of the beings of light," "the great architect," and "living spirit" to issue an *awakening call* to the trapped Primal Man. The living spirit's work of salvation results in the Primal Man's redemption. The name of the redeemer, in Persian, is Mithra.

Where the connection with John the Baptist?

Well, apart from the hypothesis that "Baphomet" referred to a "baptism" of Mithra, we may consider how in Islamic tradition, which the Templars encountered at close quarters, the prophet Idris, the *"Green*

One" or *"Evergreen,"* is commonly associated both with Elijah and with Enoch. As an "incarnation" of Elijah, and arguably of Enoch also, the prophet John is thus brought into relation with Idris. In Islam, Idris is a saint and prophet whom God raised to heaven. He may appear when miraculous help is needed. The Qu'ran describes Idris as a man of truth, sincerity, constancy, and patience. Remarkably, in this regard, the Sabians (meaning "bathers," the Islamic word for the Mandaeans) relate how they received their religion from Adam's realization of God as *Life,* passed on to the prophets Seth and Idris (Enoch).

We may recall how Muslims in Damascus and Aleppo credited the relic of John the Baptist's head with miraculous powers. Readers may draw what conclusions they will from these deeply related images and ideas, but before we leave this realm of speculation, we cannot avoid mentioning a notable painting discovered in a cottage in the village of Temple Combe, Dorset, England. The painting shows a severed head. Most who see it instinctively relate it to John the Baptist, rather than Jesus, the other obvious candidate for a bearded, long-haired icon. It has been carbon-dated to ca. 1280 CE, when the Templars held a commandery at Temple Combe. Temple Combe became the property of the Knights Hospitaller after 1307, when four knights were arrested, following the accusations of Philippe of France. The painting may have been a Templar object; it has a haunting quality.

There is undoubtedly a mythic dimension to the head of John the Baptist. It is on the *head* of Jesus, for example, that the Holy Spirit alights. From the mythological perspective, the blood of the Lord of Midsummer would have given form to ideas of rebirth and fertility, of raising and the power to return. The chaff must die, the harvest beaten on the threshing floor, winnowed in the spirit and the waste burned with fire, so the seed may live again in humankind, as food, drink, and the promise of renewal in creation. The secret is in the head of John that must be "cut" that he may live again in the spirit. John is thus lord of the season of the great Light, closest to the sun, and he is raised a Master; the "Jewel" rests on him first. We may, if we wish, conclude that the position of John has become a thing obscure to Masons either because it was hidden—and afterward forgotten—or it was suppressed and the comparatively wooden *mythos* of the slain Hiram, worker of brass, somehow nudged its way in by 1730. But if the spirit of John lives on, then we may glimpse that *through* John perhaps, the spiritual Templar has been reborn in our own times.

THE MANDAEANS

The claim of the Mandaeans that John the Baptist was their last prophet must be taken seriously. Other than the Kurdish Yezidis, whose doctrinal origins are more problematic for the historian and philosopher of religion, the Mandaeans are undoubtedly the last, attested sect to survive the first great Gnostic movement on Earth; their testimony is of inestimable value, as was recognized by the world's greatest scholar of Gnosis, Hans Jonas (1903–1993).

Mandaeans do not claim their religion began with John the Baptist, but that what John believed, they share also. Primarily, that belief is in the efficacy of water baptism as the principle mode by which purification of the faithful is effected; baptism is vital for salvation. To the Mandaeans, John is a Mandaean. But "Mandaean" is not their original name, coming as it does from their word for knowledge: *manda*. Mandaean initiates are called "Nasuraiah" in Arabic, that is, Nasoraeans. They consider themselves "Guardians" (their term) of a primal revelation, an authentic, distinct, monotheist religion.

There is no *a priori* reason to doubt that Mandaeans were once historically linked in some manner to the "church" of John the Baptist. Kurt Rudolph (*Gnosis*, Harper & Row, 1985) is convinced their origins must originally have been Jewish but that the link with anything like normative Judaism has long been effectively severed. It would make sense then if the Mandaeans' forebears dwelt in Samaria and were

Samaritans, with Samaria's closeness to those parts of the Jordan where the fourth Gospel shows both John and Jesus baptizing. Samaritans were estranged from Jerusalem and its temple cultus. Readers may recall Pontius Pilate's vicious suppression of Samaritan religious enthusiasts in 36 or 37 CE. The proto-"Gnostic heretics" Simon (called "Magus," *fl.* 50s CE) and his disciples Satornilos and Menander came from Samaria and taught in Syria and Syro-Phoenicia.

We read in the fictional "Pseudo-Clementine romance" (ca. third century), an anti-Pauline, Jewish-Christian polemic in the Jamesian tradition, the astonishing story that Simon Magus was not only an Alexandrian Jew (like Apollos) but also John the Baptist's *leading disciple,* so gifted indeed that John would have chosen Simon to succeed him but for the fact Simon was in Egypt when John was executed. Instead, according to the romance, John's disciple Dositheos, another noted heresiarch, took over John's church until Simon returned to usurp the position. While the author of the anti-Pauline romance may have been deliberately confusing Simon with Apollos, there may be something in the Acts story of Simon trying to purchase the "gift" of passing on the Holy Spirit from the apostles, the act that gave us the word *simony.* That is to say, we may be seeing the conflict between the John water baptism and Paul's spirit baptism in an alternative form. We are clearly witnessing the surviving propaganda of rival churches.

It is especially significant then that the Nag Hammadi Gnostic text, *Concerning Our Great Power,* thought by scholar of Gnosis Kurt Rudolph to derive from "Simonian" speculative sources, begins with the words, "He who would know our Great Power will become invisible. And fire will not be able to consume him. But it will purify and destroy all your possessions." We may detect here an echo of Paul's caveat about the fire in 1 Corinthians 3 noted in chapter 10, here reappearing in a suggestively Johannite setting.

The church father Hyppolitus (*Refutatio* VI, 9–18) records a remarkable self-designation of Simon as "he who (formerly) stood, stands and (again) will stand." Other sources give Simon the honorific title "he who stands," a remarkable instance of "pillar language" based on the Malachi prophecy that asks, "Who will stand?" when the Lord comes into his temple, as well, perhaps, as a nod in the direction of the Syrian pillars of Seth. Seth was himself claimed by Gnostics as a patriarch and redeemer figure whose "three steles," that is pillars, give us the title of another Nag Hammadi Gnostic composition, *The Three Steles of Seth.*

Standing and facing the sun is a persistent motif of what we may call broadly the John tradition. Lucian of Samosata in the second century apparently observed descendants of north Syrian "Nazerini" formerly noted by Pliny in the early 70s CE. Lucian's "Daily Bathers" in the north Syrian Euphrates prayed to the sun, conducted dawn baptisms and ate honey, milk, and wild fruit.

The sun is the visible god whose radiance, as it were, hides the invisible God of the Gnostic, the Gnostic being he who will "become invisible. And fire will not be able to consume him." The spirit of the Gnostic is redeemed into the invisible image of the Primal Man after a succession of ascent-trials; this is the Mandaean-Nasorean redemption also.

Unlike the Mandaeans, the Pseudo-Clementine romances take the Primal Adam (Man) to be Christ, though, following the Gnostic view, the Primal Adam is still the "great power above the creator," an ideology associated with Dositheos, derived through Simon from his alleged master, John the Baptist. Paul was also aware of the "Primal Adam" theory. Paul held Jesus to be the "Second Adam," a restoration of the primal or heavenly Adam whose link to humankind had been sundered by Adam's "original" sin in the garden (*paradeisos*) of Eden, according to Paul. The Mandaeans found that the Primal Adam concept did not require a Jesus figure. The Man is the *Man.*

The Mandaeans' "Secret Adam" is identified with the third descendant of Adam, Enosh, son of Seth: "And to Seth, to him also there was born a son; and he called his name Enos: then began men to call upon the name of the LORD" (Genesis 4:26). Enosh in Genesis restores the link between humankind and what the Mandaeans call the "Life." "Enosh" is the Aramaic for "Man" and the Mandaean language is of an Aramaic type, though Mandaean employs its own distinct script, examples of which have been found on bowls from as long ago as the fifth century CE.

The Qu'ran accords respect to "Sabians" and while the precise origin and reference of the Qu'ranic term *Sabian* is debated, the fact that the Syriac root *Sabu'a* ("Washed Ones") appears in Arabic as "the Subba" has ensured until recently that the "Sabaeans of the marshes" or Mandaeans have been protected by Muslim authorities in Mesopotamia and Persia, though accorded *dhimmi* or inferior status, like Jews and Christians under strict Islamic law.

To Mandaeans, John the Baptist is "Yahya Yuhana" or "Yahya as-Sabi" whose father was Abba Saba Zachariah. John's teacher was Enosh, or "Man" (Hebrew: Adam), that is, the heavenly Man. This is consistent with my assessment of the term "Son of man" as denoting a person who has seen the divine image of Man in the Light of God.

Since the Allied invasion of Iraq in 2003, the largest Mandaean centers in Iraq, in Baghdad and Basra, whose priests have conducted their baptismal rites at the Shat al-Arab marshes where the Tigris and Euphrates join for well over fifteen hundred years, have suffered continual persecution and human-rights violation. Extremists have murdered and are murdering Mandaeans. Occasionally, the killings are opportunistic. The Mandaeans have long survived by organizing the gold and silver markets in Basra and Baghdad. Sectarian murders for ostensibly religious reasons are often inspired by a desire to rob shops and kidnap family members for money. The result is that a community estimated before the war at some fifty thousand souls has been reduced by exile to about five thousand. Mandaeans have found asylum in Jordan, Syria, Australia, Canada, the United States, Sweden, and the United Kingdom.

In July 2004, Yuhana Nashmi, a "Tarmida" or first-stage

Mandaean priest, gave a talk at the Liverpool Museum in England to highlight the plight of Mandaeans—problems, which I might add, that are also shared by the Yezidis in northern Iraq—and to give an insight into the Mandaean religion and the challenges to Mandaean survival in the modern world.

It had taken nearly two thousand years for a member of an authentic John tradition to speak about his religion in the West, for the Mandaeans do not proselytize. One wonders how many devotees they might find today if they did.

According to Yuhana Nashmi, Mandaeans believe in one God, Haii Rabi, meaning the *Great Life,* or the Great Living God. His universe has many mansions, of which life on Earth is only a part. Mandaeans understand that a conflict between good and bad characterizes our world. The good is the light (Nhora) and is represented in flowing, living water (Maia Haii); the bad is the dark (Hshokh) and represented as dead and salty water (Maia Tahmi). These principles achieve a balance on Earth, where there is a mixture to be found in all things.

After this life, the soul has the opportunity to enter the "world of light." The soul (Neshemtha; the Hebrew *Neschama*) belongs to the Great Life and will return to it. On returning to God, the soul receives a body of light and life (Damotha). To reach the world of Light, it is necessary to render an account of one's life on Earth.

Mandaeans believe in repeated baptism (Masbuta). Baptism cleanses the Mandaean faithful of their sins, preserving the soul from the negative effects of earthly life. In Iraq, little tributaries were traditionally taken off the Tigris for the purposes of baptism in flowing water. The tributaries, called "Jordans," further testify to the ancient presence of the *"nasuraiyi"* (Nasoreans) or "elect of righteousness" (*bhiri zidqa;* Hebrew *zedek*) in ancient Palestine. Mandaeans can still be seen on special occasions in their white robes and turbans immersing their fellows *three times* and crowning their heads with myrtle. This is probably a more accurate picture of the real John the Baptist than that provided by either Hollywood or Renaissance masters.

Yuhana gave an interesting account of the role of "manda," knowledge, in the contemporary Mandaean scheme of life. Rather than speak of manda or gnosis as an initiated mode of spiritual salvation, or special esoteric knowledge, he spoke of knowledge in its conventional sense of education. Education and knowledge of the universe, along with a commitment to peace and nonviolence were ways to reach God. The Great Life, he said, is a "significant resource of knowledge."

The first to realize Haii's existence was Adam, the first prophet. His son Shetel (Seth) was the second prophet, followed by Sam (Shem) son of Noah, and finally the last prophet Yahya Yuhana, John the Baptist. John was the last Rabi, that is, the highest rank of Mandaean priest, to have lived on Earth. The second rank is the Reshama, or "Head of the Nation," of whom there can be only one (and no one in the role at present). Below this rank is the Ganzbra (or "Treasurer," for Mandaean knowledge is a treasure). The Ganzbra is someone of distinguished religious education and perception. Currently, four Ganzbras live worldwide. The Tarmida is the initial rank of priest. He can perform ceremonies such as weddings but is regarded still as a student of the Mandaean religion. In 2004 Yuhana Nashmi was one of about thirty Tarmidas alive in the world. Tarmidas are assisted by the Shkanda whose presence is needed for important rituals.

The Mandaeans possess a surprisingly extensive literature, of which the most important work is the *Ginza*, "Treasure" or "Great Book." The "Right Ginza" contains much theology and mythology. The smaller "Left Ginza" contains hymns for the mass of the dead, devoted to the soul's ascent through the "kings" (*melki*) or angels. I saw a video recently of a Mandaean priest in Sweden who was upset because he experienced great difficulty in carrying out the baptismal mass of a dead Mandaean on account of the corpse having been consigned to a Swedish state hospital morgue. Mandaean custom requires the swift washing of the body with proper rites and prompt burial; the priest was frustrated at not being able to take control of the dead person's body due to state bureaucracy. Mandaeans in England have found it hard to find suitable places of flowing water appropriate for regular baptisms.

The Baptist par excellence is of course Yahya, or John. The Book of John is important to Mandaeans. It is also known as the Books of Kings. The "Kings" refers to "angels"; we seem to be in analogous mythological territory to that of Enoch and the Watchers. John himself is credited with a number of beautiful discourses. These are expressed purely in the language of Mandaean mythology and cannot be regarded as records of the utterances of the historical John, though there is clearly a conviction that the spirit of the discourses is inwardly authentic. Here are some examples of a John long lost:

Yahya proclaims in the nights and says:

Through my Father's discourses I give light and through the praise of the Man, my creator. I have freed my soul from the world and from the works that are hateful and wrong.

The Seven [rulers/planetary spirits] put the question to me, the Dead who have not seen Life, and they said unto me; "In whose strength dost thou stand there, and with whose praise dost thou make proclamation?" Thereupon gave to them answer: I stand in the strength of my Father and with the praise of the Man, my creator. I have built no house in Judea, I have set up no throne in Jerusalem. I have not loved the wreath of the roses, nor had commerce with lovely women. I have not loved the deficiency, nor loved the cup of the drunkards. I have loved no food of the body, and envy has found no place in me. I have not forgotten my night-prayer, not forgotten the wondrous Jordan. I have not forgotten my baptizing, nor forgotten my pure sign. I have not forgotten Sunday, and the Day's evening has not condemned me. I have not forgotten Shilmai and Nidbai, who dwell in the House of the Mighty. They clear me and let me ascend; they know no fault, no defect in me.

When Yahya said this, Life rejoiced over him greatly. The Seven sent him their greeting and the Twelve made obeisance before him. They said to him: "Of all these words, which thou hast spoken, thou hast not said a single one falsely. Delightful and fair is thy voice, and none is equal to thee. Fair is thy discourse in thy mouth and precious is thy speech, which has been bestowed upon thee. The vesture, which First Life, did give unto Adam, the Man, the vesture, which First Life, did give unto Râm, the Man, the vesture, which First Life did give unto Shurbai, the Man, the vesture First Life did give unto Shum Bar Nû [Shem, son of Noah] has He given now unto thee. He hath given it thee, O Yahya, that thou mayest ascend, and with thee may those descend. . . . The house of the defect (thy body) will be left behind in the desert. Everyone who shall be found sinless, will ascend unto thee, in the Region of Light; he who is not found sinless, will be called to account in the guardhouses."

John appears significantly in another Mandaean text: the *Diwan of the Great Revelation, Called "Inner Haran,"* also known as the *Haran Gawaita*. From its confused text we can discern that the community of Nasoreans was persecuted in Jerusalem, for which the city was destroyed, presumably a reference to the conflagration of 70 CE. Interestingly, the account features John as "the envoy of the king of light" and he is presented as an adversary of Christ. We may speculate that we have here the distant echo of a conflict with Paul's particular version of messianic Christocentricity. However, the text gives no ground for conviction on this score. The "Right Ginza" speaks of persecution and, not surprisingly, is full of invective against "Christ the Roman," a reference to the Byzantine Orthodox Church that dominated the Near East following the early fourth century.

John is never presented as the community's founder, only as a disciple of the Mandaean revelation and a "priest" of the religion. Rudolph has suggested that the Mandaeans may have taken their idea of John from other heretical Christian or Gnostic groups, though it is difficult to see why John should have risen in their estimation to "rabi" status on such a basis alone. Taking John and dismissing the Christian interpretation would have won them few friends by itself. The John texts exhibit more than ordinary respect or reverence. Rudolph is, however, convinced that the Mandaeans belong in the world of first-century baptismal sects close to the Jordan, while the *Haran Guwaita* refers to Nasoreans fleeing Jewish leaders in Palestine during the reign of Parthian King Ardban (Artabanus). If this was Artabanus II, then we should be talking about the conflict in which Lucius Vitellius, governor of Syria took part after 35 CE, and shortly before John's and Jesus's executions. According to the Mandaean text, Nasoreans made their way to the Median hill country or "inner Haran" between Harran and Nisibis in north Persian territory (Harran and Nisibis are now in Turkey). Harran was the home of the Harranian astro-magi, or "Sabians" as they would call themselves after Islamification. Mandaeans today regard these Mesopotamian "Chaldaeans" with their magic and their astrology and their Hermetic writings as their own ancestors, whose interest in learning they maintain.

After the first sojourn in "inner Haran," [*sic*] Nasoreans established themselves in Baghdad and became governors and built temples. These were destroyed during the consolidation of the Zarathushtrian state under the Sassanid Shapur I (241–272 CE). The Mandaeans had contacts with Mani in the third century, but found themselves more and more forced to look inward, a process intensified after the Islamic conquest of Mesopotamia in the seventh century.

The Mandaeans now face a new struggle for survival, a struggle of adaption to the modern world. It has been mooted among Mandaeans that, contrary to years of custom, conversion to Mandaeism may yet be permitted. What if a Mandaean man or woman should want to marry outside of the faith while both parents agree they want their children raised as Mandaeans? Once conversion of spouses is permitted, what then? Might we see these spiritual descendants of John the Baptist standing by our flowing and hopefully not overpolluted rivers and once more issuing to a world gone mad a sacred call that the time has come for the world to clean up its act?

Then we might wonder whether John is not long dead after all, but liveth, on our own doorstep.

BIBLIOGRAPHY

Anderson, James. *Anderson's Constitutions of 1723*. Introduction by Lionel Vibert. Reprint. Kila, Mont.: Kessinger Publishing, undated.

———. *Anderson's Constitutions of 1738*. Reprint. Kila, Mont.: Kessinger Publishing, undated.

The Bible in Hebrew. British and Foreign Bible Society, 1907.

Blair, Harold Arthur. *The Kaleidoscope of Truth: Types and Archetypes in Clement of Alexandria*. Worthing, West Sussex: Churchman Publishing Ltd., 1986.

Burns, Robert. *The Works of Robert Burns*. Ware, Hertfordshire: Wordsworth Poetry Library, 1994.

Charles, Robert Henry, trans. *The Book of Enoch*. London: SPCK, 1994.

Churton, Tobias. *Freemasonry—The Reality*. London: Lewis Masonic, 2007.

———. *The Missing Family of Jesus*. London: Watkins, 2010.

Copenhaver, Brian P., trans. *Hermetica: The Greek Corpus Hermeticum and the Latin Asclepius*. Cambridge: Cambridge University Press, 1995.

Dibelius, Martin. *From Tradition to Gospel*. London: James Clarke & Co. Ltd., 1971.

Ehrman, Bart. D. *Lost Scriptures: Books that Did Not Make It into the New Testament*. Oxford: Oxford University Press, 2005.

Eisenman, Robert. *James the Brother of Jesus*. London: Watkins, 2002.

Eisenman, Robert, and Michael Wise. *The Dead Sea Scrolls Uncovered*. London: Penguin, 1992.

Eusebius. *Ecclesiastical History*. 2 vols. Translated by Kirsopp Lake. London: Loeb Classical Library, 1973.

Fenton, John. *St. Matthew.* Pelican New Testament Commentaries. London: Penguin, 1978.

Fowden, Garth. *The Egyptian Hermes.* Cambridge: Cambridge University Press, 1986.

Η ΚΑΙΝΗ ΔΙΑΘΗΚΗ [The New Testament, in Greek]. London: The British and Foreign Bible Society, 1965.

Herodotus. Translated by Canon Rawlinson. London: John Murray, 1897.

The Holy Bible. Authorized King James Version. Oxford: Oxford University Press, 1969.

Hughes, David. *The Star of Bethlehem Mystery.* London: J. M. Dent & Sons Ltd., 1979.

Jöckle, Clemens. *Encyclopaedia of Saints.* London: Parkgate Books, 1997.

Josephus, Flavius. *Antiquities of the Jews.* Translated by William Whiston. Edinburgh: William P. Nimmo, 1865.

———. *Jewish Wars.* Translated by William Whiston. Edinburgh: William P. Nimmo, 1865.

Kelly, John Norman Davidson. *Early Christian Doctrines.* London: A & C Black, 1977.

Liddell, Henry George, and Robert Scott. *A Greek-English Lexicon.* Oxford: Oxford University Press, 1901.

Mason, Rex. *The Books of Haggai, Zechariah, and Malachi.* Cambridge Bible Commentary on the Old Testement. Cambridge: Cambridge University Press, 1977.

May, Herbert G., ed. *Oxford Bible Atlas.* Oxford: Oxford University Press, 1975.

More, St. Thomas. *Utopia.* Ware, Hertfordshire: Wordsworth Classics of World Literature, Wordsworth Editions Ltd., 1997.

Pliny. *Natural History.* 2 vols. London: Loeb Classical Library, 1989.

Robinson, James M., ed. *The Nag Hammadi Library in English.* Leiden: E. J. Brill, 1984.

Rudolph, Kurt. *Gnosis.* Translated by Wilson R. McLachlan. San Francisco: Harper & Row, 1985.

Suetonius. *The Twelve Caesars.* Translated by Robert Graves. London: Folio Society, 1964.

Throckmorton, Burton H. Jr. *Gospel Parallels—A Synopsis of the First Three Gospels*. London: Thomas Nelson & Sons, 1967.

Vermes, Geza, trans. *The Complete Dead Sea Scrolls in English*. London: Penguin, 2004.

Yamauchi, Edwin. *The Stones and the Scriptures*. London: Inter-Varsity Press, 1973.

INDEX

BOOKS OF RELATED INTEREST

Gnostic Philosophy
From Ancient Persia to Modern Times
by Tobias Churton

The Invisible History of the Rosicrucians
The World's Most Mysterious Secret Society
by Tobias Churton

The Magus of Freemasonry
The Mysterious Life of Elias Ashmole—Scientist, Alchemist,
and Founder of the Royal Society
by Tobias Churton

The Gospel of Mary Magdalene
by Jean-Yves Leloup

The Gospel of Thomas
The Gnostic Wisdom of Jesus
by Jean-Yves Leloup

Founding Fathers, Secret Societies
Freemasons, Illuminati, Rosicrucians, and the Decoding of the Great Seal
by Robert Hieronimus, Ph.D.
with Laura Cortner

The Temple of Solomon
From Ancient Israel to Secret Societies
by James Wasserman

An Illustrated History of the Knights Templar
by James Wasserman

INNER TRADITIONS • BEAR & COMPANY
P.O. Box 388
Rochester, VT 05767
1-800-246-8648
www.InnerTraditions.com

Or contact your local bookseller